Alutiiq Villages under
Russian and U.S. Rule

Alutiiq Villages under Russian and U.S. Rule

Sonja Luehrmann

University of Alaska Press
Fairbanks

University of Alaska Press
P.O. Box 756240
Fairbanks, AK 99775-6240

ISBN 13: 978-1-60223-023-1
ISBN 10: 1-60223-023-4

The Library of Congress has cataloged the hardcover edition as follows:
Luehrmann, Sonja.
Alutiiq villages under Russian and U.S. rule / Sonja Luehrmann.
      p.   cm.
    Includes bibliographical references.
    ISBN-13: 978-1-60223-010-1 (hardcover : alk. paper)
    ISBN-10: 1-60223-010-2 (hardcover : alk. paper)
    1. Pacific Gulf Yupik Eskimos—History—Sources.   2. Pacific Gulf Yupik Eskimos—
Government relations.   3. Pacific Gulf Yupik Eskimos—Social conditions.   4. First contact
of aboriginal peoples with Westerners—Alaska.   5. Rossiisko-amerikanskaia kompaniia—
History.   6. Russkaia pravoslavnaia tserkov'—History.   7. Russia—Foreign relations—
United States.   8. United States—Foreign relations—Russia.   I. Title.   II. Title: Alutiiq
villages under Russian and US rule.
    E99.E7L84 2008
    979.8´40049714—dc22
                    2007016246

Text design by Detta Penna
Cover design by Dixon J. Jones, Rasmuson Library Graphics. Cover images are watercolors of
Chirikof Village in 1869 and an interior of an Alutiiq House near Kodiak, both by Vincent Colyer.
Upper image courtesy of the Beinecke Rare Book and Manuscript Library, Yale University. Lower
image courtesy of the Alutiiq Museum Archaeological Repository.

This publication was printed on acid-free paper that meets the minimum requirements for ANSI /
NISO Z39.48–1992 (Permanence of Paper for Printed Library Materials).

for Ilya

Contents

Illustrations

Figures

Maps and Table

Introduction

Alaska was a colony of the Russian Empire from the mid-eighteenth century, and when it was sold to the U.S.A. in 1867 it practically remained a colony—with no representation in the U.S. government and no influence on the commercial interests exploiting its resources—at least until it gained territorial status in 1912. Even then, the bulk of the Native population did not gain citizenship until 1924, and one could argue that Alaska, despite having achieved statehood in 1959, is still going through a decolonizing process, facing such issues as the numerical, political, cultural, and linguistic dominance of whites within the state and dependence on the cycles of the global economy, and continuing to struggle to find an equitable solution for Native land and resource rights (Berger 1985; Haycox 2002; Mitchell 1997).

This book describes and compares the effects of the two successive colonial periods on a part of Alaska that was strongly affected by both of them: the coastal region of South-Central Alaska, stretching from eastern Prince William Sound, via the southern Kenai coast and the Kodiak Archipelago, to the Pacific and Bristol Bay coasts of the Alaska Peninsula down to the isthmus at Port Moller. Its Native population shares a common language, Sugcestun (spoken in several dialects with a major divide between Prince William Sound and Kenai Peninsula on the one side and Kodiak Island and the Alaska Peninsula on the other) and a common history of close association with the Russian colonizers, reflected in the modern self-designation Alutiiq. This is the Sugcestun form of "Aleuty" (pl.), the Russian term for speakers of both Unangan (the modern "Aleuts") and Sugcestun. Widespread adherence to Russian Orthodox Christianity is also a legacy of the Russian period. Other shared historical memories of Alutiiq people include surviving disasters such as the 1837/1838 smallpox epidemic, the 1912 eruption of Novarupta Volcano near Katmai, and the 1964 earthquake and tsunami.

The Alutiiq[1] identify with ancestors who, according to nineteenth-century accounts and the archaeological record for the preceding centuries, showed certain similarities across the region, despite strong regional differences and a complex political history of largely independent villages engaged in trade and warfare. Common characteristics were the maritime orientation of their subsistence economy (with a highly developed kayak and harpoon technology), supplemented by the harvesting of yearly salmon runs in coastal rivers; their semisedentary lifestyle, with permanent villages serving as a base for seasonal moves to fishing and hunting camps; and a ranked society in which chiefly families enjoyed privileges over commoners and slaves. Today, Native and non-Native inhabitants of the region still share a strong orientation toward the sea, and the whole area, except the Bering Sea side of the Alaska Peninsula, was strongly affected by the 1989 Exxon Valdez oil spill (Crowell and Luehrmann 2001; Partnow 2001; Wooley 1995).[2]

The two colonial periods brought very different economic and political dynamics to the region. For the Russians, obtaining sea otter pelts for the China trade was the main motivation to come to Alaska, and they conscripted men from the Aleutians and Kodiak Island to hunt at increasingly remote places, such as Sitka, the Kuriles, and California. After obtaining a monopoly in 1799, the company managing the fur hunt, known as the Russian-American Company (RAC), was simultaneously the governing institution of the colony. It had the power to regulate the lives of Native inhabitants and Russian employees, exercise jurisdiction in minor cases, and take charge of defense and foreign trade in Alaskan harbors. The small, almost entirely male Russian population in Alaska relied on the Native men and women for their skills in hunting, gathering, and processing food and preparing skins and clothing, and Russians frequently took Native women as wives. Creoles, the offspring of such unions, formed a special class, some of them educated people who served as clerks, administrators, explorers, and priests (Black 1990; Tikhmenev 1978).

The U.S. period started with an administrative vacuum filled only minimally by patrols of the U.S. Army and Revenue Service. The fur trade was taken over by several competing companies, one of which, the Alaska Commercial Company, had purchased the assets of the RAC. Competition sometimes meant better prices for the hunters, but it also brought the fur-bearing animals close to extinction. The core of the economy of coastal Alaska shifted toward salmon canning, an industry that primarily employed Asian contract laborers and European immigrant fishermen and quickly marginalized the Native population. Marriages with these newcomers, many of them Scandinavian, created new mixed groups and introduced new economic pursuits, such as fox farming and commercial fishing. Creoles lost their special status and, like all Natives and offspring of mixed unions, faced strong racial discrimination. Protestant missionaries started arriving in the 1880s, creating a racially segregated school system, as well as rifts between Orthodox and Protestant Alutiiq that persist to the present day. World War II brought an influx of soldiers and new military bases, to Kodiak Island in particular.

Following statehood and the negotiation of land claims by representatives of Alaska's Native people, three separate regional corporations were established under the 1971 Alaska Native Claims Settlement Act: Chugach Alaska Corporation (Prince William Sound), Koniag, Inc. (Kodiak Island), and Bristol Bay Native Corporation (northern Alaska Peninsula, including Yup'ik areas). The corporations did not create a representative body for all Alutiiq, but the distribution of shares provided the first positive incentive in a long time for people of mixed ancestry to think of themselves as Natives. Starting in the 1980s, increasing efforts to revive and record Alutiiq heritage have led to the establishment of dance groups, craft and language classes, oral history projects and museums, and to a struggle with the Smithsonian Institution for the return and reburial of human remains that were excavated near Larsen Bay, Kodiak, in the 1930s (Bray and Killion 1994; Davis 1984; Mishler and Mason 1996; Pullar 1994:30).

The project through which I became involved with Alutiiq history was connected to the struggle of Alutiiq and Alaskan, or national, institutions to come to terms with each other. In 1995, the Anchorage office of the Smithsonian Arctic Studies Center began collaborating with the Alutiiq Museum in Kodiak City and an advisory board of Alutiiq elders in preparing an exhibit called *Looking Both Ways—Heritage and Identity of the Alutiiq People*, which toured museums in Alaska as well as New York and Washington, D.C. between 2001 and 2003. The exhibit brought back to Alaska pieces from the collection of William H. Fisher, tidal observer and trader on Kodiak Island in the 1880s (Crowell, Steffian, and Pullar 2001). During the summers of 1998 and 1999, I was able to work at the Arctic Studies Center as a research fellow working with Russian-language documents relevant to Alutiiq history. Even for the first decades of U.S. rule, the most detailed written sources are in Russian, from priests and traders resident in the region. The most important collections for the nineteenth century as a whole are the correspondence of the RAC and the archives of the Russian Orthodox Church in Alaska.

The RAC correspondence came into the possession of the U.S. government with the treaty of purchase of 1867. The collection consists of the books into which the staff at Sitka copied letters received from the Main Office in St. Petersburg (communications received, 1802, 1817–1866) and letters sent to that office and the subordinate offices in the various Alaskan districts (communications sent, 1818–1867). The incoming correspondence from the districts was not included with these papers and has not been located in Russia either. But the letters, especially the communications sent, still contain detailed information on colonial policies as well as living and working conditions.

The Russian Orthodox Church archives are far more heterogeneous. Of particular importance to my research were the confessional records, clerical registers, vital statistics, and reports and travel journals of parish priests. Confessional records (*ispovednye rospisi/ispovednye vedomosti*) are lists of the names of all parishioners prepared each year for the purpose of noting who came to confession and who did not. These exist, in varying degrees of completeness, for Kodiak parish for 1830–1921, for Afognak (formerly part of Kodiak parish) intermittently between 1895 and 1911, for Kenai parish from 1846 to 1919, for Nuchek and Tatitlek between 1882 and 1916, and for Nushagak from 1842 to 1929.[3] Clerical registers (*klirovye vedomosti*) contain information on parish property, employees, and activities as well as the numbers of parishioners. I made extensive use only of the Kodiak (1840–1921) registers, which break down population figures by villages. Priests' reports and journals are mainly from the period after 1867, especially between 1880 and 1910.

Another type of church record are the vital statistics, which list baptisms, chrismations,[4] weddings, and deaths in individual parishes. For Kodiak parish, these are preserved from 1826 to 1918, for Kenai parish from 1845 to 1933, for Nuchek and Tatitlek from 1894 to 1907. I also used the statistics for Sitka parish for information on the Alutiiq population there.

All types of documents contain a wealth of information on the names, periods of existence, and ethnic composition of villages. Abandoned villages are an important issue in Alutiiq history—by one account, there were sixty-five villages on Kodiak Island alone in the 1830s; today there are seven (Tikhmenev 1978:200). From Russian documents and published accounts, U.S. census records, and historic maps,[5] I began to put together maps of the region for different historical periods. In the process it became apparent that the shift of village locations in response to population decrease and changing colonial policies provided a good basis for discussing differences between the two colonizations and their impact on the Alutiiq population.

Since the Russian-language sources are richest for the period between 1805 and 1920, I concentrate on this period. Soon afterward, events such as the 1924 Native Citizenship Act, the 1931 transfer of responsibility for Alaska Natives from the Bureau of Education to the BIA, World War II and statehood, along with the rising Native land claims movement, added dynamics to the economic and legal status of the Alutiiq population that would take the scope of this book beyond the comparison between Russian and U.S. colonial practices. Within the given time period I have more to say about Kodiak Island than other parts of the Alutiiq region, since the influence of the RAC and the Orthodox Church was strongest there and the records are most detailed.

Although the place of villages in colonial political economies is the common focus, every chapter of this book approaches the written record from a different angle. Chapter 1 starts out with an analysis of recent trends in the portrayal of the history of Native Alaskans in North America and Russia, with special consideration to the influence of such developments as the end of the Cold War and the movement toward greater control over cultural heritage by Native groups. By analyzing some of the frameworks from which comparisons between the Russian and U.S. colonial periods have been made, this chapter lays the groundwork for my own subsequent interpretation of archival sources.

Chapter 2 presents a chronologically organized narrative of the Russian colonial period and the first decades of U.S. rule in the Alutiiq region, organized along a series of maps that trace the changes in locations and types of settlements from 1805 to 1930. The documents on which I relied to construct the maps also yielded rich information on life in these villages during the two periods, which I lay out more extensively in the remaining three chapters.

Chapters 3 and 4 form a pair, focusing on the organization of labor first in the Russian period and then in the American period, and proposing a largely economic argument about changes in the social position of Alutiiq over time. Chapter 3 also addresses a question that has exercised scholarship on Russian America for some time—how a few hundred Russians managed to exert control over the relatively dense and quite well-armed populations of the Alutiiq region.

Chapter 5 shifts gears somewhat toward a discursive analysis of documents and travelers' accounts, asking how the legal and social categories into which the population was divided by each colonizing power mattered in such areas of life as education and citizenship. Rather than reading colonial statistics for the information they were intended to convey, I read them both for the categories they employ and for traces of the difficulties faced by administrators in compiling them. Some of the records contain evidence of how hard it was to make complex social realities—about which the record keepers were sometimes inadequately informed—conform to the expectations about family size, kinship, and gender that were encoded in statistical conventions.

I hope that my interaction with archival and published sources has created or assembled some historical objects that others will find useful for pursuing their own questions. As far as my maps are concerned, matching names in documents with actual locations always involves some guesswork, and more intensive use of archaeological and oral sources might have brought different results, although I consulted the published results of archaeological investigation where available (Clark 1987; Crowell 1997; Crowell and Mann 1998; Knecht, Haakanson, and Dickson 2003; Knecht and Jordan 1985; Woodhouse-Beyer 2001). My emphasis on the influence of colonial policies and economies on Alutiiq village life might seem to downplay the importance of people's interaction with their environment and its resources for village locations as well as for processes of sociocultural change or persistence. Such issues will probably loom larger for people more engaged with local conditions than I, who visited Kodiak Island and Kenai Peninsula only briefly in 1998 and have never seen most of the sites mentioned in this book. I leave it to them to reinterpret the sources from colonial archives with their own questions in mind.

Neither do I reproduce the attempt of the *Looking Both Ways* exhibit to include the voices of Alutiiq elders and search for alternative modes of telling history, since the story I am telling is squarely shaped by the standards of truth and interests of documentation of the colonial archives. What I hope to contribute is an account that places the history of South-Central Alaska and its Native and non-Native inhabitants in the context of two empires that crossed paths in this region. Knowledge of these wider imperial contexts, I argue, can help enrich and complicate our understanding of the experience of the people who lived in Alaska during the past centuries. Conversely, people interested in colonial legacies elsewhere can benefit from knowing more about the history of South-Central Alaska.

Some of the materials used in this book were previously published in different form. A short summary of Chapter 2 appears on pages 54–66 of Aron Crowell and Sonja Luehrmann, "Alutiiq Culture: Views from Archaeology, Anthropology and History," in *Looking Both Ways: Heritage and Identity of the Alutiiq People*, edited by A. Crowell, A. Steffian, and G. Pullar (Fairbanks: University of Alaska Press, 2001, pp. 21–71). Core arguments of Chapter 3 were first elaborated in Sonja Luehrmann, "Russian Colonialism and the Asiatic Mode of Production: (Post-)Soviet Ethnography Goes to Alaska," *Slavic Review* 64 (4) 2005, pp. 851–871. Materials from Chapter 5 have appeared, in Russian, in Sonja Luehrmann, "Ot aleutov i kreolov k chernym i belym: IUzhnaia Aliaska mezhdu dvumia imperiiami," *Ab Imperio* (3) 2001, pp. 169–190. My thanks to the publishers for permission to reuse these materials here.

My research in Anchorage in 1998 and 1999 was supported by funding from the Smithsonian Institution, the German National Merit Foundation (Studienstiftung des deutschen Volkes), and the German Academic Exchange Service (DAAD). The research resulted in maps and other materials for the *Looking Both Ways* exhibit (Crowell and Luehrmann 2001, Figures 51 and 60), as well as in a master's thesis in anthropology completed at Johann Wolfgang Goethe University in Frankfurt, Germany, in 2000. I am grateful to Christian Feest, my advisor in Frankfurt, for his inspiring breadth of knowledge, contagious enthusiasm, and unfailing encouragement, and to Aron Crowell, director of the Arctic Studies Center's Anchorage office, for helping to make my stays in Anchorage possible and for permission to republish the map research.

Sharon Bohlen, Janelle and Leslie Matz, Gail and Joe Kelley, and Helen and the late John Szablya sheltered me in Anchorage, Kodiak, and Seattle. A number of people in the United States, Germany, and Russia discussed various aspects of this project with me and gave helpful information and insights. I list them in roughly chronological order of their involvement with the project: Olga Nyrkova, Andrei Nyrkov, Shauna Lukin, Dee Hunt, Lydia Black, Ronald Inouye, Rory Ong, Robert Ackerman, Jessica Gienow-Hecht, April Laktonen, Gordon Pullar, Ann Fienup-Riordan, Carola Lentz, Burkhard Schnepel, Gisela Welz, Oya Ataman, Peter Schweitzer, Julie Cruikshank, Ann Stoler, William Rosenberg, and Andrei Grinev. Ilya Vinkovetsky, Donald Clark, and Mina Jacobs were especially generous in pointing out useful sources and providing information and feedback across continents and library systems. Erica Hill was a supportive and knowledgeable editor at University of Alaska Press. Special thanks are due to Richard Knecht and a second, anonymous reader for thoughtful comments on the manuscript.

I am also thankful to Mark Matson, illustrator at the Arctic Studies Center, who designed the map graphics, to Anna Petrova and Polina Degen for advice on Russian translations, and to my parents, Renate and Dieter Lührmann, for attentive readings and many other forms of moral and material support. For the pleasures of reading archival documents and of the Russian language, I am indebted to two of my high school teachers, Gudrun Westphal and Ingrid Müller-Mennenöh.

ENDNOTES

1. In Sugcestun, the grammatically correct plural is "Alutiit." However, I will follow the current usage of the mainly English-speaking population and use "Alutiiq" as the plural as well as the singular form.
2. The Chugach of Prince William Sound are the only Alutiiq group on which an

ethnographic monograph has been published (Birket-Smith 1953). Relatively detailed descriptions of Kodiak Island's ethnography were provided by eighteenth- and nineteenth-century Russian travelers (Black 1977b; Davydov 1812, 1977; Gedeon 1994, 1989; Holmberg 1856). More recent syntheses are in Clark 1984; Davis 1984; and Crowell, Steffian, and Pullar 2001.

3. Some of the villages on the Alaska Peninsula were part of Belkofsky parish in the late nineteenth century. Owing to time constraints, I did not look at records from this parish but refer to Morseth (1998), who consulted some of them, for information on these places.

4. Chrismation (Russian *miropomazanie*) is the act of anointing a recently baptized person with consecrated oil as a sign of the seal of the Holy Spirit. It is often performed immediately after baptism in the Russian Orthodox Church, but if the baptism was carried out by a layperson, chrismation must be done at a later time by an ordained cleric.

5. Elmer E. Rasmuson Library, University of Alaska Fairbanks, has an important collection of historic Alaskan and Arctic maps.

A Note on Citation, Transliteration, and Translations

In this book archival materials are cited in the following format. The first three collections are held by the Library of Congress, Manuscripts Department, and were viewed on microfilm at Consortium Library, University of Alaska Anchorage.

1. Russian-American Company correspondence

"RAC cs 15: 151–151v, Feb 26, 1838, to Kodiak office" means: "Correspondence of the Governors-General of the Russian-American Company, communications sent, volume 15, folios 151–151 verso, letter of February 26, 1838, to the Kodiak office of the RAC." Sender is always the RAC Chief Manager (*glavnyi pravitel'*) residing at Novoarkhangel'sk/Sitka. "To Main Office" means "to the main office of the RAC in St. Petersburg" (*glavnoe pravlenie*).

2. Documents of the Russian Orthodox Church in Alaska

"ARCA D248/172: report from Fr. Tikhon Shalamov to the Sitka Consistory, Kodiak, June 9, 1894" means: "Archives of the Russian Orthodox Church in Alaska, series D, container 248, microfilmed on reel 172," followed by information on the kind of document, author and addressee (where applicable), place, and date. The microfilm reel number is added because material from one container may appear on two or more reels.

3.   Russian Orthodox Church vital statistics

"VS E33, Kodiak, baptisms 1885" means: "Russian Orthodox Church vital statistics (Archives of the Russian Orthodox Church in Alaska, series E), container 33, Kodiak parish, baptismal records (as opposed to records of chrismations, weddings or deaths) of the year 1885." The microfilm reel number is not indicated, since the correct reel can be easily located according to the parish name and year.

4.   U.S. census records

The census forms up to 1920 are available on microfilm at branch offices of the National archives across the United States. In referring to them I identify the year and the location, spelled as on the form. For example, "1910 census, Nenilchuk" refers to the 1910 form for Ninilchik. All census references are from Alaska.

Dates in the Russian documents cited in this book follow the Julian, or old style, calendar, which was used in Russia up to the October Revolution of 1917. The difference to the Gregorian calendar (new style) was 12 days in the nineteenth century: October 14, 1897, old style, is October 26, new style. Since precise dates are rarely relevant in the present narrative except for the identification of archival documents, I have not adjusted old style dates to new style. Dates from Vladimir Stafeev's journal (Stafeev ms.) are new style.

Russian terms and names are transliterated following the Library of Congress system, omitting diacritics.

I have generally tried to locate published travel accounts and other materials in the original language (Russian or German). Sometimes I also refer to English translations, but the absence of such a reference should not be taken to mean that none exists. All translations are my own unless otherwise noted.

A great limitation is placed on this work by my ignorance of the Alutiiq language. All Alutiiq names (both of individuals and of places) are transcribed as they are spelled in the documents, with no attempts to adjust them to contemporary Alutiiq orthography. Place names vary over time, and I have tried, without complete consistency, to use the spellings appropriate for a given period. For instance, "Aiakhtalik" or "Aekhtalik" are older Russianized forms of the village name Aiaktalik. For a concordance of place names as they appear in different nineteenth-century records, see Table 1 in Chapter 2.

1

Masks and *Matrioshkas:* Memorabilia from Alutiiq Historiography

When tourists in South-Central Alaska visit a souvenir store, they are presented with a range of items to remind them of the natural and cultural riches of the forty-ninth state: from gold nugget jewelry to various products made of moose "nuggets" (feces); from birch syrup and sea otter beanie babies to plastic miniature totem poles; from Native crafts such as ivory carvings, Athabaskan beadwork, ulu knives, and Yup'ik masks to Russian Orthodox icons and nesting *matrioshka* dolls featuring Lenin, Stalin, Brezhnev, Gorbachev, Yeltsin, and Putin. Finally there are the *Tundra* cartoons by Chad Carpenter making fun of the whole tourist business in Alaska.

The articles of Native art in these stores still recall the kinds of souvenirs sold to the first waves of tourists visiting the territory around 1900, when, in the interpretation of Molly Lee, Native artworks served as metonyms (attributes standing for the whole) for Alaska (Lee 1999:268). If the range of objects selected as metonyms seems to have widened in the course of the century, the whole that these detached attributes refer to also has multiple shapes: Do carved walrus tusks represent Alaska as the Last Frontier rich in wildlife or as home to a fascinating Native population? Do icons belong together with *matrioshkas* in an Alaskan version of the post-Cold War trade in Russian/ Soviet curios, similar to what one might find on the opposite side of the world, in places such as Berlin or Prague? Or do they, together with ulus and masks, point to the religious practices of Alaska Natives and offer an image of deeper and richer cultural roots than 140 years of U.S. presence could convey?

If recognizably Russian souvenirs sell well in contemporary Alaska, this indicates certain shifts in the way Alaskan history has been portrayed and presented both to Alaskan residents of various origins and to outsiders with relatively little personal stake in its telling. Especially since the end of the Cold War, the fact that Alaska was a Russian colony before it was sold to the United States in 1867 has increasingly been portrayed in a positive light, giving the state the kind of uniqueness and distinctiveness that tour operators look for. For those parts of Alaska's Native population whose history was deeply intertwined with the Russian presence, this change has opened up new possibilities of telling their history and articulating their identity. The Alutiiq, whose experiences under two successive colonial powers form the subject of this book, are a group that has gained public visibility in recent years partly thanks to the increased attention to the Russian period in Alaska, partly to a growing interest in the "hybrid" or "creolized" cultures that resulted from colonization in many parts of the world. The purpose of this chapter is to introduce the background of historical and anthropological scholarship, both in English and in Russian, out of which this renewed attention emerges and to outline some of the reasons why Alutiiq history should matter to Alutiiq and non-Alutiiq readers.

Whose Colorful Past Is It?

For a long time, Alutiiq history was marginal to popular and scholarly accounts of Alaska Native culture owing to this group's long history of intermarriage and economic interdependence with Russian and Anglo-American newcomers. Gordon Pullar, former president of Kodiak Area Native Association (KANA) and later director of the Department of Alaska Native and Rural Development at the University of Alaska, tells of a woman from Kodiak Island who looked at objects elaborately crafted by her ancestors and excavated at Karluk in the 1980s:

> Her facial expression reflected both confusion and sadness. Finally speaking, she said, "I guess we really are Natives after all. I was always told that we were Russians." (Pullar 1992:183)

As Pullar elaborates in his article, the "baggage" (Pullar 1992:182) accumulated over generations of being colonized by two successive powers whose institutions—Russian Orthodox and American Protestant schools—directly competed for a while, leaves many Alutiiq today with unresolved issues of shame, guilt, and humiliation and a sense of lacking knowledge of and authority over who they are.

As inhabitants of the southern coastline, relatively accessible and rich in sea otter and salmon, the Alutiiq were among those Alaskan peoples most strongly affected by Russian and early U.S.-American activities in Alaska. The very designation "Alutiiq" shows the marks that this history has left on the self-identification of the people of Kodiak Island and South Alaska. Since the Russians extended their name for the Unangan population of the Aleutian Islands to the people they encountered and subdued further to the east, these people began themselves to identify as "Aleuts." Heinrich Johann Holmberg, a Finnish traveler who visited Kodiak Island in 1851, claims that the younger generation at that time did not know any other name for themselves than "Aljutik" (Holmberg 1856:282), their pronunciation of "Aleut." On the Alaska Peninsula, where precolonial ethnic boundaries are subject to much debate, people speaking Unangan and various dialects of Sugcestun and Yup'ik came to call themselves "Aleut" as a mark of their close affiliation with the Russians in the area and to distinguish themselves from those Yup'ik groups to the northwest who lacked such contacts (Morseth 1998:7–9; Oswalt 1967a:4–5, 8).

Today, the term "Alutiiq" is used as a self-designation by speakers of Sugcestun (an Eskimoan language closely related to Yup'ik) living on the Kodiak Archipelago, the Alaska Peninsula, and Prince William Sound. By adopting the local pronunciation of the Russian word, they distinguish themselves from the linguistically and culturally distinct "Aleuts" (Unangan) of the southwestern tip of the Alaska Peninsula and the Aleutian Islands. The Alutiiq are also known as Sugpiaq, meaning "real person." The terms "Koniag" (from an Unangan designation) and "Chugach" are used for the inhabitants of the Kodiak Archipelago and Prince William Sound, respectively. The term "Pacific Eskimo," introduced by twentieth-century anthropologists on the basis of close linguistic ties to Yup'ik, is often taken as an insult. Under Russian colonization, "Aleuts" had grown accustomed to regarding "Eskimos" as dirtier and less civilized, and telling people who thought of themselves as Aleuts that they were really Eskimos did little to foster relationships of mutual respect with scholars (Clark 1984:195–196; Crowell 1997:35; Pullar 1992:185).

Throughout much of the twentieth century, the widespread intermarriage in the Alutiiq area, first with Russians, then with Scandinavians, was used to deny their descendants claims to "nativeness." The Creoles, descendants of Russian men who had married Native—mainly Unangan and Alutiiq but also Yup'ik, Denaina, and Tlingit—women, had formed a special class in the social order of the Russian colony. Under the U.S. system that distinguished mainly between "white" and "colored" and that frowned on or actually prohibited miscegenation, there was no conceptual space for such a group of people. For Creole families, identifying as Russian may have been a strategy to gain status and opportunities denied to Natives in the early twentieth century, but for the woman Pullar describes, her family's decision had become a cause of shame and regret at having lost touch with the past that is presented to her in the

Group portrait of seven men at Kodiak, ca. 1892. This portrait, featuring Orthodox priest Aleksandr Martysh (front row center) surrounded by prominent Kodiak Creoles such as Ivan Semenov (front row left), Timofei Demidov (back row first from left), and Innokentii and Vasilii Chechenev (back row second and fourth from left), gives an idea of the long-standing Russian influences that have sometimes made it difficult for people in the Alutiiq region to claim their Native heritage. *Courtesy of Alaska State Library, Michael Z. Vinokouroff Collection, p243-1-079.*

museum (Partnow 2001:143–144, 203). Even today, identifying/being identified as Native in Alaska has two sides: it can provide a sense of pride, bring certain economic benefits, and provoke a benevolent interest from non-Natives, but it can also mean being discriminated against, labeled as a lazy alcoholic or a quaint remnant of the past, and belonging to communities that still have to fight for their economic and cultural rights.

Pullar argues for a historic understanding of the roots of this sense of disempowerment and uncertain identity—dealing with the "pain and confusion" in family histories along with celebrating the "valuable knowledge" of elders (Pullar 1992:188). Assuming "that a Native community made up of people with a strong sense of who they are is in a much more powerful position to assert its rights," even though the outcome of that struggle for awareness might be a totally new culture, he points to the way in which historical research by or in traditionally disadvantaged communities will always be incorporated into debates over how to achieve justice in the present (Pullar 1992:183, 189). In the Alutiiq region, this interest in the revitalizing effects of historical knowledge has resulted in several collaborative projects between regional or village corporations and Alutiiq and outside researchers, such as the excavations at Karluk carried out in collaboration between KANA and Bryn Mawr College, oral history projects, and the *Looking Both Ways* exhibit project. Between 1993 and 1998, Afognak Native Corporation ran the "Dig Afognak" archaeological field school for Kodiak and outside students at precontact and Russian-period sites on Afognak Island codirected by Katherine Woodhouse-Beyer from Brown University and Patrick Saltonstall from the Alutiiq Museum and Archaeological Repository in Kodiak (Crowell, Steffian, and Pullar 2001; Kodiak Area Native Association 1987; Pullar 1992:183; Woodhouse-Beyer 2001).

Such initiatives were enabled in part by the 1971 Alaska Native Claims Settlement Act, which created Native corporations with ownership over land and economic resources and thus gave representatives of Native communities a certain financial and institutional power that researchers cannot simply ignore (Berger 1985; Case 1984:14–28). But these new collaborations were also spurred by a new interest in the colonial society that had existed in Alaska under Russian colonial rule, precipitated by political changes in the Soviet Union, which made Russian archives and Russian scholarship available to Anglophone scholars.

North American Historiography: East of the Cold War Border

Nowadays objects made to stand for Alaska's Russian past, whether icons, *matrioshkas*, or Orthodox Churches, have a positive value for tourism, and the Russian past is celebrated. Sitka, for instance, reminds visitors of the time when it was capital of Russian America—"The Paris of the Pacific"—as proof of its "colorful history" (National Park Service 1997). But this has not always been so.

In the decades following the sale of Alaska to the United States in 1867, Russian Orthodox religious practices, literacy in the Cyrillic alphabet, allegiance (real or suspected) to the Russian tsar, and other signs of Russian influence among the Native (including the Creole) population were attacked as vigorously by Protestant teachers and missionaries as indigenous languages and religions. Protestants alternately accused Russian Orthodox priests of focusing on empty ritual and not having done anything to convert the Natives in earnest and of exerting too much control over them (Dauenhauer 1996:84–85; Jacobs 1997:38–39). Charles Elliott, on an inspection of the Alaskan salmon fisheries, reported from Kodiak in 1899:

> The Indians are under the domination of the Russian Church, and the personality of the priest in charge determines to a considerable extent the condition of the Indians. The priest at Kadiak preaches sedition against the United

States, his influence being distinctly for evil. [. . .] The [U.S.] Government seems so remote to the Indians that it is not surprising they still look to Russia, through its clergy, for protection. (Elliott 1900:741)

In texts from the period after World War II, Cold War fears enter into the description of extremely brutal, drunken Russians invading the Aleutian chain in the eighteenth century, enslaving the defenseless Natives:

The cowed Aleuts never again found the courage to resist the Russians [after an uprising in 1764]. So thoroughly were these easy going people broken that they became but bondsmen, slaves, and concubines to the Russians as the Muscovites continued their expansion eastward along the coasts of Alaska. (Hulley 1958:61)

Such an attitude is not only anti-Russian (and usually accompanied by a failure to be equally critical of U.S. policies in the region) but also demeaning to the people who were supposedly so weak that they were "cowed" into absolute submission. Persisting Russian elements in Native cultures were seen as evidence of the destruction of former cultural purity, and the contribution of institutions such as the Orthodox Church to giving Native communities strength and resilience was seldom acknowledged.[1] This inability to imagine Russian heritage as part of a Native identity must have been part of the difficulty experienced by the woman observed by Pullar. Lydia Black, the scholar who contributed greatly to changing this image of Russian rule, responded in 1977 to claims that Native culture had disappeared owing to colonization:

It is true that in the course of the last two centuries Aleut culture has changed. Aleuts are predominantly members of the Orthodox branch of the Christian Church, are participants in the modern economic and political order, and have been *literate in their own language for over 150 years*. The Aleuts are concerned with their heritage; they take great pride in their literary legacy. As far as the alleged lack of interest in history is concerned, the problem may lie [. . .] among the investigators who look for the wrong kind of history—a history that is no longer pertinent to the Aleuts. (Black 1977a:95, emphasis in the original)

Lydia Black (1925–2007) has done much to provide scholars with a broader source base to assess the organization of Russian rule in Alaska and the interaction of Russians and Natives. She and colleagues such as Richard Pierce, Barbara Smith, Katherine Arndt, and Michael Oleksa have published translations from Russian sources and interpretations of research in Russian and U.S. archives. During the same period, the growing field of ethnohistory challenged the view of colonized people as victims in an inevitable process of acculturation by emphasizing the dynamics of mutual accommodation and the creative strategies with which the colonized protected and reshaped their own spheres of life (Berkhofer 1974:124–126). Historians of Russian America have also come to realize that mere brutal force would not have allowed the Russians to exploit such a large area, given the small numbers of Russians present in Alaska and their dependence on Native hunters (Gibson 1996). Much of the late-twentieth-century scholarship on the Russian period emphasizes peaceful coexistence, cultural exchange, and the contributions of benevolent individuals such as Saint Innocent, formerly Father Ioann Veniaminov, priest at Unalaska and Sitka, later bishop and Metropolitan.

In her last work on the history of Russian Alaska to appear during her lifetime, Lydia Black criticizes the first chief manager Aleksandr Baranov and other individual administrators but points out the beneficial effects of medical and educational facilities built by the RAC and the church. She uses the example of the Creole class to demonstrate the opportunities of social advancement for educated Natives and people from mixed families and stresses the ongoing veneration of Orthodox missionaries such as Saint Herman and Saint Innocent (Black 2004).

This positive image of Russian Alaska fits in with a growing fascination in scholarship and popular culture with hybrid, creolized histories created through intermarriage and social interaction in the contact zones of colonial empires, the globalizing economy and cyberspace culture (Brah and Coombes 2000). This current interest has made the histories of previously almost forgotten populations visible again, for instance that of the Alaskan Creoles or their Siberian counterparts (Vakhtin, Golovko, and Schweitzer 2004). Things become more problematic when some scholars use the current positive image of the Russian period, especially the alleged irrelevance of racial barriers and the use of Native languages in church services and education, as a positive contrast with later U.S. policies (Black 1990:153; Dauenhauer 1996; Oleksa 1987:20–25). Rather than going from the extreme of vilifying Russian rule in Alaska to the opposite extreme of glorifying it, the new accessibility of sources and possibilities for scholarly exchange across the Bering Strait may provide the opportunity to understand the Russian Empire and the late-nineteenth-century United States in their respective historical contexts. In this way, students of Alutiiq history could learn something about the ways in which people live through successions of social and economic changes, without having to decide which colonial period was better or worse than the other.

Ironically, some of the more idyllic pictures of the Russian period painted in current Anglophone scholarship echo the portrayals of Russians as benevolent partners rather than colonizers that became mandatory in Stalin's Soviet Union after a short period of more critical historiography in the 1920s and early 1930s. One of the benefits of the opening of borders to the former Soviet Union for ethnohistorical research on Alaska is the possibility to learn about the trajectory of research on Alaska carried out in the Russian language. Scholarship in Russia draws on different approaches and intellectual traditions and developed under other kinds of political pressure. Therefore, the perspectives of Russian and North American scholars complement each other's strengths and blind spots in important ways.

Views from Across the Bering Strait

The succession of leaders portrayed on the nesting dolls for sale in Alaska, and the very presence of their Russian sellers, can be read as additional signs of Alaska's colonial past and unique geographical position, but they simultaneously attest to the changes occurring in the postsoviet Russian Federation, changes that have given rise to a revision of scholarly perspectives on many aspects of Russian history. Since some of the most interesting scholarship on Russian Alaska is in Russian, and only parts of it are available in English translation, I introduce it at some length in this section.

In an article on tendencies in the historiography of the Russian colonization of Alaska, the Russian ethnohistorian Andrei Grinev (1994) divides Soviet scholarship on the topic into a prewar and a postwar period. The most important prerevolutionary work, Petr A. Tikhmenev's *History of the Russian-American Company*, which appeared in 1861, commissioned by the company to help in the negotiations to renew its imperial charter, is left out of Grinev's considerations (Bolkhovitinov 1997:7; Tikhmenev 1978 [1861]). Grinev characterizes prewar Soviet scholarship, exemplified by the work of Semën Okun', as using an "unmasking approach" (*oblichitel'nyi podkhod*), aiming to uncover the connection of the Russian colonization of Alaska to reactionary tsarist policies as well as to the interests of the rising Russian capitalist bourgeoisie. In the postwar period, the antagonism between the Soviet Union and the United States, as well as the need to justify the persistence of the Soviet empire in the face of liberation movements in colonies worldwide, led to an emphasis on positive consequences of Russian rule. Even Okun' already softens his generally negative representation of the activities of the Russian-American Company in his conclusion, when he mentions the civilizing role of Russia in the North Pacific:

Under its supervision a certain part of the native population received specialized knowledge. This region, thanks to the intensive trading activity of the
company, was connected to all progressive countries, to the whole industrial
world. (Okun' 1939:258)

In closing, Okun' stresses the lasting contributions of the Russian-American Company not only in the discoveries made in the North Pacific and its civilizing role but mainly in strengthening the Russian presence—and not so much
on the American shores of the Pacific but also on the Asian, on "those natural
borders where even now the USSR, the great Pacific power, vigilantly watches
over the vital interests of her peoples" (Okun' 1939:259).

With the general turn toward increased Russian nationalism under Stalin and the accompanying emphasis on the leading role of the Russians over
other Soviet nationalities (Slezkine 1994:303–309), studies of Russian activities in Alaska emphasized the "democratic" character of the Russian colonial
population, supposedly composed mainly of freedom-loving individuals flee-
ing from the oppression of Russian feudalism and entering into friendly relations with the local population. Russian colonialism was portrayed as more
"humane" and "progressive" than its Spanish or English counterparts; even the
word "colonization" (*kolonizatsiia*) disappeared from scholarly vocabulary in
favor of "appropriation" (*osvoenie*; for example Shunkov 1968). Conflicts with
Natives in Alaska were often blamed on British or American agitators (Grinev
1994:163–164). It is remarkable how close some aspects of this portrayal are
to the view promoted by some Anglophone Alaskanists today, namely, in the
emphasis on the Russians as the more humane power that did not oppress the
Natives but entered into fruitful exchange and brought them education and
contact with the outside world.

The positive portrayal of the Russian role in Alaska continued well after
Stalin's death. The complex analysis of the different groups involved on the Russian side—government, merchants, nobles, officers, employees—that made the
earlier work of Semën Okun' more than just a politically opportune indictment
of tsarist imperialism is replaced in A. I. Alekseev's *Sud'ba russkoi Ameriki*
(The Destiny of Russian America, 1975) by a summary indictment of the RAC
for merely being a "cover" for tsarist politics and capitalist expansion, after
which the author, having fulfilled the requirements of Marxist orthodoxy, goes
on to write a traditional history celebrating the achievements of the company's
upper-class leaders (Alekseev 1975:176, 321).

Grinev remarks that the political climate caused a divorce between historical and ethnographic studies of Alaskan materials. Many Soviet historians

avoided the subject of Russian-Native relations and focused on the organization of the RAC and its relations with other colonial powers, while many ethnographers scrutinized written sources and museum collections for the ethnographic information they provided, ignoring the historical context of contact with the Russians (Grinev 1994:164–165). However, like their U.S. colleagues, Soviet/Russian ethnographers have also published and interpreted sources that contain historical as well as ethnographic information (for example, Dridzo and Kinzhalov 1994; Dzeniskevich 1977; Liapunova 1977).

Concluding his review of the existing literature, Grinev calls for an "objective" portrayal of "the positive as well as the negative" traits of the colonial period and its dynamics, praising the work of Nikolai Bolkhovitinov, Svetlana Fedorova, and Aleksei Istomin in this respect (Grinev 1994:165). Writing such an objective history is also the explicit aim of the recent three-volume history of Russian America that appeared in Russia under the editorship of Nikolai Bolkhovitinov, a respected historian of Russian-American relations. Russian and American scholars, among them Grinev, contributed chapters to the three volumes that appeared in 1997 and 1999. In the words of the editor, it is intended to fill the need for a study incorporating the whole breadth of international scholarship, "free from fashionable tendentiousness" (Bolkhovitinov 1997:11).

These volumes present what is probably the richest collection of scholarship on Alaska's Russian period to date. At the same time, in their desire to avoid the pitfalls of ideologically inspired interpretations, the authors of individual chapters keep to a strictly chronological framework and assemble a wealth of data, while offering few interpretations of their findings. Most chapters create an event-centered narrative that says little about social conditions or cultural processes. But not all contributors seem to find it possible, or desirable, to leave their ideological commitments out of their interpretations. The closing words of Lydia Black's essay on the activities of the Russian Orthodox Church in Alaska in the first volume show her to be as openly Orthodox and pro-mission as any Soviet scholar could have been anti-tsarist and Marxist:

> And, when the Orthodox of Alaska gather at church, they remember all the monks of the first mission, but with special love and reverence our first saint, the humble Herman, who did not abandon his flock in his lifetime, and does not abandon it now. (Black 1997:277)

Though far removed from Lydia Black in ideological commitments, Andrei Grinev also shows in articles published outside the three-volume history that objectivity for him does not preclude a distinctive theoretical perspective. As we will see later, unlike some other post-Soviet scholars, he freely uses his own version of Marxist theory, incorporating his archival findings into an over-arching theory whose claims to universality many of his American colleagues might find discomforting, but that complements some of their own searches for explanations of the Alaskan colonial economy. If a theoretical or moral per-spective on history inevitably involves some "tendentiousness," the value of col-laboration between different groups of people interested in how the history of Alaska is told—Native and non-Native, inside and outside academia, working in different national traditions—may be that each group brings its own rules and assumptions, and is sensitized to different pitfalls.

Placing Village Histories in Context: Nuchek and Geography

One possible pitfall of an approach to Native history that attempts to address Native experiences of colonial encounters is an excessively localized focus, one that emphasizes the unique perspectives of whatever population is at the center of the analysis. A challenge for this book is to approach Alutiiq history through village sites and changes in settlement patterns while simultaneously placing these sites into a wider context that can be helpful to readers who know and care about the Alutiiq region as well as to those who need other reasons to be interested in its history. By using written sources on Alutiiq villages to address larger questions of comparative colonialism and the economic history of the circumpolar north, I hope to make these outside perspectives available for a variety of reading publics.

An incident related by Andrei Kashevarov, Orthodox psalmist in the Chugach village of Nuchek on Prince William Sound in the 1890s, shows that placing villages into larger contexts is never an innocent undertaking. At the same time, the anecdote suggests the complex web of local and translocal con-nections in which members of Alutiiq societies have participated for a long time. Kashevarov was born on Kodiak in 1863, into a Creole family long in-volved in Orthodox Church work. He spoke Alutiiq, Russian, and also English, which he learned when he attended a Russian Orthodox school in San Fran-cisco. Having worked for the church in the Sitka parish intermittently since 1980, he was transferred to Nuchek in 1893 as a punishment for marrying in a civil ceremony against the wishes of the parish priest and remained there until he was allowed to return to Sitka in 1900 (Kan 1999:353–355; Pierce 1990:215). Apart from leading church services, his duties included teaching in the Or-thodox parish school, the only school in Nuchek at the time. Reporting from his backwater parish to the dean of the Sitka district of the Alaskan diocese, Kashevarov writes that the parents of his students objected to his introduction

Chugach house in Nuchek, 1907–1909. The mixed log-and-sod building technique of this house, along with the more Europeanized wooden houses in the background, illustrate the mix of life-styles and economic pursuits in the village a few years after Andrei Kashevarov worked there. The wooden frame leaning against the right side of the house is intended for drying sealskin, suggesting the persistent importance of a local subsistence economy. *Courtesy of Alaska State Library, Ray W. Moss Collection, p11-227.*

of new subjects, namely, English (as a foreign language added to Russian) and geography:

> They tried to persuade their children not to study Geography, that it was of no use to them, that they were not going to measure the earth, that they were not going to be captains either, that they were just wasting their time for nothing. Luckily the children told me about this and I immediately tried to convince the people that it is very useful to study Geography, that there is not only Nuchek on earth, but many, many other places. At the same time I emphatically asked them not to interfere with my teaching, otherwise it would be better if there was no school at all. The teacher knows better what is necessary to learn and what is unnecessary. (ARCA D305/203: Andrei Kashevarov to Archimandrite Anatolii, Dean of the Sitka district, Nuchek, April 11, 1898)

This argument between teacher and parents seems to be about the usefulness of placing their village home into the kind of global world to which, as Russian historians claimed, Russian colonialism first introduced them. While the teacher interprets the parents' objections to geography as stubborn provincialism that insists that there is nothing beyond their little village, the objections of the parents, as he reports them, seem to focus on the connection of geographic knowledge with contexts that are inaccessible to Nuchek children anyway. The parents do not deny that there are surveyors or sea captains, but they do not imagine Nuchek people in such positions. Issues of unequal access, of the prestige of different forms of knowledge, and of authority over the children and their future have to be part of any discussion of the relation between an Alutiiq village and the outside world. At the same time, there are different levels of "outside" and "inside" in this story. Andrei Kashevarov, member of a prominent Kodiak Creole family, would be considered a member of the Native elite by today's standards but was a short-time sojourner in Nuchek. In this report to his Russian superior at least, he clearly portrays himself as different from the Chugach villagers, and less limited in his horizons.

On the background of such longstanding disdain for the expertise and capacities for self-governance of Native communities, the work that Natives and non-Natives are doing in the Alutiiq region to study and promote long-neglected local histories, local knowledge, and strategies of local development takes on special urgency. In addition to the projects and publications referred to already, much of the recent scholarship on the ethnohistory of the region, encompassing the Russian as well as the U.S. period, has focused on particular places and the resources people have used and continue to use there, and on the meaning these places and their histories have for elders and coming generations. Some of this information was generated in discussions over current and future use in National Parks or in connection with the clean-up after the Exxon Valdez oil spill (Cook and Norris 1998; Crowell and Mann 1998; Mobley et al. 1990; Morseth 1998). Other projects focus more on the preservation of cultural memory (Partnow 2001) and on mitigating the effects of being governed from far away by bringing information and objects back to rural Alaska. The *Looking Both Ways* exhibit temporarily returned objects that had been stored in Washington, D.C. for over a century, in order to begin to address the problem that people in Washington, Seattle, Berlin, and St. Petersburg can see more—and older—Alutiiq art than can people in Kodiak or Perryville. Village corporations gather the information on their past that is dispersed in remote archives or unknown languages. All these projects also involve considerable travel for various Alutiiq individuals. For marginalized and dispossessed communities, localization can mean asserting rights within the globalized world rather than withdrawing from it.[2]

At the same time, and even before such people as Andrei Kashevarov could travel to California for their education, Alutiiq villages have long been part of trading, raiding, and diplomatic networks that spanned the southern Alaskan coast, the Bering Strait region, and, with the advent of the Russians and later Anglo-Americans, the kind of global world that Kashevarov may have taught about in his geography classes. Given the entanglement of Alutiiq identity with their position at the crossroads of two colonial empires, scholarship on the last 250 years of Alutiiq history also needs a framework for comparing and contextualizing these two colonial periods, a framework that merely local perspectives cannot provide.

In his interpretation of excavations at the Three Saints Bay site, the historical archaeologist Aron Crowell works with approaches to the capitalist world-system developed by the economic historian Immanuel Wallerstein and the anthropologist Eric Wolf (Wallerstein 1974, 1989; Wolf 1982). Adapting Wallerstein's question of how the world-system of capitalist trade and production expanded to incorporate ever greater parts of the globe into its peripheries, Crowell investigates links between social hierarchies in the emerging colonial society and degrees of access to the goods of the world-system brought by the Russians. Excavation results confirmed Crowell's expectation that access to imported goods declined with lower status in the colonial hierarchy but also brought to light a general scarcity of imported goods for anyone who was not part of the Russian elite. Crowell links this finding to Russia's own semiperipheral position in the world-system dominated by the rapidly industrializing western Europe. As a semiperipheral power, Russia had difficulty providing its expanding trade networks with sufficient trade goods, and this fact is reflected in the archaeological record of Russian sites in Alaska (Crowell 1997:29, 232–233).

When it comes to comparing the Russian colonial economy with those of its British and American rivals, Crowell follows Eric Wolf in contrasting the Russian "tributary" extraction of fur from subjugated peoples with the market-driven fur trade of the Hudson's Bay and other companies in Canada. The problem with taking Eric Wolf as a guide for understanding Russian colonialism in Alaska is that he develops his model of tributary fur extraction with relation to Siberia, without taking into account that the legal and administrative situation was quite different in Alaska. As Crowell points out, the administration of Alaska was not based on tribute collected by the state, as in Siberia, but was assigned to a private, monopolistic company (Crowell 1997:10–16, 233; Wolf 1982:183–184).

In general, neither Wolf nor Wallerstein provides a sophisticated basis for understanding the Russian colonial empire, since both are interested in imperialism as a western European phenomenon spreading from Portugal and Spain via Holland to Britain and France in connection with the rise of capitalism. In this context, the vast but economically backward Russian empire appears either as a survival of older forms of empire-building or, notably in its new efforts of expansion in the second half of the nineteenth century, as a derivative form of western European imperialism. Wolf claims that the Pacific fur trade was taken over by the Americans, French, and British once the Aleutian sea otters were depleted in the late eighteenth century, ignoring the continuing Russian presence in Alaska up to 1867 (Wolf 1982:184), and Wallerstein has little to say about the Russian Empire after he declares European Russia incorporated into the European world-economy in the eighteenth century. Russia's autocratic political system and slow industrialization does indeed make it hard to compare to western European empires (Geyer 1973; 1977:13), as does the largely continental character of its expansion, where Alaska was the only overseas colony. But the latter factor may present an opportunity for comparison with another anomaly among empires, the continentally expanding United States (Kaplan 1993; Limerick 1987).

To make such a comparison fruitful, one must understand the political and economic traditions for dealing with Native populations that each colonial power brought to Alaska. On the question of politics and cultural knowledge, recent work on Russia as a multiethnic empire has argued that Russia had important distinctive features as a state premised on dynastic principles, whose agents were often more interested in collective loyalty to the tsar than in individual assimilation, but that Russian elites also asked themselves the same kinds of questions of how to place people on scales of savagery or civilization that animated the scientific and political endeavors of western imperial powers, including the United States (Kappeler 2001; Knight 1998; Slezkine 1994).

Concerning economics, Andrei Grinev, the Russian ethnohistorian whose review of the historiography of Russian America I cited earlier, has presented his own theory of the Russian empire as having been not a feudal state with a tributary economy but one characterized by a political and economic order Grinev calls "politarism"—something Karl Marx referred to as the Asiatic mode of production. In this social order the state apparatus itself, rather than a class of feudal or capitalist property holders, forms the exploiting class and exercises power through control over the redistribution of resources among the population (Grinev 1996, 2000; Luehrmann 2005). Although this theory at first sounds far removed from Alaskan history, it enables Grinev to propose an answer to the question raised by Crowell's excavations: how, given the scarcity of trade goods, were the Russians able to keep much of the Alutiiq population engaged in hunting sea otters for them? I will come back to Grinev's ideas in Chapter 3, when I address the question of the foundations of Russian colonial authority in the Alutiiq region, showing how the Russian historian's work provides an alternative to Wolf's idea of tributary and mercantile modes of fur extraction.

As far as the United States administration of Alaska is concerned, we will see that its early decades were characterized by a near-absence of government institutions and by unregulated economic competition, allowing for a coexistence of old and new institutions that sought to govern and reshape Alutiiq villages—for instance, Orthodox parish schools such as the one where Andrei Kashevarov taught and schools sponsored by the U.S. government but led by Protestant missionaries. Different from the dynastic Russian empire, the U.S. had no tradition of incorporating Native communities into its body politic as communities, which led to important differences in the meaning of the term "village" in each period that will be the topic of the last section of this chapter.

Villages and Communities

When this book uses the term "village" with reference to Alutiiq residential groups across historic time periods, readers should be aware that this term has different meanings in different sources. U.S. census records, which form an important source for Alutiiq history around the turn of the nineteenth and twentieth centuries, list people where the census taker finds them, even on ships, in hunting and prospecting camps or in bunkhouses for migrant workers (1900 census, hunting party from Kodiak Island and Afognak in steamers St Paul and Lydia; 1910 census, Red River Beach, Shelikoff Strait, Kodiak; 1910 census, Karluk Village and Cannery). A named village in these records is a collection of people who happen to be together in one place at a certain time.

The Russian records, by contrast, present lists of people who are supposed to reside permanently at a given place and have obligations to fulfill there, such as coming to confession regularly or helping to fill the village's quota for hunting expeditions. For instance, after a smallpox epidemic wiped out one third of the population of Kodiak Island in 1837–1838, the Russian American Company created seven consolidated villages for the survivors to move into. It also created an office of appointed village chief, one of whose responsibilities was to make sure no one left the village without permission. But it is difficult to say whether, and for how long, people lived together in these villages or whether some of them existed more for purposes of record keeping, while people spent most or all of the year at their accustomed sites. As a reverse side to possibly listing people at a place where they did not in fact live, Russian records leave out those who do not officially belong in a place, such as visitors or transient workers. Non-Orthodox residents of a settlement are included in confessional records up to 1867, because the church had to account for all Russian subjects, including Finnish and German Lutherans. After 1867 only those non-Orthodox residents married to Orthodox women appear in Orthodox church records (ARCA D414/265: Sitka parish confessional records, 1867; D261/180: Afognak parish confessional records, 1897).

These differences in definition of what a village is and who counts as a resident point not only to the different purposes for which statistics were collected but also to the different political traditions of the two countries. In feudal Russia, each person had his or her assigned place in a village or town, and mobility was subject to legal restrictions. The records of the RAC attest to its concern with controlling the movements of Russian and Alutiiq subjects. Village chiefs were ordered not to let anyone settle in the village from outside nor leave for any length of time without good reason, and everyone, at least in theory, needed permission from the Chief Manager's office to move from one post or island to another (RAC cs 20:78-78v, March 22, 1841; 16:57v, May 18, 1838; 16:174v, Oct 31, 1838, all to Kodiak office). In the United States, personal freedom of movement has been both a legal right and a part of national mythology, and a census that enumerates people wherever they happen to be seems to be an appropriate and practical form of record keeping for such a polity.

To what degree the villages recorded in either Russian or U.S. records corresponded to their residents' ideas of what a village was and who was part of it is a different issue. As I mentioned in the introduction, Alutiiq throughout the historic period practiced a system of seasonal migration between large, permanent winter villages and summer fish camps used by small kin groups. Early Russian observers also noted that several villages could have a common chief, and residents of such villages considered themselves to be of common descent, perhaps indicating processes in which villages split when the resources at one location could not support all residents (Davydov 1812:113). My general assumption is that Russian records represent the larger winter villages (cf. Clark 1987:107), whereas U.S. records, as noted above, sometimes list families at temporary camps or at cannery locations where they spent the summer fishing.

The question of what different meanings villages may have had to those who lived there and those who made statistical records of their populations leads to a larger question of the limits of written records as evidence of the history of people who largely did not write. This book does not take the route of putting contemporary Alutiiq accounts of their past alongside the perspectives of nineteenth-century Russians and Anglo-Americans, because, important as such work is in beginning to fill some of the gaps in scholarly debates resulting from current imbalances of power, I am not convinced that it solves the problem of the silence of dead generations of Alutiiq. One example of the dilemmas involved when living descendants are expected to speak for their ancestors is the debate about the appropriate form of reburial for the human remains returned to Larsen Bay from the Smithsonian Institution. Not all the people whose remains were returned had been Christians, but most of their descendants were, and many of them wanted a Christian burial service for their ancestors. For others, the presence of Orthodox priests at the ceremony was a further reminder of colonization (Bray and Killion 1994).

With all due respect for the project of recovering community-based ways of telling histories, my aim in this book is more modest and perhaps more conventional. I have used my Russian skills to present and interpret information contained in sources that, though available at several locations in Alaska on microfilm, are not easily accessible to Alutiiq and other present residents of South-Central Alaska. It is one of the ironic consequences of South Alaska's history of dual colonization that many of the richest written sources on Native history well into the U.S. period are in a language few contemporary residents of Alaska can understand. Recent scholarship has begun to use these sources not only for the Russian but also the U.S. period, when for several decades some of the closest observers of Native life were still the Russian Orthodox priests (Kan 1999; Znamenski 2003); but equivalent work has not been done for the Alutiiq region. I also use my training in Russian and U.S. history to suggest how the information from these sources may gain in richness when understood in a framework of imperial histories taking their momentum from places far away from Alaska.

Readers with greater local knowledge and a greater personal stake in its interpretation may find fault with my narrative, but, as James Clifford points out in a critical reading of *Looking Both Ways* and related projects, it may be deceptive to think that a single account, even a multivocal one, can harmonize perspectives that are uttered with conflicting aims and for conflicting reasons (Clifford 2004:19). It is worth keeping in mind that those few Russian observers who quote Alutiiq voices in reported speech tend to be those whose narrative is full of antagonism and sometimes disdain, such as psalmist-teacher Andrei Kashevarov and Gavriil Davydov, a naval officer whose work I will use later on. Both quote Alutiiq speakers as adversaries in disputes, whereas more benevolent observers describe their plight but have them remain silent.

Reading Alaskan colonial archives offers, then, no escape from Euro-American traditions of writing history, but it does offer a more complex view of what that history was, and what possibilities of interaction and transformation it held for all concerned. It is to such a reading of archives that I turn in the remaining chapters, trusting in the openness of maps, quotes, and bits of data, like souvenirs, to accommodate many meanings and serve many purposes.

ENDNOTES

1. For a relatively early example of ethnographic work recognizing the importance of the Orthodox Church among the Alutiiq, see Rathburn 1981.

2. See Fienup-Riordan 2005 for an example involving Yup'ik elders traveling all the way to Germany to bring knowledge about museum collections back to the descendants of those who made the objects.

2

Village Locations and Colonial History: Map Essays

Maps are a powerful medium for focusing on particular places while simultaneously placing them in larger contexts. Maps of the Alutiiq region, such as those in this book, cut out and enlarge an area that occupies a very marginal position on most world or continental maps, owing to its proximity to the North Pole and its position at the far western edge of America, a cut-off point for those world maps that place Europe in the center. This enlarged fragment can center attention on the area inhabited by the people who came to be known as Alutiiq. At this scale, Kodiak Island forms the center of regional activities of trade, hunting, colonial administration, and education. The Alaska Peninsula, Kenai and Prince William Sound take a peripheral position relative to it.

But even this fragment of a world map, try as it may to make central what the map usually marginalizes, is designed to be intelligible to people who can place it within the whole map in their heads. Regional maps may perhaps induce viewers to look at the world map in a different way: a map of Russian expansion into Alaska and California challenges the East-West direction that many North Americans associate with the conquest of North America; maps of subsistence territories may be used by those who are threatened with dispossession to mark and assert their own claims and set limits to outsiders' dreams of conquest (Brody 1988). The maps in this chapter, for their part, are designed to make visible and accessible the information that is contained in the historic maps and records compiled by Russian and American visitors and administrators. Chronologically, they cover shorter intervals than those included in the *Looking Both Ways* exhibit, based on the same research (published in Crowell and Luehrmann 2001:Figs. 51, 64).

For reasons connected to their interest in the natural and human resources of the region, civilian and church institutions kept lists of village names and population figures as an important part of their records. This chapter asks what these lists and historical maps can tell us about the impact of successive colonizations on the ways in which Alutiiq lived together, the places where they lived, and the means of subsistence they had at their disposal. Especially for the early decades of the nineteenth century, deducing information from sparse records involves much conjecture, and large parts of the sections devoted to the first three maps are taken up by discussions of the evidence that led me to identify a village name in a record with a certain location. Readers who do not appreciate this look inside the historian's craft will find easier reading from mid-century (section accompanying Map 4) onward, where a more plentiful source base makes for a livelier narrative focusing on the economic, epidemiological, and political factors that caused Alutiiq to move their villages, rather than on the locations themselves.

The maps in this chapter seek neither to make Alutiiq sole builders of their unique history nor to portray them as victims of the expansion of Russian and U.S. spheres of influence into their territory. Rather, they tell a hybrid story of a succession of encounters that had very destructive consequences—disease and population decline will be a constant theme, as well as dangerous and exploitative working conditions—but that also created new patterns of life and new groups of people living together.

Map 1. Kodiak Island in 1805: Center of a Periphery

The first decade of the nineteenth century is the earliest period in Kodiak Island's career as center of the Alaskan periphery of the Russian Empire for which Russian accounts provide detailed geographical information.[1] The first Russian map of the archipelago to show a significant number of named Alutiiq villages was drawn by IUrii Lisianskii in 1805 (Lisianskii 1812).[2] Lisianskii came to Kodiak on a round-the-world expedition under the command of Adam von Krusenstern, sponsored by the Russian government as part of the effort to establish and secure a far-flung empire. Russia's claim to its share of the sea otter trade and to scientific and military authority over the Pacific region had to withstand competition from the French, British, and Spanish expeditions under La Pérouse, Cook, and Malaspina, and the remoteness of the Alaskan possessions inspired a search for a sailing route quicker than shipping supplies overland across Siberia to Okhotsk and from there to Alaska (Gibson 1976:51–52; Khisamutdinov 1993:25; Vinkovetsky 2001).

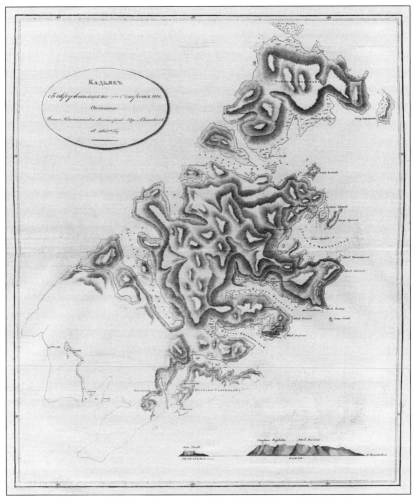

IUrii Lisianskii's map of Kodiak and surrounding islands, 1805 (Lisianskii 1812). *Courtesy of Alaska and Polar Regions Collections, Elmer E. Rasmuson Library, University of Alaska, Fairbanks.*

At the time, the Russian tsar claimed sovereignty over Alaska, but the colony was not governed by imperial officials. Instead, the Russian-American Company (RAC), a private joint-stock company, held the exclusive privilege to hunt furbearing animals, utilize natural resources, found settlements, and conduct explorations along the American coast north of fifty-five degrees latitude for a period of twenty years, granted by an imperial decree of 1799 (Dmytryshyn, Crownhart-Vaughan, and Vaughan 1989:18–23). With this arrangement the

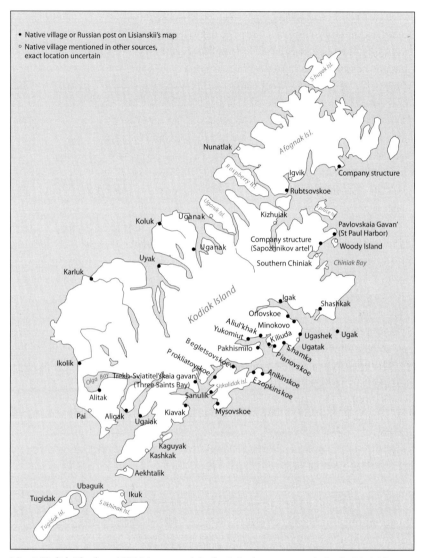

• Native village or Russian post on Lisianskii's map
○ Native village mentioned in other sources, exact location uncertain

S'huyok Isl.

Afognak Isl.

Nunatlak

Raspberry Isl.

Igvik

Company structure

Rubtsovskoe

Koluk

Uganak

Uganik Isl.

Kizhujak

S'pruce Isl.

Pavlovskaia Gavan' (St Paul Harbor)

Company structure (Sapozhnikov artel')

Woody Island

Uganak

Uyak

Southern Chiniak

Chiniak Bay

Karluk

Kodiak Island

Igak

Shashkak

Orlovskoe

Minokovo

Aliul'khak

Yukomiut

Kiliuda

Ugashek

Ugak

Begletsovskoe

Pakhismilo

Shamka

Ugatak

Prokliatovskoe

Pianovskoe

Ikolik

Olga Bay

Trekh-Sviatitel'skaia gavan' (Three Saints Bay)

Anikinskoe

Sitkalidak Isl.

Ezopkinskoe

Alitak

Sanulik

Pai

Aligak

Ugaiak

Kiavak

Mysovskoe

Kaguyak

Kashkak

Aekhtalik

Ubaguik

Ikuk

Tugidak

Sitkhinak Isl.

Tugidak Isl.

Map 1. Kodiak Island, ca. 1805. Map research by Sonja Luehrmann, map design by Mark Matson.

competition between several companies for the exploitation of Alaska was settled to the advantage of the heirs of Grigorii Shelikhov, the man who had established the first permanent Russian post on Kodiak at Trekh-Sviatitel'skaia gavan' (Harbor of the Three Prelates, modern Three Saints Bay) in 1784.

For the imperial government, the administration of overseas territories by a private company was an attractive alternative to integrating Alaska into the political structure of the Russian empire, as had been done with Siberia: it was both cheaper to do and a less direct challenge to other powers with pretensions in the North Pacific, namely, the United States and Britain (Dmytryshyn, Crownhart-Vaughan, and Vaughan 1988:356–358; Okun' 1939:19–29; Pierce 1990:454–455). Indirect rule through a chartered company was also in conformity with the practices of the western European colonial powers, which members of the Russian elite were trying to emulate in their drive for modernization—the Dutch East India Company and the British Hudson's Bay Company were also private trading companies carrying out administrative functions in overseas colonial ventures (Vinkovetsky 2004).

When Lisianskii arrived in Alaska in the summer of 1804, Pavlovskaia gavan' (St. Paul Harbor, modern Kodiak City) on Kodiak Island, where the RAC headquarters had moved in 1793 after two earthquakes had demonstrated that Three Saints Bay was unsafe, was just losing its status as colonial capital to Novoarkhangel'sk (Sitka) in Tlingit territory. Lisianskii assisted in the move but also spent considerable time on Kodiak (Lisianskii 1947:142–143). His map (Lisianskii 1812) is especially rich in detail for the southeast coast of the island, which he visited in March/April 1805 on a round trip between St. Paul Harbor and Three Saints Bay. Map 1 presents the information from his map with some additions from other sources.

Donald Clark has compared Lisianskii's map and travel account with archaeological information on Alutiiq village sites and was able to identify many of the locations shown on the map with sites that had probably been occupied continuously from pre-Russian times (Clark 1987; Lisianskii 1947:165–175). Nineteenth-century accounts document a seasonal pattern of movement between settlement sites: there were large winter villages of semisubterranean, sod-roofed houses (*ciqluaq* in Alutiiq, called *barabara* by the Russians) with a central room for cooking and storage and attached sleeping compartments for individual families (*zhupan*). In the spring their inhabitants spread out to various sealing and fishing camps. Some of these camps consisted of a single *barabara*; at other sites people lived in tents (Davydov 1977:154–155; Erlandson et al. 1992:45). Given the season of Lisianskii's trip and his description of villages with several *barabaras*, Clark concludes that he encountered the population in their winter villages, before they left for the summer camps.

Comparing the villages shown on the map with archaeological sites from the late precontact period, Clark finds that, at least for the southeastern part of the island, settlement patterns had not changed much during the first decades of Russian presence. The sparse indications of settlements along the west coast raise some questions. Did Lisianskii, not having visited this area personally, simply lack information, or was the western part so much less populated during this period (Clark 1987:107, 121, 124)? There is some evidence that Lisianskii may have been quite well informed about the geography of at least some parts of the west coast. On Uyak Bay, where there are several large precontact village sites, the only site that has yielded Russian-era artifacts is a small settlement at the northern tip of the peninsula that shields off the bay to the east. Lisianskii shows Uyak village precisely at that location (Dumond 1994:47). In general, although there are many late precontact sites on the west coast, archaeological evidence indicates that the southeastern coast tended to be more densely inhabited, probably because of its proximity to sea mammal migration routes. This would mean that on the west coast as well, the settlement patterns of Lisianskii's time continued trends from before the arrival of the Russians (Crowell and Luehrmann 2001:Fig. 20; Richard Knecht, personal communication, November 2006).

Additional sources do not significantly alter the picture provided by Lisianskii. The naval officer Gavriil Davydov, who spent the winter 1802/1803 on Kodiak, mentions visiting at least three Native villages not indicated on Lisianskii's map: a village on Woody Island, opposite St. Paul Harbor (Davydov 1810:208), a "Southern Chiniak village" on Chiniak Bay[3] (1810:218), and Kizhuyak (*Kizhuetskoe*) on the bay of the same name (1810:213). Cape Chiniak, later the site of a Creole settlement, is described as uninhabited by Davydov (1810: 235). On Uganik Bay he seems to refer to two villages, one on the shore of the bay and one on Uganik Island, both inhabited in March 1803 (1810:222–223). Aiakhtalik, on the island of the same name, is described as a populous village at the time of Russian arrival and a good location for sea otter hunting by Georg Heinrich von Langsdorff and Gedeon, a monk from Alexander Nevskii Monastery in St. Petersburg who came to Kodiak together with Lisianskii's expedition and stayed until 1807 to take charge of the Orthodox mission in Alaska. From one of Gedeon's letters written in 1805, we also know of a village called Ubaguik on Sitkhinak Island off the south coast of Kodiak (Gedeon 1994:67, 86; Holmberg 1856:412).

Langsdorff, physician on Krusenstern's ship, quotes lists of villages compiled by the RAC in 1795 and 1804. They contain a number of names that do not appear on Lisianskii's map (see Table 1). Some of them may be Alutiiq terms for eastern villages that have Russian names on the map (such as Pianovskoe, Mysovskoe, and Prokliatovskoe).[4] Others may refer to locations that were abandoned by the time of Lisianskii's visit. But there are two additional names from Langsdorff's lists that recur in later Russian records. One of them is Kaguik in the southern part of Kodiak, which may be the Kaguyak (see Map 2) of later records, the other one is Pai, which reappears repeatedly in pre-1840 Russian records as Paiskoe or Piaiskoe but is not indicated on any maps. A Pai River is shown by Bocharov and Izmailov on the southwest shore of Kodiak Island, west of Cape Alitak, apparently referring to what is known today as Sukhoi Lagoon. This location would fit in with the fact that survivors from Paiskoe moved to Akhiok after the 1837 smallpox epidemic (VS E27, Kodiak 1832, baptisms; ARCA D255/175, Kodiak parish confessional records, 1844; Efimov 1964:Map 178; Langsdorff 1812:53–54).

With a possible second village in Uganik Bay, and Pai on the southwest shore, these sources do not add any significant number of villages on the western side to Lisianskii's account. It is possible that smaller west coast villages escaped the notice of early Russian observers. Russians also prized the rich maritime resources of the east coast and concentrated their activities there. Of those places Lisianskii labels "company structure"[5] or that are known to be Russian posts through other sources—St. Paul Harbor, Igak, possibly Minokovo,[6] Three Saints Bay, Alitak or Aligak, Karluk, and Rubtsovskoe—only Karluk is on the west coast of the island. Although it may well be that Russian knowledge of some parts of the archipelago was less than complete in the early nineteenth century, overall it seems that the east coast was indeed more densely settled at the beginning of the nineteenth century, whatever the prior demographic situation may have been.

Turning to Afognak Island, an attempt to combine information from different sources creates some riddles. Lisianskii's map suggests that Rubtsovskoe is the main Russian post. However, if the 1786 map reproduced by Lydia Black (1991:175, Figure 4b) is correct, the post founded on Afognak Island on Shelikhov's orders in 1785 or 1786 may have been located further to the north, perhaps in the vicinity of Cape Izhut, at the site of Lisianskii's "company structure." Davydov, who visited Kodiak two years before Lisianskii, distinguishes *Rubtsova odinochka*, inhabited by just one Russian and several *kaiury* (slaves), from the "main *artel*" (workstation, post) located 16 verst (approximately 10 miles) from the former and manned by eight or ten Russians and many *kaiury* engaged in catching and drying halibut. Elsewhere, he says that there are two *arteli* on Afognak, Igvetsk or Afognak and Malinovskoe (Davydov 1810:233, 220; 1977:192). If Igvetsk is the "main *artel*," it may correspond to the location of the "company structure" at Cape Izhut, the later site of Little Afognak.

Contemporary Afognak elders interviewed by archaeologists identify the name Igwik with that location, although others remember Igvak as the name of

Table 1 Correspondences Among Village Names in Nineteenth-Century Sources

RAC lists quoted by Langsdorff (1794 and 1805)	Lisianskii map[i] (1805)	1820 confessional records quoted by Prisadskii	1832 vital statistics	1849 consolidated villages	1880 census
On Kodiak Island:					
Uganak	Uganak	Uganok	Uganak		Ooganak North & South
	Uiak	Uiak	Uiak		Ooiak
	Koluk				
Karluk	Karluk	Karluk	Karluk	Karluk	Karluk
Askolik	Ikolik	Aiakolik	Aiakolik		
Pai		Piai	Pai		
Alitok	Alitak	Alitak	Alitak		
Ischiok		Akhiok	Akhiok	Akhiok	Akhiok
	Aligak				
	Ugaiak				
Kaschkack		Kashkak	Kashkak		
Kaguik		Kaguiak	Kaguiak		Kaguiak
Kijawik	Kiavak	Kiiavik	Kiiavik		
	Three Saints Bay		Three Saints Bay	Three Saints Bay	Three Saints Bay
	Pakhismilo				
	Yukomiut				
Aduguak	Aliul'khak[ii]				
Kilüda	Kiliuda	Kiliuda	Kiliuda		
	Pianovskoe				
	Shamka				
Ugatak		Ugatak	Ugatak		
Ugashik	Ugashek				
	Minokovo				
	Orlovskoe			Orlovskoe	Orlovsk
Igak	Igak	Igak	Igak		
Scheschkak	Shashkak		Shashkak		
		Sredniaia odinochka			
		Kal'sivskaia odinochka			
Kischujok		Kizhuiak	Kizhuiak		
Unknown location:[iii]					
Schettak					
Itnak					
Ak					

See table notes on page 30.

RAC lists quoted by Langsdorff (1794 and 1805)	Lisianskii map (1805)	1820 confessional records quoted by Prisadskii	1832 vital statistics	1849 consolidated villages	1880 census
Unknown location (continued):					
Nukalik					
Tschukak					
Naschkukak					
Kaschilok					
Taüchtalik					
Schaschkachok					
		Pesiutniakovskoe			
		Nezamaika			
On Afognak:					
Naschkuchalik				Afognak	Afognak
	Rubtsovskoe		Rubtsovskoe		
Igwik		Afognak	Afognak[iv]		
Nunatlak			Malinovskoe		
On Spruce Island:					
	village on Narrow Strait				Oozinkie
	Elovskoe				Spruce Island
On Woody Island:					
Tschiniak		Chiniiak	Chiniiak	Woody Island	Wood Island
On Ugak Island:					
Ugak		Ugakskoe	Ugak		
On Sitkalidak Island:					
	Anikinskoe	Anikinskoe	Anikinskoe		
	Ezopkinskoe	Ezopninskoe	Ezopkinskoe		
	Begletsovskoe	Begletsovskoe	Begletsovskoe		
	Prokliatovskoe	Prokliatovskoe	Prokliatovskoe		
Schanulik	Sanulik	Sapulik	Sanulik		
	Mysovskoe	Mysovskoe	Mysovskoe		
		Razbitovskoe	Razbitovskoe		
		Kolpakovskoe	Kolpakovskoe		
On Aiaktalik Island:					
Agajachtalik		Aekhtalik	Aiakhtalik	Aekhtalik	Ayakhtalik
On Sitkhinak Island:					
Ikuk		Sitkhinskoe	Sitkhinak		
Ubaguik		Ubachvig	Ubagvik		
On Tugidak Island:					
Tukhidok		Tugidak	Tugidak		

Table 1 Correspondences between village names in nineteenth-century sources: notes

[i]Except in the case of Slavic place names, I leave out the –skoe or –tskoe endings that Lisianskii and the Russian confessional records add to most Alutiiq place names (see note 8 in this chapter).

[ii]The correspondence between these two names is uncertain.

[iii]Some of these unidentified names from Langsdorff's lists may correspond to Russianized names on Lisianskii's map, for instance to villages on Sitkalidak Island.

[iv]Woodhouse-Beyer (2001: 77) concludes from her excavations that the main Russian post on Afognak Island was located on the north side of Afognak Bay up to the late 1830s, when it was moved to the later site of Afognak village in the wake of the smallpox epidemic. Since Russian sources which mention an Alutiiq village named Afognak do not specify where it was located at any given time, I follow her in assuming a shift of location in the 1830s.

---

a site across the bay from Afognak village, where excavations led by Katharine Woodhouse-Beyer located the site of a late-eighteenth century Russian *artel'*. The RAC lists quoted by Langsdorff show three Alutiiq villages on Afognak— Nunatliak, Igwik, and Naschkuchalik (Langsdorff 1812:53). Nunatliak, reportedly the biggest of the three, may be the same as Malinovskoe (Davydov gives Nunuliak as the Alutiiq name for Malinovskoe). Igwik, as we have seen, may either correspond to Little Afognak or the *artel'* site on the north side of Afognak Bay. Naschkuchalik or Nashqualek, according to the same elders interviewed by archaeologists, refers to the site of Rubtsovskoe, and is obviously the name of a Native village next to the Russian post (Woodhouse-Beyer 2001:60, 68).

Whereas the distribution of the population across the Kodiak archipelago may not have changed much over the first decades of Russian presence, Russian sources point to a sharp decline in population numbers. Lisianskii estimates the Native population at 4,000 men, women and children, adding that the old people say that it was twice as much before the arrival of the Russians. Langsdorff's lists give the population as 6,519 in 1795, and 4,834 in 1804. Exact population figures for the time prior to Russian arrival are unknown, but if the number of pre-Russian village sites is compared with those indicated by Lisianskii, the population loss looks even greater. It is possible that contagious disease set off this decline even before the physical arrival of the Russians (Erlandson et al. 1992:53; Lisianskii 1947:178).[7]

In other ways as well, Russian rule had already begun to affect Alutiiq life by the time of Lisianskii's visit. Free men and women were drafted for compulsory service in sea otter hunting, food procurement, and production of tools and clothing, and the slaves whom wealthy families had kept before the arrival of the Russians had been expropriated (Davydov 1977:114, 190–191). Since the

Tlingit inhabiting the environs of the new capital of Novoarkhangel'sk were too strong militarily to be pressed into similar services, Russians continued to rely on Alutiiq and Unangan labor—and even on their fighting strength for protection against the Tlingit—even as their main hunting grounds shifted to Southeast Alaska (Gibson 1996:27, 1998:71). For this reason, St. Paul Harbor remained central to RAC operations as the place from which hunting parties were dispatched and where furs were collected. Other Russian posts (*arteli*, *odinochki*) strewn about the archipelago were a new kind of human habitation in addition to Alutiiq summer fish camps, which continued to be used. In each *artel'* one or more RAC employees lived among a group of slaves and hired Alutiiq workers and supervised their work. These posts served the dual purpose of organizing hunting parties and gathering and processing food stores for the colony (Fedorova 1971).

Among the outlying posts, Karluk with its rich salmon run was especially important for the production of *iukola* (dried fish)—twenty men and eighteen women lived there year-round during Gedeon's time, and more women came from other villages during the salmon season. At Igak, Three Saints Bay, and Alitak whale and seal blubber was rendered in blubbering stations. Simple Russian hunters lived mainly on local food such as seal and whale meat and fish, but for its higher-level employees the RAC made efforts to recreate the Russian lifestyle and diet. For this purpose, company employees experimented with cattle raising and horticulture at the Sapozhnikov *artel'* (Crowell 1997:214; Gedeon 1989:36–39; Langsdorff 1812:64).

Map 2. Kodiak Island in 1830: Records to Supplement the Maps

Orthodox Church confessional records and vital statistics contain information on village names and population figures, but the earliest records preserved in the archival collection, from the 1820s and 1830s, often seem to list only the Russian inhabitants of the island and those Alutiiq who lived at Russian posts. The Alutiiq population of the island was not fully baptized until the 1840s, making church records spotty at best (RAC cs 17:14v–15, Feb 20, 1839, to Kodiak office; Mitropolit Innokentii 1888:371). A century later, a priest publishing in the *Russian Orthodox American Messenger,* referring to a document not preserved in the collections of the National Archives, quotes the names of thirty-seven villages belonging to the Kodiak parish from the 1820 confessional records (Prisadskii 1939:76).

I reproduce this list of villages in the third column of Table 1. As the table shows, most of the names can be identified with places on Lisianskii's

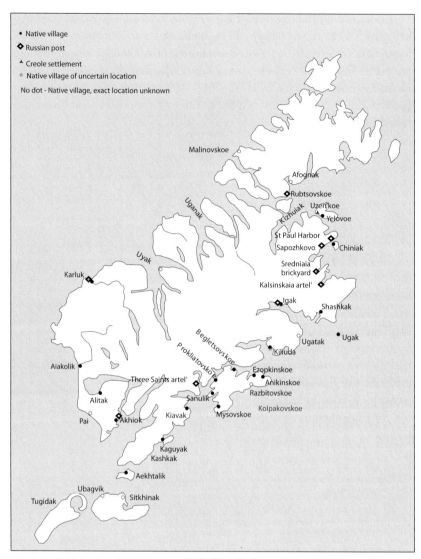

• Native village
◆ Russian post
▲ Creole settlement
○ Native village of uncertain location
No dot - Native village, exact location unknown

Malinovskoe

Afognak

◆Rubtsovskoe

Uzen'koe

Kizhuiak

Yelovoe

Uganak

St Paul Harbor

Sapozhkovo ◆ ○Chiniak

Uyak

Sredniaia
brickyard ◆

Karluk ◆

Kalsinskaia artel' ◆

◆Igak

Shashkak

• Ugak

Ugatak

Begletsovskoe

Kiluda

Prokliatovskoe

Aiakolik •

Ezopkinskoe

Three Saints artel'

Anikinskoe

Razbitovskoe

Alitak

Sanulik

Kolpakovskoe

Pai

◆Akhiok

Kiavak

Mysovskoe

Kaguyak

Kashkak

•Aekhtalik

Ubagvik

Tugidak

○ Sitkhinak

Map 2. Kodiak Island, ca. 1830. Map research by Sonja Luehrmann, map design by Mark Matson.

map. Two names from the list not included in the table are Kanikhliukskoe and Tkhatilikskoe,[8] probably corresponding to Kiniklik and Tatitlak on Prince William Sound (see Map 3), an area apparently considered part of the Kodiak parish at that time. Sredniaia and Kal'si[n]skaia odinochka are Russian posts on Chiniak Bay (Liapunova and Fedorova 1979:240, 247). Ugatak may be located near the Ugashek on Lisianskii's map, judging from a 1784 map by Bocharov and Izmailov (Efimov 1964:Map 178), which shows the mouth of the Ugatak River close to that location. Although it might seem that Ugaschik and Ugatak are merely two versions of the same name, Langsdorff lists both (1812:54). Kashkak is mentioned in the 1832 vital statistics. That year, Father Frumentii Mordovskii from Kodiak visited it on the way between Kiiavik/Kiavak and Kaguyak, indicating that it was located in the southwestern part of the island (VS E27, Kodiak, baptisms).

Kolpakovskoe and Razbitovskoe are probably villages on Sitkalidak Island, although Lisianskii does not show them on his map. The former is always mentioned in connection with other villages on this small island off the southeast coast of Kodiak; the latter is obviously located close to a fortified refuge rock that had been the site of a decisive defeat of the local inhabitants by Shelikhov's men in 1784, and for which Bocharov and Izmailov recorded the name *Razbitoi kekur* (Broken/Crushed Rock, Crowell 1997:46). Archaeological evidence confirms that there was a village close to the site up to the mid-nineteenth century, although Holmberg was told in 1851 that no one had lived on the rock since the battle (Holmberg 1856:417; Knecht, Haakanson, and Dickson 2003; Richard Knecht, personal communication, November 2006).[9]

I place Chiniak on Woody Island because maps from the 1850s call the village there Chiniak/Tschinjagmjut, and the 1850 confessional records list "Chiniiak on Woody Island" (*Chiniiak na ostrove lesnom*, ARCA D255/176: Kodiak parish confessional records, 1850; Holmberg 1855; Teben'kov 1981 [1852]). By the end of the nineteenth century, Chiniak was the name of a village on Cape Chiniak (Petroff 1884), but this was a Creole settlement founded later (see Map 4). The name Chiniak recurs at various places because it is the Russian form of the Alutiiq word for cape, *cingiyaq* (Gordon Pullar, personal communication, August 1999).

All names mentioned by Prisadskii reappear in the 1832 vital statistics, with the exception of Pesiutniakovskoe and Nezamaika—place names I have not been able to find anywhere else—and Uzen'koe and Elovskoe, two villages on Spruce (*Elovyi*) Island. An 1839 map of *Uzen'kii* (Narrow) Strait (Anonymous 1839) shows two settlements close to each other, one called zhilo Terent'eva, the other zhilo Skvortsova, probably the names of Creole families (Russian *zhilo*—dwelling place). Alutiiq from Elov[sk]oe are mentioned in the 1826 vital statistics (VS E27, Kodiak, baptisms 1826). On this evidence, the map identifies Elovoe as an Alutiiq village and Uzen'koe as a Creole village, as it was later, although there is no concrete evidence that there were Creole settlers on the island as early as 1830 (see the text for Map 4).

A village listed in the 1832 vital statistics but not mentioned by Prisadskii is Malinovskoe. The vital statistics of 1826 and 1832 mention Alutiiq from Malinovskoe, some in company employment, being baptized at the church in St. Paul Harbor. I identify this village with Nunatlak on Afognak (see Map 1) rather than with the *odinochka* on Raspberry (*Malinovyi*) Island, which Teben'kov shows in his 1852 atlas, because there is no mention in Russian sources of a Native village on that island.

Comparing Lisianskii's map with the information from the 1820s and early 1830s, one can say that no great changes in settlement patterns occurred. Some villages are no longer mentioned, most notably several on Kiliuda Bay, but since even a combination of all the names mentioned in Russian sources for that time never adds up to the 65 villages that existed prior to the 1837 smallpox epidemic according to RAC sources (RAC cs 22:233, May 10, 1843, to Main Office; Tikhmenev 1978 [1861]:200), it seems likely that some of the places shown by Lisianskii still existed at the time as small, perhaps seasonal, villages but were overlooked by Russian priests or subsumed under other village names. By now, it is no longer likely that Russian ignorance of the region could be the reason why the northwest seems less densely inhabited than the southeast. During the 1837 smallpox epidemic, the medic sent to the northwest side of the island finished his tour in two months, whereas the one in charge of the southeast took twice as long to visit all villages (RAC cs 15, 249, May 1, 1838, to Main Office).

Left out from this map are the communities of Kodiak Alutiiq that had been created by the RAC at increasingly remote places: Katmai on the Alaska Peninsula, founded in 1786 and manned in part by people relocated from Kodiak (Morseth 1998:37); Ukamok on what is now Chirikof Island, where Alutiiq men and RAC employees hunted sea otters and ground squirrels (Liapunova and Fedorova 1979:46); Novoarkhangel'sk (present-day Sitka), which was conquered and built with the help of Alutiiq manpower and where 146 male "Kad'iak Aleuts" were living in 1825, and a large percentage of the women must have been from Kodiak as well (Khlebnikov 1994:69); Fort Ross in California, maintained for hunting and agriculture from 1812 to 1841, whose population of 260 men and women was about half Alutiiq in 1820 (Istomin 1992:9); and Urup Island in the Kurile chain, where 49 Kodiak Islanders and 12 Russians were sent for sea otter hunting in 1828, and some stayed on beyond the sale of Alaska to the United States in 1867 (Shubin 1992:63–65). At all these places, Alutiiq from Kodiak were more numerous than Unangan from the Aleutians. The latter were resettled in considerable numbers to the Pribilof and the Commander Islands and also, especially in the early years of RAC activities in the area, to Kodiak (Liapunova 1987:102–103).

In its recruitment of Alutiiq workers and hunters for long-distance assignments, the RAC drew heavily on east coast villages. In vital statistics of the 1830s and 1840s, the villages on Sitkalidak Island and the southeast of Kodiak, along with Chiniak, are the ones most commonly named as villages of origin of people in company service at St. Paul Harbor, Afognak, Novoarkhangel'sk, and Fort Ross (VS E27, Kodiak; VS E72, Sitka; Osborn 1997:389–407). This does not mean that people from the west coast of the island were free from labor for the company—they worked out of Karluk in hunting or *iukola*-production, and people from Karluk may have manned the posts at Katmai and Sutkhum.

To summarize the picture emerging from Russian records of the 1820s and 30s, they indicate a situation in which the RAC's knowledge of Alutiiq settlements and ability to demand Alutiiq labor power for company business extended through the whole archipelago. At the same time, the fluctuating, but overall stable, number of village names, as well as the sporadic nature of the surviving records, indicate that the Russians as yet lacked power to change Alutiiq settlement patterns. The population continued to live spread out over numerous villages whose locations probably changed with the seasons and that were difficult for the Russians to keep track of. Surviving church records from this period contain lists of villages visited by the Kodiak priest on his tour of the island and the names of people who were baptized, married, or buried by the priest but not the comprehensive lists of inhabitants that the church kept in later years (see Chapter 5). The priests rarely ventured on tours as extensive as the one taken by Father Mordovskii in 1832, so that many villages must have remained without contact with Russian clergy for years at a time. Among the inhabitants of such villages, only men who participated in hunting parties or those who visited Russian posts had personal contact with Russians. Population decline through Russian-introduced diseases and the absence of significant numbers of male hunters for months and sometimes years must have forced Alutiiq to reshape their village life, but direct Russian influence on their community affairs remained limited.

Map 3. The Alutiiq Region in 1850: A Wider Picture

The RAC never had as strong a presence on the mainland as on Kodiak Island and the Aleutians. Indeed, its concentration on the maritime fur hunt and reliance on the labor power of sedentary island populations that were relatively easy to control may have constituted its decisive advantage over rivals such as the more land-based Lebedev-Lastochkin Company in the struggle for dominance and, eventually, monopoly. Accordingly, information on Alutiiq villages

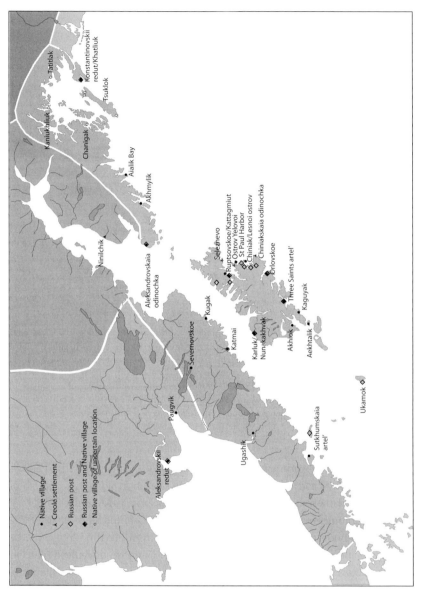

Map 3. Alutiiq Region, ca. 1850. Map research by Sonja Luehrmann, map design by Mark Matson, reproduced courtesy of Smithsonian Arctic Studies Center.

outside Kodiak Island is relatively scarce in Russian-era sources. Some Chugach hunted for the company out of Konstantinovskii redut on Nuchek (Hinchinbrook) Island, founded in 1793 by the Lebedev-Lastochkin Company and taken over by Shelikhov's men in 1797, and at Aleksandrovskaia odinochka (English

Bay/Nanwalek), founded on Shelikhov's orders in 1786. A shipyard had existed at Voskresenskaia gavan' (Resurrection Bay, at the present location of Seward, not shown on the map) from 1793 until the early nineteenth century, but the company later moved its shipbuilding operations to Novoarkhangel'sk. There is no mention of a Native village near the shipyard (Gibson 1976:67, 39; Grinev 1994: 166; Ketz & Arndt 1990:X–XI; Pierce 1990:302–303; Sarafian 1970:228).

For the outer coast of Kenai Peninsula, Russian records mention only Natives living at or near Aleksandrovskaia odinochka and at a place called Akhmylik on Nuka Bay, perhaps identical with the Yalik shown on Petroff's map for the 1880 U.S. census report. There is archaeological evidence for a mid-nineteenth-century village at the Denton Site on Aialik Bay, where, according to recorded oral history, people lived seasonally and possibly year-round in the 1880s (ARCA D291/196: Kenai parish confessional records, 1846; Cook and Norris 1998:27; Crowell and Mann 1998:111–112). The outer Kenai coast is very rocky and strongly dented by fjords, so it is likely that some villages there escaped the notice of the Russians, who largely bypassed the region on voyages from Kodiak and Aleksandrovsk to Nuchek and Novoarkhangel'sk. On an archaeological survey in the 1930s, during which she interviewed local residents about former village sites, Frederica de Laguna heard about villages in Day Harbor, east of Resurrection Bay, as well as some on the Cook Inlet side of the peninsula, near English Bay. She gives no dates of habitation for any of them (de Laguna 1956:35–36).

On Prince William Sound, some more names appear in the sources, but locations are largely uncertain. Maps show only the redoubt on Nuchek Island; church records mention five villages: Khatliuk near the redoubt, Tatitlak, Kani-ukhliuk, Chanigak, and Tsuklok. Tsuklok was the Russian name for Montague Island; Tatitlek, Kiniklik, and Chenega are names of villages that existed into the twentieth century. Their locations seem to have shifted several times even in the late nineteenth/early twentieth centuries, so that they can be only tentatively located at the places where the earliest maps show them. For Tsuklok, I indicate the location of archaeological village sites identified but not dated by de Laguna, one of which may have been the site of the Russian-period village. De Laguna's informants remembered more village sites, and again it is likely that the Russians did not have a full overview of the region (ARCA D291/196: Kenai parish confessional records, 1846; RAC cs 28:169, July 3, to the manager of Konstantinovskii redut; de Laguna 1956:24–33).

On the Alaska Peninsula, recorded village locations are equally scarce, although at least the Pacific side was frequently visited by Russian expeditions and hunters in the early nineteenth century. The archaeological record also suggests that the region was thinly inhabited at the time of Russian arrival, perhaps because resources were less diverse and reliable compared to those

available on Kodiak Island. There is no evidence for permanent villages between Katmai and Sutkhum or south of Ugashik. Kugak/Kukak, Katmai, and
Severnovskoe/Ikak on the portage across the Peninsula apparently had sizeable populations at the time the Russians first arrived. A map drawn by the
navigator I. IA. Vasil'ev as a result of an exploring expedition in 1830 (Litke
1835:286) shows a pair of villages, Alinnak and Ikak, at the general location
of Severnovskoe. The Russian post at Katmai served as a trading center and
also sent out its own hunting parties. North of Kukak, Vasil'ev and Teben'kov
(1981 [1852]) both show a village called Kaiaiak at the approximate site of late
nineteenth-century Douglas. Sutwik Island was visited in the summer by hunting parties from Kodiak and Katmai, but there also seems to have been a year-
round *artel'*, most likely on Cape Kumliuk on the mainland. The *artel'* was used
intermittently in the nineteenth century: reestablished in 1830 after temporary
abandonment, it was ordered closed by Chief Manager Etholen in 1842. A village may have remained on Cape Kumliuk, where Sutkhum village is indicated
on an 1847 map. The 1850 vital statistics for Kodiak parish still mention people
baptized at Sutkhum (RAC cs 21:202–202v, May 9, 1842, to Main Office; VS
E29, Kodiak, baptisms 1850; Hussey 1971:128, 162–165; Morseth 1998:12, 37;
Morskoe Ministerstvo 1847).

The Bristol Bay side of the Peninsula, whose waters are devoid of sea otters,
was of less interest to the RAC. But in the course of northern and interior expansion, (Novo-)Aleksandrovskii redut on the mouth of the Nushagak was founded
in 1819, for trade with the local Yup'ik-speaking population. The RAC lacked the
power to organize compulsory hunting parties among these people, but some
groups, notably the Aglurmiut, seem to have welcomed the post as a source of
protection from enemies (Gibson 1976:16; Morseth 1998:23; Sarafian 1970:219).

As noted earlier, on the Alaska Peninsula the ethnic label "Alutiiq" or
"Aleut" applies to people of different linguistic groups. The people of Ugashik
and Severnovskoe seem to have spoken a distinct dialect that was closer to the
language of the Kiatagmiut, a Yup'ik group on the northern peninsula, than
to the Sugcestun dialect spoken at Katmai, which was closely related to the
language of Kodiak Island. The confessional records for Nushagak parish distinguish several Yup'ik groups in most villages, designated by ethnonyms ending in -*miut*. But they always identify the majority of people at Ugashik and
Severnovskoe as "Aleut," suggesting that, for whatever reason, Russians perceived a greater closeness of these people to those of Kodiak and the Aleutians
than to Aglurmiut or Kiatagmiut (ARCA 146, Nushagak parish confessional
records, 1855–1879; Morseth 1998:22; Partnow 2001:37). By contrast, Paugvik,
also called Kuchugmiut (Vasil'ev in Litke 1835:286) or Kinghiak (Petroff 1884),

and known as Naknek today, was considered an Aglurmiut (Yup'ik) village by Russian priests. Alutiiq appear to have moved there only in the early twentieth century to work in canneries, mixing with the more established Yup'ik population (1910 census, NacNic; Dumond and VanStone 1995:6).

Map 4. Kodiak Island in 1850: After the Epidemic

Compared to the peninsula and Prince William Sound, Kodiak Island, depicted here on the basis of a map published by the RAC in 1849, former chief manager Mikhail Teben'kov's 1852 atlas, and the Finnish traveler Heinrich Johann Holmberg's map of 1855, still appears densely settled (Holmberg 1855; Russian-American Company 1849; Teben'kov 1981). But a comparison with 1830 shows a dramatic decrease in the number of villages. This is due to the smallpox epidemic that struck the region in 1837–1838. The virus came from Novoarkhangel'sk on RAC ships, and it proved especially disastrous on Kodiak Island, where 738 people died, bringing the combined Alutiiq and Creole population of the island down to under 2,000. Although mortality seems to have been lower on the mainland, owing to the more dispersed population, the Russians' spotty knowledge of the region leaves open the possibility that some villages there may have been abandoned at that time without ever appearing in written sources. The RAC made efforts to inoculate the population, but the disease spread more quickly than medical help could travel. In some villages people even refused the vaccine, out of the suspicion that the Russians had brought the illness and were trying to make them even sicker (ARCA D252/174: Kodiak parish clerical register, 1843; RAC cs 15:248v-253, May 1, 1838; 16:224v–226, Nov 4, 1838, both to Main Office; Dumond 1986:31; Fortuine 1989:230; Tikhmenev 1978 [1861]:200).

The RAC, concerned about losing its hunters, took measures to make Alutiiq life at once more secure and easier to control. Starting in 1840, the survivors of the epidemic from reportedly sixty-five small villages were concentrated in seven places, most of them located near Russian posts: Woody Island/Chiniak, Orlovskoe (Eagle Harbor), Three Saints Bay, Aiakhtalik, Akhiok, Karluk, and Afognak. According to the 1844 confessional records, which identify families by current residence and village of origin, families from Igak, Ugak, and Kiliuda were settled at Orlovskoe; families from Kiavak and the villages on Sitkalidak Island (Anikinskoe, Begletsovo, Mysovskoe, Kolpakovskoe, and Orininskoe, a village name I have not encountered in any other sources) moved to Three Saints Bay; those from Kaguyak, Sitkhinak, Ubachvik, Tugidak, and Kashkak to Aiakhtalik; those from Alitak, Aiakolik, and Paiskoe to Akhiok;

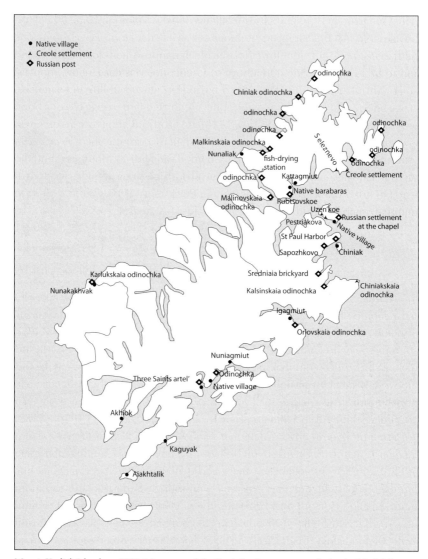

Map 4. Kodiak Island, ca. 1850. Map research by Sonja Luehrmann, map design by Mark Matson.

and those from Uyak and Uganak to Karluk (ARCA D255/175:Kodiak parish confessional records, 1844). The confessional records for Chiniak and Afognak do not identify any residents as having resettled from other places, but an RAC report states that the population of these two villages formerly lived at fourteen different places—among them probably Kizhuyak, Malinovskoe, and villages on Chiniak Bay. Each of the new villages had a *toion* (chief) whose election had to be confirmed by the company administration. His duties included assigning men to hunting parties and planning the hunt in consultation with company employees, but also mediating disputes in the village and taking care of orphans and poor people (RAC cs 20:73v–81, March 22, 1841, to Kodiak office; 20:170v–173, May 1, 1841; 22:233, May 10, 1843, both to Main Office; ARCA D255/175:Kodiak parish confessional records, 1844).

Feeding the relatively large populations of the consolidated villages—about 250 people in most of them—proved a problem. The naval officer Pavel Golovin, who inspected the colonies in 1860–61, reported that some villages had requested permission to split up (Dmytryshyn and Crownhart-Vaughan 1979:24). Kaguyak reappears on mid-century maps (Russian-American Company 1849:Kaniiagmiut; Holmberg 1855:Kanjagmjut/Kawujagmjut), although the survivors from this village were initially listed as living at Aiakhtalik (ARCA D255/175:Kodiak parish confessional records, 1844).

This discrepancy raises the question if the relocation measures were actually enforced or if they remained administrative fiction. The above-mentioned petition for permission to split up larger villages indicates that village consolidation had at least some practical consequences. Besides Kaguyak, the names of other purportedly abandoned villages also recur in later vital statistics but, as far as I could see, only as the home villages of parents and god-parents at baptisms and chrismations (VS E29, Kodiak, chrismations 1849), perhaps referring to their place of birth rather than current residence. I have found no clear mention of church rites performed at such villages. In general, Orthodox Church records become far more detailed in the years following the epidemic, beginning to list the individual names of parishioners in each village systematically and consistently. This also suggests that actual changes in Alutiiq settlement patterns occurred at this time, making it easier for Russian record keepers to keep administrative control (see Chapter 5). None of this diminishes the likelihood that old village sites and summer campsites continued to be used at least seasonally for hunting and fishing.

It was even the expressed purpose of the RAC not to allow relocation to interfere with Alutiiq hunting patterns. But one should keep in mind that after the epidemic more than before, what the Russians list as "Aleut villages" is an administrative unit that implies certain political institutions and obligations that did not always correspond to an actual residential community. Aiakhtalik and Akhiok, listed separately in the confessional records in 1844 and later, were apparently not considered independent villages by the RAC but are counted together with Three Saints Bay as three villages administered by the Three Saints *artel'* under the responsibility of a single *toion* (RAC cs 18:126–127, Apr 21, 1840, to Kodiak office; 22:233, May 10, 1843, to Main Office).

The rise of several Creole settlements between the 1830s and the 1850s is another consequence of the decline of the Alutiiq population, as well as of the difficulty for the RAC of bringing enough employees from Russia. Since very few Russian women came to Alaska, many Russian hunters married Native women. Their descendants should legally have been registered at their father's place of origin and as members of his estate, thus becoming full Russian citizens entitled to accompany their father to his home at the end of his service. Some RAC employees registered their Alaska-born children in that way, but many others either never returned to Russia because they were in debt to the company when their normal seven-year term of service ended or had a Russian wife at home and did not intend to take their Alaskan family back with them.

The RAC, for its part, had an interest in creating a colonial population that could perform such duties as manning posts, overseeing Native hunting, keeping records, and sailing the ships. RAC officials hoped that such an Alaskan-born labor pool would help alleviate the difficulties of recruitment in Russia and Siberia, where there was a shortage of free men willing to go to Alaska in the face of less strenuous and more rewarding opportunities for migration within Siberia. So Creoles, people born in the colony of Russian fathers and Native mothers, were recognized as a special class in the second charter of the RAC, granted in 1821. They were Russian subjects equal in status to the burgher estate (*meshchanskoe soslovie*) but free from state taxation as long as they lived in Alaska. Creoles educated at the expense of the RAC were obliged to serve the Company for at least ten years. Creoles free of that obligation, or those who had retired from the service, as well as Russian retirees who were unwilling or unable to leave Alaska after their term was up and who registered as "colonial citizens" (*kolonial'nye grazhdane*, a rank created in 1835), were encouraged to establish agricultural settlements (Black 1990:143–145; Dmytryshyn and Crownhart-Vaughan 1979:14; Sarafian 1970: 12, 63, 147–149).

By the 1830s, Creole families had settled on Afognak and Spruce Island, where wood for construction was readily available, different from the treeless southern part of Kodiak Island. In 1835, the company administration decided to establish a settlement for retirees on Kenai Peninsula, but plans were disrupted by the smallpox epidemic and the ensuing troubled relations with the Denaina neighbors of the proposed site, who blamed the Russians for bringing the disease. But providing for elderly employees and their families remained a major problem for the RAC, and the first family was settled at Ninilchik, on the

Cook Inlet side of Kenai Peninsula, in 1842 (see Map 3). The settlement persists until this day, but soil conditions and the remoteness of the location, as well as lack of enthusiasm among prospective settlers, kept it from growing beyond a handful of families during the Russian period (Arndt 1996:240–246). In 1846, the Creole Koriakin was given permission to settle on Cape Chiniak south of St. Paul Harbor on Kodiak Island with his family. This seems to be the origin of the Chiniak village listed in the 1880 census. On a map drawn in 1863, Verman calls it a village of "settlers" (*poselentsy*), suggesting that it was a Creole rather than an Alutiiq village (RAC cs 27:79, Oct 4, 1846, to Kodiak office; Liapunova and Fedorova 1979:plate between pp. 16 and 17).

None of these Creole settlements became self-sufficient, nor did any of them contribute much to supplying the Russian colony as a whole. The climate was such that only potatoes and turnips could be grown with some success, and the RAC correspondence describes the economy of settlers on Spruce Island as relying on a number of sources besides horticulture: cattle raising, fishing, clamming and hunting, and ongoing dependence on pensions from the RAC (RAC cs 29:244–247v, May 10, 1848, to Main Office; Gibson 1976:100).

Agricultural settlements were not the only attempt by the RAC to achieve economic self-sufficiency, and not the only ones to meet with limited success. The brickyard at Sredniaia Bay and the *artel'* at Kal'sinsk, still shown on Map 4, were closed before the sale of Alaska. An ice plant on Woody Island, founded in the 1850s for the export of ice to California, was a final example of the RAC's bid to diversify its economic base, but it failed to make much difference in the balance of trade (ARCA D255/176:Kodiak parish confessional records, 1865; Gibson 1976:42; Kushner 1975:7–8; Verman's map in Liapunova and Fedorova 1979:between pp. 16 and 17).

By the mid-nineteenth century, then, various types of permanent settlement coexisted in the Alutiiq region. Afognak Island offers examples of all of them. At this point Rubtsovskoe was definitely the main RAC station on the island. Maps distinguish between the fort, surrounded by a Creole or a Russian village, and an Alutiiq village, sometimes called Kattagmiut, on the other side of the bay, at the site of the earlier Russian *artel',* which had been abandoned in the 1830s, perhaps in connection with the smallpox epidemic (Woodhouse-Beyer 2001:77). This village may have been the Afognak village that is mentioned as a relocation center for survivors of the 1837 smallpox epidemic (RAC cs 22:233, May 10, 1843, to Main Office). The 1849 RAC map also shows some "Aleut barabaras" immediately north of the post. On his tour of the island in 1832, the Kodiak priest recorded five baptisms at "Afognak village" (Kattagmiut?). Those baptized were all children of "Aleuts," apparently born into resident families with the exception of one, whose father came from Chiniak. At Rubtsovskoe, seven children were baptized, three of them children of Creoles, two children of Alutiiq company employees from Ugatak and Razbitovskoe, and the other two the offspring of an Alutiiq couple whose origin is not mentioned (VS E27, Kodiak, baptisms 1832). So it seems that the post and its vicinity were inhabited by Russians, Creoles, and Alutiiq in company service, some of whom came from other parts of the archipelago, while there was an Alutiiq village across the bay to the north. It is unclear whether Alutiiq villages in other parts of the island persisted beyond the epidemic. Nunaliak is still mentioned by Teben'kov in 1852, but Malinovskoe, apparently the Russian name for the same village, disappears from church records after the epidemic.

The pattern of some Alutiiq living as workers at a Russian post, while most lived in a nearby, separate village, was common throughout Russian-dominated Alaska since Shelikhov's time, who settled families captured by him near the new settlement at Three Saints Bay (Clark 1987:112; Shelikhov 1981 [1791]:40). Population figures for St. Paul Harbor and Konstantinovskii redut on Prince William Sound indicate that no or very few Alutiiq were living at the post, while there is a Native village near each of them, Chiniak on Woody Island and Khatliuk. A plan of Kodiak town made by the U.S. military in 1868 shows a single "Aleut House for Aleuts from villages around the island" (Curtis 1868), obviously a *barabara* that housed hunters and workers who had come from remote villages and who lived separately from the Russian and Creole townspeople. Zagoskin reports the same for the RAC forts Mikhailovskii and Kolmakovskii in the Yukon-Kuskokwim area, where Creole and "Aleut" workers had barracks inside the fortifications, while Yup'ik lived in villages at some distance (Michael 1967:96, 100, 252).

In addition to exemplifying this pattern of a Russian post paired with a Native village, Afognak was also a site of Creole settlement. The site of Lisianskii's "company structure" to the north of the main Russian post is called Seleznevo on the mid-century maps, after Makarii Seleznev, a Russian with an Alutiiq wife and several grown sons who had settled there by the 1830s (ARCA D255/175: Kodiak parish confessional records, 1831; RAC cs 27:72–72v, Oct 4, 1846, to Kodiak Office). The 1849 RAC map and Verman show an additional settlement of free Creoles a short distance to the north, on the other side of Cape Izhut. In 1847, Khristofor, the oldest of the Seleznev sons, was appointed supervisor responsible for the discipline of all Creole settlements on Kodiak and Afognak (RAC cs 28:147v–148, June 22, 1847, to Kodiak office).

The 1849 RAC map also shows a great number of *odinochkas* around Afognak island. There is no information on them in other sources, and they may not have been permanently manned but just huts or *barabaras* erected for hunters, fishers, and loggers.

Spruce Island was another preferred place for Creole settlement, where they seem to have formed the majority of the population. The various settlements shown on the island on different maps are usually listed as one in Russian statistics, referred to as Ostrov Elovoi (Spruce Island) or Selenie Uzen'koe (Narrow Village/Village on Narrow Strait). Several families of retired Creoles and Russians lived on the island, as did some Alutiiq near the chapel at Novyi Valaam, the site where the hermit monk German, a member of the first Orthodox mission sent to Alaska in 1794 and canonized today as Saint Herman of Alaska, had lived until his death in 1836. The Alutiiq population was quite small according to Russian statistics. The clerical register lists no "Aleuts" on the island in 1843, nine in 1849, and eleven in 1853. These people apparently lived in a separate village, shown at the southeast corner of the island on the 1849 RAC map (ARCA D252/ 174:Kodiak parish clerical registers, 1843, 1849, 1853; Black 1997:276).

In addition to Rubtsovskoe on Afognak, four posts on Kodiak Island supervised nearby villages of smallpox survivors: St. Paul Harbor, Orlovskoe, Three Saints *artel'*, and Karluk. The names *odinochka* and *artel'* are often used interchangeably, although strictly speaking *artel'* implies a bigger Russian population. The Igak *artel'* had been moved across the bay to Orlovskoe in 1837, a place that offered better conditions for cattle raising. The odinochka at Akhiok (alternative name: Alitak) had apparently been abandoned by 1840, and the villages of Akhiok and Aiakhtalik were administered from the *artel'* on Three Saints Bay (ARCA D255/176:Kodiak parish confessional records, 1846; RAC cs 14:278v, May 16, 1837, to Kodiak office; 22:233, May 10, 1843, to Main Office; Liapunova and Fedoroya 1979:44).

The various villages and posts in the vicinity of Three Saints Bay shown on Map 4 may or may not all have existed at the same time and appear to represent the gradual shift of the population from the old location near the original *artel'* to that of late-nineteenth century Old Harbor (Nuniagmiut on the map). Some of the villages may also have been seasonal camps. In 1847, seeing that the buildings were in need of repair, the RAC decided to move the *artel'* to a more convenient location (RAC cs 28:156, June 22, 1847, to Kodiak office). The 1849 RAC map shows the *artel'* slightly north of the original site, where a village with the old name of *gavan' Trekh Sviatitelei* is still indicated, either for historical reasons or because some people remained at the original site. The map also shows an Alutiiq village called Ukshivikhkagmiut just north of the entrance to Three Saints Bay. Teben'kov shows the *artel'* at the same site but places the

Alutiiq village further north, at the bottom of Three Saints Bay (not shown on my map). Holmberg shows no settlements in the bay at all, just an *odinochka* and the village Nunjagmiut (near the present location of Old Harbor) on Sitkalidak Passage. In 1863, Verman shows a settlement at the site of the *artel'* in Three Saints Bay, and Odinochka Sviatitel'skaia (Saint's post) at the location of Holmberg's Nunjagmiut. In 1880, the U.S. census enumerates 4 Creoles and 3 "Eskimos" at Three Saints Bay, and 155 "Eskimos" and 5 Creoles at Old Harbor, a name originally given to the Three Saints Bay post when the RAC offices moved to St. Paul Harbor, but that seems to have moved along with the bulk of the population (Clark 1989:3; Crowell 1997:71–72; Petroff 1884:29).

The combined effect of the shrinking number of Alutiiq villages after the smallpox epidemic and the emergence of permanent Creole settlements make the map of Kodiak Island in 1850 appear quite different from what it looked like in 1830. For the first time, the RAC tried to control not only the time and labor power of those Alutiiq who were drafted into company service each year but also the physical location of the whole population year-round. The extent to which these attempts were successful is difficult to gauge, but there is evidence that life in the consolidated villages was different in important aspects from what it had been before the epidemic. I discuss some aspects of this life in more detail in Chapters 3 and 5. As far as the settlements of Creoles and colonial settlers are concerned, they could potentially create problems of competition for resources between Native villages and new settlers, and with their modest horticulture, Russian-derived architecture, and dependence on goods purchased from the company with pension money they were residential spaces that were clearly different from Alutiiq villages and not open to settlement by Alutiiq households (RAC cs 42:157–157v, Sep 5, 1860, to Kodiak office; Arndt 1996:239).

At the same time, it is unclear whether newly established Creole villages would have been seen by Alutiiq neighbors as strangers usurping their territory or relatives setting up households. The classification of a village, as far as Russian administrators were concerned, was determined by the ethnicity of the male heads of the households. In each "Creole" village or "Russian" post, Alutiiq as well as Creole women were present. These women, especially given the chronic shortage of European goods, must have brought much of Alutiiq material and intellectual culture to the Creole settlements. They also created alliances and trade connections to their Alutiiq relatives and villages of origin (Knecht and Jordan 1985:32–33; Tikhmenev 1978 [1861]:171; Woodhouse-Beyer 2001). It may thus be more fitting to speak of Kodiak Island in the wake of the smallpox epidemic as having become a more thoroughly colonial place rather than a Russianized one: a society was taking shape whose constituent parts were profoundly shaped by Russian colonial policy but developed their own patterns of interaction, in which Russian administrators did not necessarily play a central role.

Map 5. The Alutiiq Region in 1895: Competitive Fur Trade and Canneries

Alaska was sold to the United States in 1867.[10] According to the treaty of cession, Russian subjects had the right to return to Russia within a period of three years. Those choosing to remain in Alaska would become U.S. citizens, "with the exception of uncivilized native tribes" (Dmytryshyn, Crownhart-Vaughan, and Vaughan 1989:546). According to Svetlana Fedorova (1971:243), 748 Russians and Creoles registered in Russian tax roles had the right to be repatriated to Russia. Of these, 537 can be shown to have left Alaska in 1867–1868. The Russian population of St. Paul Harbor, or Kadiak as it came to be called by Americans, numbering 28 men and 13 women in 1867, had entirely disappeared by 1870, and the Creole population had decreased from 190 men and 165 women to 104 men and 102 women. Of the seven Russian men and two women living at Afognak, however, all or almost all seem to have remained, suggesting that these were permanent settlers who had formed stronger bonds to the island and its Alutiiq population. All other posts in the parish, including Katmai and Ukamok, were staffed by Creoles rather than Russians before the sale, and the numbers of these Creoles did not change perceptibly. A closer comparison of the names in confessional records across years and locations in the years immediately following the sale might make it possible to say with more certainty who left Alaska. It would also be interesting to see how many Alutiiq women accompanied their husbands to Russia. However, since most of them are identified only by a Russian first name in the records, those who stayed on Kodiak and returned to their Alutiiq family or remarried would be extremely difficult to trace (ARCA D253/174:Kodiak parish clerical register, 1867, 1870).

The only other RAC post in the Alutiiq region that may have had a Russian population in 1867 was Konstantinovskii redut on Prince William Sound, where eight Russians were recorded in 1858. These had disappeared by 1870, but a sizeable population of eighty-eight Creoles and Denaina (known as *Kenaitsy* in Russian) remained at the trading post, which was still distinguished from the Chugach village Khatlik (ARCA D292/196, D294/199, confessional records, Kenai 1858, 1870).

By 1870, most of the buildings and stores belonging to the RAC had become the property of the San Francisco-based Alaska Commercial Company

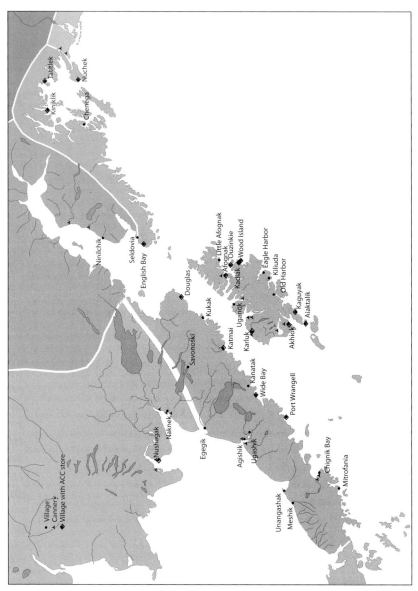

Map 5. Alutiiq Region, ca. 1895. Map research by Sonja Luehrmann, map design by Mark Matson, reproduced courtesy of Smithsonian Arctic Studies Center.

(ACC), founded in October 1868 as a consortium of several businessmen who had individually acquired RAC assets (Lee 1996:23–29; Sloss 1977; Sloss and Pierce 1971). But the ACC neither had monopoly rights excluding competition from other American companies (except for the fur seal harvest on the Pribilofs) nor did it inherit the RAC's administrative functions and judicial power over the population of Alaska. This may explain why many new village sites appeared in the Alutiiq region in the first decades of U.S. rule, and old sites that had been abandoned after the smallpox epidemic were resettled. On Kodiak Island, Kiliuda and Uganok reappear in the 1880 census and are listed again in the church records from 1872 and 1883, respectively. In both cases, the village reappeared before canneries were established at these locations (VS E31, Kodiak 1872; ARCA D257/178:Kodiak parish confessional records, 1883; Befu 1970:30; Petroff 1884; Roppel 1986:187).[11]

It seems likely that these villages were reestablished for the purpose of subsistence hunting, because people felt that the consolidated villages were too big. Contradictions among different types of church records—the vital statistics mention baptisms and weddings at Kiliuda in 1872, the confessional records start listing the village again only in 1881—suggest that people were occasionally listed among the population of larger villages visited by the priest rather than at the place they were actually living. Some places may have been used as seasonal camps even under the RAC and perhaps slowly regained the status of year-round villages until at some point the church recognized their existence.

Shifting village names and locations point to the mobility of the population across seasons and years. Petroff's map accompanying his report of the 1880 census (Petroff 1884) shows two village sites at Uganok, one near the western mouth of the bay, the other further east, south of Uganik Island. He does not say whether these were seasonal sites used by the same people or whether both were year-round villages. The agent of the 1900 census found the village population "on Uganak Island," possibly in a summer camp. A village called Pokrovskoe, not shown on any maps, appears in Kodiak parish records between 1894 and 1905. It apparently split off from Aiaktalik, where most of its residents are listed in confessional records for 1893. In 1903, no population figures are given for Pokrovskoe, but Aiaktalik has twenty more people than in 1902 and 1905. Pokrovskoe may have been a seasonal site used by people from Aiaktalik, or shifting patterns of resource use may have caused some families from Aiaktalik to live in Pokrovskoe during certain years, moving back to Aiaktalik in others (ARCA D258/179:Kodiak parish confessional records, 1893, 1894; D259/179: Kodiak parish census, 1902–1905).

The late nineteenth century was a time of considerable population movement and relative growth on the Alaska Peninsula, an area that apparently still offered better sea otter and subsistence hunting than Kodiak did, where overhunting had been more pronounced during the Russian era. People from Katmai, Bristol Bay, and Kodiak spread out along the southern coast of the peninsula and established new villages. The ACC and rival companies opened stores in many villages and fitted out small, local hunting parties, different from the more centralized operations of the RAC. It was probably the combined effect of the increasing scarcity of sea otters and of competition among trading companies that forced hunters and traders to exploit the coast more evenly. Although Douglas/Kaguyak apparently grew on a site already inhabited during the Russian period, its population increased considerably during its time as main trading post of the ACC on the peninsula. Father Nikolai Kashevarov of Afognak parish, who was responsible for the Pacific coast of the peninsula, says that people moved to Douglas from Katmai and Severnovskoe and that a chapel existed there since 1876 (Kashevarov 1898:508). Both the village and the post may have moved several times. In the records of Kodiak parish[12] a village "on Kamysh'iak Bay" appears from 1876 to 1881; later the same people are listed at Cape Douglas, which juts out at the south end of the bay. Petroff's map for the 1880 census shows a village called Ashivak on Kamishak Bay, and the trading post of Douglas on the cape, but he reports population figures only for Ashivak. Later maps show Douglas, or Kaguyak, south of the cape (ARCA D256-257/177–178:Kodiak parish confessional records; Hussey 1971:160–162, 235-243; Petroff 1884; Porter 1893).

South of Katmai, the villages of Kanatak, Wide Bay, and Port Wrangell were founded in the 1880s and 1890s. The priests who visited them write that all were founded by immigrants from Nushagak parish, that is, the interior and Bristol Bay side of the northern Alaska Peninsula, who were coming to hunt sea otters and escape oppressive traders at Nushagak. Others came over for the hunting season only, many of them from Yup'ik villages such as Egegik. At Sutkhum the ACC maintained a trading post in the 1880s and 1890s, but there apparently was no permanent village (ARCA D262/181:travel report of Father Tikhon Shalamov for 1895, Kodiak, March 4, 1896; Kashevarov 1898:508; Morseth 1998:75–82; Oswalt 1967b; Partnow 2001:158–159; Stafeev ms., June 22, 1889).

On the Bristol Bay side of the peninsula, there also seems to have been a migration movement toward the south, although the attraction here cannot have been sea otters, which do not live in the bay. Since that coast was less visited by Russians, the likelihood that Unangashak/Inangashak and Meshik/ Mashkhik had simply escaped the notice of previous observers is greater than for the Pacific side villages. Both are mentioned for the first time in Petroff's census report, their population designated "Aleut." Nushagak parish priests occasionally mention visiting them in subsequent years. Unangashak was reportedly established by people from Ugashik, attracted by the abundance of caribou. The location of Meshik is ambiguous, but most reports before the turn of the century seem to indicate that it lay to the west of Unangashak, different from the early twentieth century, when the name referred to Port Heiden further east, by then the site of a cannery (Morseth 1998:71–74).

Not all new villages were established by people from the peninsula. Mitrofania was a settlement of Kodiak Creoles who also moved there for sea otter hunting, an occupation not reported for Creoles before 1867. This change was probably due to the end of the special relationship between Creoles and the RAC, which had offered Creoles opportunities for company employment and provided aid for Creole families in agricultural settlements. The "Russian-Aleut" population of Mitrofania continued to speak Russian until the early twentieth century (Morseth 1998:85–86; Partnow 2001:157).

There is no evidence for a similar dispersal of settlements on Prince William Sound and the Kenai Peninsula. The more advanced decline of the sea otter population in that area may have forced people to move to the vicinity of white settlements to make the money they needed for store-bought goods. On the Kenai coast, the village of Yalik, recorded by Petroff in 1880 and probably the same as the Akhmylik of Russian records, had disappeared by 1890 following the closure of the ACC store. Residents reportedly moved to English Bay (former Aleksandrovskaia odinochka) to be near the church and work odd jobs for traders and prospectors and later at the Kachemak Coal Mines, founded in 1900. According to elders' memories recorded in the twentieth century, the village in Aialik Bay had become a mere seasonal camp by the 1890s (Bortnovskii 1901:275; Cook and Norris 1998:69–70, 77; Crowell and Mann 1998:112).

The principal ACC stores in this region, English Bay and Nuchek (former Konstantinovskii redut), were located at former Russian posts. But even after merging with the biggest competitor, the Western Fur & Trading Company, the ACC was obliged to establish small stores at Tatitlek and Kiniklik in order to retain its share of the dwindling trade. Sea otters remained more plentiful in remote bays than in the vicinity of Nuchek, where they were almost extinct by 1890 (Cook and Norris 1998:73–74; Lethcoe and Lethcoe 1994:40–41; Stafeev ms.).

While the trade in sea otter furs was generally on the decline in the late nineteenth century and the numbers of trading posts decreased accordingly, salmon canneries were the expanding business of the time.[13] Starting in 1882, when the first cannery was founded at Karluk, cannery locations began to influence the seasonal routes of Alutiiq families, and increasingly even their places of permanent residence (Davis 1986:119; Roppel 1986:6). Chignik Bay, site of a small village called Kaluiak (population 30) in 1880, grew into a major population center on the peninsula after a saltery was founded there in 1883, followed by canneries in 1889. Places such as Naknek, Kasilof (Kenai Peninsula), and Odiak (Prince William Sound), located outside the area historically inhabited by Alutiiq people, began to attract some of them for summer work. Akhiok and Aiaktalik residents gradually put less emphasis on sea otter hunting and spent their summers fishing for the Alitak canneries on Olga Bay, the first of which was also established in 1889. The 1890 census lists Alitak as populated by 107 white males, 177 "Mongolian" males, 80 "Indian" (probably Alutiiq) males and 54 females, and two "mixed" (Creole) males. The nearby village of Akhiok is not listed in this census, which probably means that virtually the entire population was over in Alitak fishing for the cannery when the census taker arrived (Befu 1970:30; Cook and Norris 1998:78; Davis 1986:89–114; Moser 1898; Partnow 2001:156; Porter 1893:4; Rostad 1988:45).

Such figures notwithstanding, canneries did not become attractive to Alutiiq immediately. Most of them employed few Natives at first, preferring to bring in Scandinavians and Italians as fishermen and Chinese and other Asian contract laborers as cannery workers. Alutiiq fishermen were seldom put on the payroll, but the packing companies bought their catch from them on a piece-by-piece basis. In the 1890 census, Chignik Bay has only 5 "Indian" residents, compared to 121 Asians and 66 whites. By 1900, the village has 63 resident "Aleuts," 22 "mixed" people, 33 whites, and 1 Japanese, in addition to the workers living at the canneries. Statistics of the Alaska fishing industry from 1900 confirm that by then, all canneries were hiring at least some Natives (probably mostly women) as shore workers, and some were hiring Native fishermen (1900 census, Chignik Bay; Elliott 1900:739; Freeburn 1976:49; Moser 1898:23–25). But generally speaking, salmon canning was the first large-scale economic enterprise in the area in which Alutiiq labor played a marginal role and that brought such an influx of outside workers that the Alutiiq became a minority. At first this effect was felt mainly during the canning season, then year-round as more and more European fishermen stayed in Alaska as trappers and prospectors. Where canneries were located near existing Native villages, as at Karluk, Alutiiq families had to compete with the fish traps in their own subsistence fishing (ARCA D262/181:Travel report from Father Tikhon Shalamov for 1895, Kodiak, March 4, 1896; Morseth 1998:87, 99; Pracht, Luttrell, and Murray 1898:409).

In the 1890s, the white population of the region was concentrated at a few centers. Except for the cannery towns, only Kadiak, Afognak, and Ninilchik had more than ten white residents in the 1890 census; Nuchek and Eagle Harbor had seven each (Porter 1893:4–5). Among these whites, the Baptist missionaries who opened a school in Kadiak in 1886 and an orphanage on Woody

Island in 1893 represented a new kind of presence. The Baptist mission society was in charge of Native education in this part of Alaska under contract with the Bureau of Education, whose Alaska division was headed by Presbyterian missionary Sheldon Jackson between 1884 and 1906 (Haycox 2002:193–194). As we will see in Chapter 5, the Protestant missionaries often came in conflict with the Russian Orthodox Church, which, in spite of financial difficulties after the end of RAC support, was expanding its activities with newly created parish seats at Nuchek (from 1894) and Afognak (from 1895), splitting the older Kodiak and Kenai parishes. Orthodox parish schools teaching Russian and sometimes English were maintained in many villages (Antonii 1900; Bishop Innokentii 1905:104, 126, 129; Jackson 1898:556; Roscoe 1992:105). Russian remained the second language of a large part of the Alutiiq population during this period; even Anglo-American traders were forced to learn it or find an interpreter to communicate with their Creole or Alutiiq employees and hunters (Jacobs 1997:53; Roscoe 1992:4).

Map 6. The Alutiiq Region in 1930: After an Eruption and an Epidemic

Sea otter hunting came to its definite end in 1911, when an international treaty prohibited even Alaska Natives—the last group that had still been allowed to do so—from killing the animals. The ACC closed many stores, independent traders reoriented toward retailing food and manufactured goods, and sea otter hunting villages such as Aiaktalik, Nuchek, and Douglas shrunk as people looked for new ways to earn a cash income (Lee 1996:29; Lethcoe and Lethcoe 1994:40–43; Morseth 1998:57–58).

The villages of sea mammal hunters on the Alaska Peninsula had thus already begun to shrink before Novarupta Volcano near Katmai erupted on June 6, 1912. Kukak had apparently been abandoned not long after the turn of the century. The villages of Katmai, Savonoski, and Douglas were destroyed by the eruption, as was the saltery at Kaflia Bay where most families were working for the summer. A thick layer of ash covered the ground as far away as the east coast of Kodiak. Katmai and Douglas residents were taken to Afognak by the U.S. Revenue Service cutter. A few weeks later, the revenue cutter took them to a place southwest of Chignik, where they founded the new village of Perryville. The location was chosen on consultation between U.S. officials and Alutiiq leaders, apparently most of all for its subsistence resources. Savonoski people resettled in South Naknek and a little upstream of it, at a location that came to be called New Savonoski. They contributed to the multilingual Yup'ik-Sugpiaq environment that contemporary elders remember as typical for the

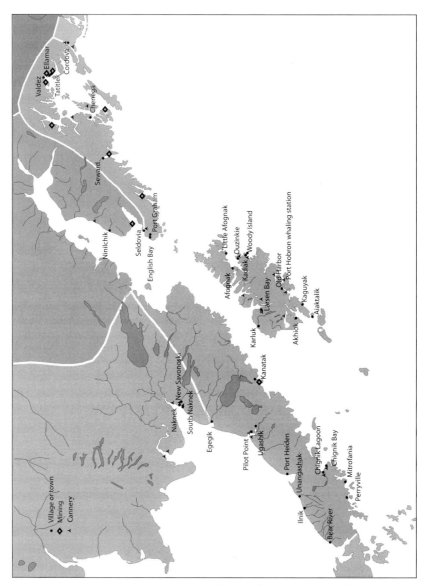

Map 6. Alutiiq Region, ca. 1930. Map research by Sonja Luehrmann, map design by Mark Matson.

Naknek, Egegik, and Ugashik area. Perryville has since split; a group of non-Orthodox families moved out in 1965 and established Ivanof Bay at a nearby location (Davis 1986:8–21; Hussey 1971:248–256; Morseth 1998:25–26; Partnow 2001:181–201).

The villages of Port Wrangell and Cold (or Puale) Bay were also abandoned at the time of the eruption or in the years following it.[14] Of the villages on the Pacific side of the Alaska Peninsula, only Kanatak experienced a boom in the 1920s, when oil drilling in the vicinity brought a sudden influx of white residents. With its school and store and access to a trail across the peninsula to the Pilot Point and Naknek canneries, the town attracted Alutiiq families from the area. It was abandoned in the late 1940s, after the end of oil drilling operations. Residents moved to Ugashik, Egegik, and Chignik (Davis 1986:94–95; Morseth 1998:77–79, 94–95).

Mitrofania was also in the process of being abandoned in 1930, if it was still inhabited at all—the last known record is from 1926. Families moved from there to Perryville or Chignik. The latter location, with its canneries, had established itself as an enduring population center, with two villages connected to different cannery locations. The younger one, Chignik Lagoon, existed by 1897 as a community of hunters who spent their summers working for the cannery. In the 1950s, a third winter village was established on Chignik Lake, away from the coast. Residents spent the winter trapping and came down to their summer cabins at Chignik Lagoon for the salmon season (Davis 1986:43–88; Morseth 1998:82–86; Partnow 2001:215).

The Bering Sea side became attractive to peninsula Alutiiq in the early twentieth century owing to numerous canneries at Port Heiden, Pilot Point/Ugashik, Egegik, Naknek, and at the mouth of the Nushagak. Ilnik and Bear River, two small villages on salmon streams, were both founded by mixed Kodiak-Ugashik families and maintained ties to nearby canneries. Ilnik, mentioned in the 1920 census, lay near the location where Meshik is shown on the 1890 census map, whereas another village near the cannery at Port Heiden had inherited the name Meshik by 1910. Ilnik was abandoned in the 1940s or 1950s, when residents moved to the Chigniks and Port Heiden. Bear River was almost wiped out by influenza in 1934 (1920 census, Ilnik, Bear River; Davis 1986:44; Morseth 1998:74–75).

In addition to the attraction of canneries, the worldwide influenza epidemic of 1918–1919 also had its effect on the depopulation of smaller villages. Ugashik and Pilot Point lost almost their entire Native population. Survivors moved to Bear River, Unangashak, and Meshik. The 1920 census lists only one Native woman at Ugashik, and the twenty-six Natives at Pilot Point are newcomers working at the cannery or as reindeer herders. The latter may have been Inupiaq migrating from the north for the government-sponsored reindeer industry (1920 census, Ugashik, Pilot Station; Morset:69, 71, 99).

As on the Alaska Peninsula, the growing importance of canneries in Alutiiq life was visible on Kodiak Island as well. A case in point is the reestablishment of a village in Uyak Bay, a site abandoned since the smallpox epidemic. The can-neries that had existed in Larsen Cove from 1881 had apparently not attracted permanent Native residents at first, and the village shown slightly north of that location on Petroff's census map (population 76) was perhaps a seasonal site, since Uyak never reappears in Orthodox church records after the 1830s. The 1890 census lists 15 Alutiiq at Uyak, apparently working at the cannery along with 114 whites and 117 Asians. In 1900 and 1910, even that small number of Native workers disappears, and only whites and Asians are listed. But after the Alaska Packers Association cannery was dismantled at Karluk in 1911 and transferred to Larsen Cove, a permanent village of white administrators and Alutiiq families grew nearby (1900 census, Uyak Bay; 1910 census, Larsens Bay; 1920 census, Uyak village, Uyak vicinity; Davis 1986:138–140; Petroff 1884; Porter 1893:4; Roppel 1986:26, 191, 215).

In other cases, the short distances on the island made it possible for people to remain in their old villages and merely work for one of the canneries in the summer. Being too close to a cannery could even be detrimental to a village. Karluk's dramatic population decline (from 298 Alutiiq and 23 Creoles in 1880 to 88 Alutiiq and 11 Creoles in 1900) happened in the heyday of the canner-ies there, not during their subsequent decline (ARCA D256/177:Kodiak parish confessional records, 1880; 1900 census, Karluk village). Villages like Old Harbor and Akhiok, not immediately next to a cannery but close enough for an easy move there in the summer, attracted people from more remote places such as Aiaktalik, Kaguyak, and Eagle Harbor. When the 1964 earthquake and tsunami destroyed both Old Harbor and Kaguyak, the former was rebuilt, the latter was not. Eagle Harbor had already been abandoned in the 1920s, Aiaktalik shortly after World War II (Agnot 1987:30; Befu 1970:30; Davis 1986:163, 178–179).

One effect of the canneries was the emergence of mixed Alutiiq/Scandi-navian families with a strong orientation toward commercial fishing. Some of these families continue to occupy important positions in such communities as Kodiak or Old Harbor to the present day. The Asian cannery workers in the early twentieth century intermingled less with Alutiiq communities. As I elaborate in Chapter 5, only Japanese can be shown to have married into Native villages, where they stayed as storekeepers or cooks (Agnot 1987:30; Mishler and Mason 1996:263–264; Rostad 1988:26).

The strong Russian influence in the northwestern part of the island contin-ued to be recognized by Orthodox priests and Anglo-American observers alike. The inhabitants of Ouzinkie on Spruce Island and Little Afognak (the former Seleznevo, abandoned by 1939) were usually described as "Creole" or "Rus-sian," as was the non-Anglo-American population of Kadiak town. In Afognak village, the Russian-era division between "Russian town," inhabited by Creoles, and "Aleut town," the Native village, remained. Afognak Island as a whole became a favorite place for Scandinavian fishermen to settle, who married into local Creole families. But gradually many residents left the island, where no cannery remained after 1883, and moved to Karluk, Ouzinkie, and Kadiak. A salmon hatchery was operated by the U.S. Government in Litnik Lake early in the twentieth century, but it employed only a few people. After the destruction of Afognak village in the 1964 earthquake, the population left the island and founded Port Lions on Kodiak (1920 census, Afognak village vicinity—Salmon hatchery; Jacobs 1997:13, 50; Khotovitskii 1916; Martysh 1902:434).

On Woody Island, an Alutiiq village existed near the Baptist orphanage until the latter moved to Kodiak City in 1939. Only a few Alutiiq families remained after that, sharing the island with a Federal Aviation Agency communications station established in 1941. By now, the island is abandoned (1920 census, Woody Island village, Woody Island orphanage; Chaffin, Krieger, and Rostad 1983:115, 119, 125).

The former Russian posts on Ukamok Island and at Sapozhkovo/Sapascovia south of Kadiak remained locations for cattle ranching and trapping by mixed American-Creole families. The experimental cattle station established by the U.S. government had its headquarters in Kadiak, with a subsidiary station in Kalsin Bay, where the RAC had already raised cattle (1900 census, Sapashkovia, U-ka-mak Island; 1910 census, Sapascovia nr Kodiak, Chiricoff Island; 1920 census, Kodiak vicinity; Chaffin, Krieger, and Rostad 1983:45; Porter 1893:4).

Ninilchik on the Kenai Peninsula also remained recognizable as a community with roots in the Russian era. Many residents had Russian surnames and parents who were born in Russia. Gardens and fields seem to have played a minor role even in this former agricultural colony; the occupation of male residents is usually listed as "hunting and fishing" (1900 census, Nenilchik; 1910 census, Nenilchuk; 1920 census, Ninilchik).

The Alutiiq population of the Kenai Peninsula, concentrated around English Bay, earned cash through cannery work at Seldovia (whose Native population was mixed Alutiiq and Denaina), winter trapping, and occasional work in logging camps. The village of Port Graham first appears in the census records in 1920 (in 1910, only six whites and five Tlingit [Eyak?] are listed, all designated coal miners), but de Laguna claims that it was an old Chugach village site. In the early twentieth century, it grew faster and attracted more white residents than English Bay did, owing to its better harbor and the cannery in operation from 1912. Villages in Dogfish Bay and Port Chatham appear in the

View of Ouzinkie, 1913. On this picture, taken by members of one of the National Geographic Society's Katmai expeditions more than four decades after the RAC left Alaska, Ouzinkie still has a distinctly "Russian" feel to it: gabled log houses, outbuildings for keeping livestock, and wooden fences could very well stand in a Siberian village. The fish drying near the house on the right reminds the viewer of the mixed maritime/horticultural economy of the village. *Courtesy of Archives and Special Collections, University of Alaska Anchorage, National Geographic Society Collection, hmc-0186-volume1-210.*

1920 census, although the latter seems to have been merely a sawmill where Alutiiq speakers of "mixed" race worked alongside white men. The occupation of the men at Dogfish Bay is also given as "loggers" (1920 census, Dog Fish Bay Village, Pt Chatham; Cook and Norris 1998:79; de Laguna 1956:36).

Mining in the Kenai/Prince William Sound area was often carried out by individual white prospectors and offered little employment to Natives, who were excluded by law from staking their own claims. Some areas with intensive prospecting are marked on Map 6 (based on Barry 1997; Lethcoe and Lethcoe 1994). Where such prospecting camps are mentioned in the census, few contain any Native workers. Only the coal mines in Kachemak seem to have employed Natives occasionally, and the copper mining town of Ellamar attracted Chugach residents during its brief existence between 1898 and the 1930s. The 1898 gold rush also created the town of Valdez/Hang Town, which replaced Nuchek as port of entry into the Sound, owing to its more sheltered harbor and its location at the beginning of a route toward the interior gold fields. Tatitlek grew into the biggest Chugach village because it was close to Valdez and offered opportunities for earning money as guides and porters for prospectors. The Orthodox parish church had moved to Tatitlek by 1907.

Nuchek people also moved to be near canneries in the vicinity of Tatitlek and Cordova. The numbers of Chugach throughout the eastern part of Prince William Sound were further reduced by the 1918 influenza epidemic. In the 1920 census, Chugach speakers living in Orca Inlet (that is, near Cordova and the canneries), Langston and Sheep Bay, and on Hawkins and Hinchinbrook Island make up a total number of fifty-nine people. The last Nuchek family moved to Cordova in 1929/30 (ARCA D305/204:report from Andrei Kashevarov to Vladimir Donskoi, Nuchek, Apr 8, 1898; D306/205:village census of Tatitlek parish, 1907; de Laguna 1956:12; Lethcoe and Lethcoe 1994:40–43).

Kiniklik was also abandoned by 1930. Today the only Chugach village besides Tatitlek is Chenega Bay, where people from Chenega relocated after their village was destroyed by the 1964 earthquake (see Map 7). The villages in the sound were particularly strongly affected by the 1989 oil spill near Valdez, although the effects of the spill on subsistence and commercial fishing were felt as far away as Kodiak and the Pacific side of the Alaska Peninsula (de Laguna 1956:27; Fall 1993:16; Mobley et al. 1990:133).

In the 1920 census, the Alutiiq population reached what was probably its low point in recorded history. The total number of people of identifiable Alutiiq ancestry, including "mixed" people whose native language was given as "Aleut" or who lived in a traditionally Kodiak-Creole village, was approximately 2,300. As far as the range of settlement sites is concerned, the decrease in the number of villages on Map 6 compared to previous maps is slightly misleading. A more detailed map would show a proliferation of fox farms on small islands, where blue foxes could be raised without cages because they could not escape very far. This business started at the end of the nineteenth century as an alternative for the declining sea otter hunt. First on the Alaska Peninsula, then also around Kodiak, Kenai, and Prince William Sound, islands were leased to corporations or individual farmers by the U.S. Forest Service. Many of the fox farms were maintained by immigrants from Scandinavia and the United States and their Alutiiq or Creole wives, or by Creole families. Living in year-round isolation required a new kind of lifestyle different from any previous Alutiiq settlement patterns (ARCA D305/204:report from Father Konstantin Pavlov to Bishop Tikhon for 1898, Nuchek, May 6, 1899; Cook and Norris 1998:112–115; Lethcoe and Lethcoe 1994:70; Morseth 1998:100–101).

Map 7 shows those Alutiiq villages inhabited today, after the relocations in the wake of the 1964 earthquake and tsunami. Although the area occupied by Alutiiq people has not changed significantly across the two centuries spanned by the maps in this chapter, several trends can be seen. Across the period the needs of a maritime subsistence economy stood in contradiction to the

Map 7. Alutiiq Region, ca. 2000. Map research by Sonja Luehrmann, map design by Mark Matson.

wishes of Russian and American administrators for centralized control and also, increasingly, to the developing interests of Alutiiq families in being close to schools, stores, opportunities for earning a cash income, and cultural and technical amenities. By the turn of the nineteenth and twentieth centuries, the

Alutiiq had become a minority in the region, and throughout the twentieth century, human occupation contracted to fewer, more centralized places, leaving large areas of the outer Kenai coast, Prince William Sound, and the Pacific coast of the northern Alaska Peninsula entirely without permanent human settlement.

Sustaining small rural communities is a challenge across Alaska, but one thing the maps show is the flexibility with which Alutiiq people were able to spread out and contract their settlements over time, in accordance with the demands of subsistence and trading economies and political conditions. Over the past two centuries, such shifts in economic and political conditions reflected in settlement patterns occurred under the aegis of the two successive colonial powers; the remaining chapters provide a more thematically focused analysis of the different roles that the Alutiiq played in each colonial period.

ENDNOTES

1. Earlier accounts are from the Billings-Sarychev expedition, which visited Alaska in 1791–1792 (Merck 1980; Sarychev 1802; Sauer 1802) and the monks of the first Russian Orthodox mission to Alaska, notably Archimandrite Ioasaf, who stayed on Kodiak from 1794 to 1798 (Black 1977b; Dmytryshyn, Crownhart-Vaughan, and Vaughan 1988:465–484). Accounts relating to the beginning of the nineteenth century include Davydov 1810, 1812; Gedeon 1994; Langsdorff 1812; Lisianskii 1814.

2. Earlier, less detailed maps are reproduced by Black (1991:166, 167, 174, 178) and Efimov (1964:Map 178).

3. This could be one of the villages shown on Sarychev's map of Chiniak Bay, based on reports from the years 1808–1810. He indicates two "Aleut villages" on the south shore of Woman's Bay and an abandoned village on the north shore of Middle Bay. Both are arms of Chiniak Bay (Sarychev 1826:Folio XVI).

4. See Table 1 for the names of villages on Kodiak Island that I cannot identify with locations known from Lisianskii's map or other records.

5. The "company structure" a short distance south of St. Paul Harbor was obviously Sapozhnikovo/Sapozhkovo, where the *promyshlennik* Sapozhnikov raised cattle and vegetables (Davydov 1810:216–217).

6. Clark considers Minokovo to be an *odinochka*, a small *artel'* usually manned by only one Russian, but evidence for this is simply the paired arrangement of Minokovo and Orlovskoe, similar to other pairings of a Russian post and a Native village, and the fact that mid-nineteenth-century maps show Igak *artel'* (moved from the north shore of the bay in 1837) at the site of Minokovo, with a Native settlement to the west (Clark 1987:112).

7. Shelikhov claims that the combined population of the islands and coast (of the Kenai Peninsula and Prince William Sound), which he subjugated to the Russian tsar, was 50,000 people, but this is probably an exaggeration in the interest of obtaining the desired monopoly for his company (Shelikhov 1981:121).

8. The "-skoe" endings are common russifications of Native place names, formed in analogy with Russian village names; -*skoe* is a neuter adjective ending, short for -*skoe selenie*, that is, village of so-and-so. In Russian sources and maps, this ending is sometimes added to what are obviously indigenous place names, sometimes left out. To avoid unnecessary confusion, I omit it except in village names that have a Russian root.

9. The RAC correspondence once refers to Razbitovskoe as lying on Staraia gavan' (Old Harbor), as Three Saints Bay came to be called after the move of headquarters to St. Paul Harbor (RAC cs 14:289, May 16, 1837, to Kodiak office). This may indicate that it was located on mainland Kodiak or simply refer to Sitkalidak Island as located off the coast of Three Saints Bay and administrated from the Three Saints *artel'*.

10. The debate on the motivations for selling and buying is too complex to summarize here. A useful introduction are two essays reprinted in a collection on Alaskan history (Bolkhovitinov 1996; Welch 1996; also Kushner 1987; Okun' 1939:219–241). Most relevant perhaps for the understanding of subsequent Alutiiq history is the fact that American, especially Californian, businessmen in the 1860s had quite detailed knowledge of and interest in Alaska's natural resources, quite to the contrary of the famous cartoons depicting Alaska as a useless icebox (Haycox 2002:170–172; Kushner 1975).

11. Uyak also reappears in the 1880 census, but not in church records, so the census may be mentioning a seasonal village. In this case, the return of permanent settlement seems to have followed the establishment of a cannery later in the century (see the section accompanying Map 6).

12. Afognak parish, spanning Afognak, Spruce Island, the northwest coast of Kodiak, and the Pacific coast of the Alaska Peninsula, was split off from Kodiak parish in 1895. Before that date, information on those villages is included in the Kodiak parish records.

13. Map 5 shows the locations of those ACC posts from which records are preserved in the ACC archives, as indexed by Oswalt (1967b). Cannery locations are from Roppel 1986 and Moser 1898.

14. According to church records, Port Wrangell was still inhabited at the time of the eruption, but it appears in neither the 1910 nor the 1920 census (ARCA D261/180:Afognak parish census, 1912). A village on Cold Bay is listed in the 1910 and 1920 census, perhaps replacing neighboring Wide Bay, which does not appear in any records after 1900.

3

Riddles of Colonial Rule:
Fur Hunting for the Russians

Twentieth-century ethnohistorians were not the first to note that different colonial powers in northern regions used different methods of economic exploitation and that this affected their relationship to the land and its people. Russian Orthodox priests who observed the changes in Alutiiq life after 1867 often explained them in terms of the advent of capitalism. An overview of the history of Afognak village published in 1939 in the *Russian Orthodox American Messenger*, a journal published by the Orthodox Church in Alaska, portrays the Russian period as a continuation of traditional life. Tools and methods used for hunting and transportation remained much the same, the population lived "in isolation from the distant industrial centers of the mainland," received everything necessary from a friendly environment, and traded surplus pelts for items they could not produce. In the contemporary period, however, life is quite different:

> The former order of life has changed abruptly. Gone are whale and sea otter hunting; devalued by the market (for the hunter-trapper) are the products of the winter hunt on land—fox, ermine, land otter—abandoned and forgotten all local domestic industries and the creation, often artistic, of local crafts of bone, leather, etc. for home use and sale—they were pushed out by "Sears and Roebuck;" the "capitalist" fishing industry, which developed over the past decades, has created new laws of production, new centers of local life, new work methods. The native population of the islands was "proletarianized" under "new authorities, new masters" from centers on the mainland that are unknown to them. The union from San Francisco and the capitalist from the stock exchange

decide all local questions, taking away from the natives all initiative and independence, and all security of their budget, their family and social life . . . The local population instinctively, without fixed plan or guidance, tries to adapt to the new orders of life, regroups at new places of residence, not improving, not renewing that which was passed on to the natives at one place from fathers and grandfathers. (Pravoslavnyi Amerikanskii Vestnik 1939:109)

The author identifies dislocation, disruption of links between generations, and dependence on far-off centers for decisions and commodities as effects of capitalism. The consequence is a helpless disorientation in which the "natives" can only "instinctively" try to "adapt." What this article does not take into consideration is that "the former order of life" was already an adaptation to the no less abrupt changes brought by Russian rule and that throughout the nineteenth century the Alutiiq must already have found ways to deal with the discontinuity created by new places of settlement, separation of families, and the loss of many members of the older generations to epidemics.

Taking this article as a reminder how easy it is to romanticize one period over another, a comparison of the ways in which Native labor was incorporated into the different economic pursuits of the Russian and the U.S.-American colonists can help clarify differences between the two colonial periods. Students of Russian Alaska have often considered a correct analysis of colonial labor relations as a key to understanding how the Russians were able to establish their dominance over the Alutiiq region. And it is undeniable that the place of the Alutiiq in the economic system that developed after 1867 was dramatically different from before, although it would be misleading to describe those changes in terms of the proletarianization of hitherto free and self-sufficient hunters. As I discuss in Chapter 1, Eric Wolf's contrast between a Russian tributary mode of fur extraction and an American mercantile one does not quite hit the mark either. But Wolf at least makes clear that even in their relations with the RAC, the Alutiiq were not simply continuing their timeless subsistence pursuits and trading whatever surplus they happened to have with the Russian company. As Wolf's model shows, the RAC interfered in Alutiiq life as profoundly, if not from as great a geographical distance, as the unions and stock exchanges of the 1930s. But contrary to his claims, the company was not a collector of tribute for the state, but a private commercial enterprise, albeit one which employed unusual methods for recruiting and controlling the labor of Alutiiq hunters, as we will see below.

For the purpose of distingushing the Russian from the U.S. period, the contrast between the extraction of furs and the production of canned fish is in many ways more significant than differences between the Russian and American modes of fur extraction. As long as fur hunting continued in South Alaska after 1867, some of the patterns of labor and the special role of such groups as the Creoles persisted. In the developing canning industry, by contrast, the Alutiiq lost the importance of indispensable specialists because the cannery operators brought Asian contract workers up from California and Seattle along with the cannery equipment. Alutiiq were less desirable workers precisely because they were not as totally dependent as the *Orthodox American Messenger* portrays them—having subsistence fishing to fall back on, they were more liable to leave in mid-season than was a captive workforce of seasonal laborers thousands of miles from home.

The slow pace at which Alutiiq families became dependent on wage labor shows that incorporation into the capitalist world-system is not an automatic or one-sided process but has to do with the choices and developing needs of those who are incorporated. At the same time, the work of economic anthropologists in many parts of the world has demonstrated that expanding capitalism can thrive in contexts where subsistence economies help sustain the workforce, enabling capitalist employers to pay low wages (Meillassoux 1975; Roseberry 1989:145–146). As I trace the changing role of Alutiiq labor in the central pursuits of the Alaskan colonial economies in this and the following chapter, I ask how to conceptualize the different ways in which Alutiiq communities were incorporated into each colonial society. As I explain below, this is a matter of some dispute among scholars for the Russian period in particular. But in addition, we will see that the experience of nineteenth-century Alutiiq can add important facets to our understanding of colonial expansion as practiced by states with different political and economic systems.

Alutiiq Labor under the RAC

More than a century before the publication of the article quoted above, observers were already contrasting contemporary Native life on Kodiak Island with an irretrievably lost past. Hieromonk Gedeon, on Kodiak from 1804 to 1807, quotes a song he heard from Aleksei Ikuik, chief of Aiakhtalik from the south of Kodiak Island, to support this view:

> Grandfather diligently I seek
> Grandfather had baidaras Aminak I seek
> Grandfather diligently I seek, Agnak had sea otters
> Grandfather Kigiliak was a promyshlennik (hunter, provider)
> Grandfather Ukhtaiak used to shout (was shouting repeatedly)
>
> (quoted here from English translation in Gedeon 1989:47–48,
> notes in parentheses added by the translator)

Gedeon explains the significance of this song as follows:

> The Kad'iak people like this song very much and during festivities sing it often, with great sadness, because in it is mentioned: 1. formerly they possessed baidaras [umiaks] while nowadays a rare toion [chief] owns even a three-hatch baidarka [kayak]; 2. formerly, they had sea otters and wore sea otter parkas, while nowadays some have great difficulty in obtaining even a puffin parka, which in the old days were worn only by their slaves; and 3. their former Anayugak(s) [chiefs] on their arrival in baidara(s) at a settlement, or when meeting guests, shouted loudly, and immediately a multitude of people responded, ran to the beach and carried the baidara and baidarkas on their (backs, shoulders) onto the shore, while today many settlements are almost deserted, even though there had been no epidemics. (quoted from English translation in Gedeon 1989:48, additions in parentheses by the translator, in brackets my own)

At another place in his account, Gedeon contradicts the last statement by mentioning an epidemic "which raged through all of Kad'iak" in 1804 and killed many old shamans (Gedeon 1989:60). Langsdorff (1812:55) also mentions disease as one of the causes of the depopulation of the island, and Lisianskii's estimate of a 50 percent population decline within less than fifty years of the arrival of the first Russians (see Chapter 2, section accompanying Map 1) could hardly be explained without the occurrence of epidemic disease. But further causes of population decline and material impoverishment lay in the uses of Alutiiq labor by the Russian colonial administration.

The main objective of the RAC was obtaining sea otter pelts, which could be sold at great profit to the Chinese at Kiakhta. Since the Russians never acquired the necessary skills to hunt the clever animals from *baidarkas* at sea, they always relied on Aleut and Alutiiq hunters to do it for them.[1] Whereas in Siberia, private hunting by individual Russian trappers existed alongside the collection of tribute (*iasak*) from the Natives by government officials, in Alaska Russians were employed by the RAC merely to supervise Native hunters and to provision the colony. Before the RAC gained its monopoly in 1799, *iasak* collection had led to violent abuses in Alaska, where competing companies imposed *iasak* on the Natives. Besides, the practice was not very profitable even in Siberia, owing to the high costs of outfitting expeditions of tribute collectors and providing them with gifts for the tributary populations. Catherine the Great prohibited *iasak* collecting in Alaska in 1788. However, shipping trade goods to Alaska was expensive and time consuming, and the Russian companies active in the North Pacific needed to keep the costs of procuring furs down because they incurred far greater expenses transporting their furs to the Chinese border on the overland route from Okhotsk to Kiakhta than did their British and U.S. competitors, who sailed from Alaska straight to the port of Canton, from which Russian ships were excluded. *Iasak* obligations were not replaced with free trade but with the conscription of Aleut and Alutiiq hunters for organized hunting parties, although this practice was legalized only in the second charter of the RAC in 1821 (Bychkov 1992:107; Dmytryshyn, Crownhart-Vaughan, and Vaughan 1989:362; Gibson 1987:34, 1996:23, 25; Stephan 1994:36).

Alutiiq men were assigned to hunting parties by the RAC foremen, known as *baidarshchiki*, who commanded the Russian posts around the island. By the early nineteenth century, the overhunting of sea otters in western Alaska forced the parties to go ever farther distances. Gedeon and Davydov describe four sea otter hunting parties that were organized annually in the Alutiiq area, the biggest of which had numbered up to 800 *baidarkas* in past years and was at 300 *baidarkas* in 1804. It gathered at St. Paul Harbor in April and went to the vicinity of Sitka, reinforced along the way by men dispatched from posts on Kenai Peninsula (Aleksandrovskaia odinochka) and Prince William Sound (Konstantinovskii redut). This party usually returned to St. Paul Harbor in August, but it frequently got caught in storms on the open sea, leading to the death by drowning of many men. Around the turn of the eighteenth century alone, such storms and drownings occurred in 1792, 1798, 1799, 1800, and 1805.

The second party consisted of those whose *baidarkas* or skills were judged insufficient for this long and dangerous trip. From the southeast of Kodiak, such men traveled to Tugidak Island, Ukamok, and on toward the Alaska Peninsula, where the third party, from northwestern Kodiak and Katmai, also hunted. The fourth party consisted of old men and boys who were allowed to remain near Kodiak and hunt near the islands between Kodiak and Cook Inlet, although sea otters were already scarce there. As we will see below, some of these old men and boys also hunted birds and small mammals to procure material for clothing. Chugach men who were unfit for the crossing to Sitka were also required to hunt near their homes, but it is likely that only some of their villages were under strong enough Russian control to enforce this rule (Davydov 1977:194–197; Gedeon 1989:62–64, 69–70 and note 41; Sarafian 1970:228).

Payment for these long and dangerous trips and the valuable pelts they furnished was made only to a very small degree in European trade goods comparable to those offered by the HBC in Canada. Throughout its existence, the RAC had great trouble providing Alaska with even enough goods to keep its own men clothed and fed (Gibson 1976:48). Excavations at the site of the first Russian settlement in Three Saints Bay, uncovering the remains of dwellings

"Five Men in Three Kayaks, All in Costume Fishing on Water Near Shore." Although it shows halibut fishing instead of sea otter hunting, this 1872 graphite painting by the American traveler Henry Wood Elliott captures some of the drama and danger faced by Alutiiq boatmen in their subsistence pursuits. The three men in the two *baidarkas* in the center are stabilizing one another by holding on to paddles from both sides, while the front man in the two-hole *baidarka* hauls out the halibut on a string and his partner in the one-hole *baidarka* prepares to kill it with a club. To the left, two men demonstrate speedy synchronous paddling. *Courtesy of National Anthropological Archives, Smithsonian Institution, Inventory No. 08594700.*

dating to the late eighteenth and early nineteenth centuries, yielded a very limited range of possible trade goods: a few varieties of glass beads, and copper and lead finger rings. A barracks apparently inhabited by Native workers contained some metal tools but also the full range of Alutiiq lithic technology, none of which seems to have been effectively replaced by Russian goods in the first decades of Russian presence. The same scarcity of European goods was found at the slightly more recent post of Igak (features dating between 1800 and 1837; see Map 2) in present-day Saltery Cove (Crowell 1997:52, 219, 221, 230). Even adding the tobacco and cloth mentioned as payment for hunters in written sources, which cannot be expected to be preserved in the archaeological record, the material amenities islanders could hope to gain from working for the Russians were small at least through the first third of the nineteenth century. A different situation was only found in structures at Karluk dating from after the 1837 smallpox epidemic. Here, English earthenware attests to the effects of an 1839 agreement with the HBC to supply the Russian colony with provisions and trade goods (Knecht and Jordan 1985:24).

In this context, the interpretation of the RAC's economic activities advanced by the Russian ethnohistorian Andrei Grinev shows its force. Grinev argues that the activities of the RAC are best understood not as trade but as a system of administrative control over the production and redistribution of key resources (Grinev 1999, 2000). It seems that rather than entering into trade relations, the Russians managed to gain control of the redistribution of such essential goods as dried fish, clothing and *lavtaki* (split sea lion skins used to make *baidarka* covers) within Alutiiq society. They did so by forcing the most able-bodied men to spend much of their time hunting furs for the company rather than attending to their own kin group's subsistence needs, while simultaneously organizing other groups of Alutiiq to prepare the much-needed supplies that were then traded with the hunters.

For example, while most of the men were away on the sea otter hunt all summer and had little time left to provide their families with the skins needed for parkas, the RAC organized elderly and sick men into small bird-hunting parties. Bird skin parkas were light, warm, and watertight but fragile and needed to be replaced frequently. As the song recorded by Gedeon recalls, sea otter parkas had been the clothing of choice for wealthy people before the arrival of the Russians. But since the RAC had prohibited the use of sea otter pelts for clothing, only low-prestige materials such as hare, marmots, squirrels, and birds remained (Davydov 1977:192–193). The parkas, as well as waterproof gutskin coats known to the Russians as *kamleikas*, were sewn by the women on order of the RAC, then used as payment for the sea otter hunters. All observers agree that this arrangement was very profitable for the RAC:

> [A] father is sent to hunt birds, the son to hunt sea otters, or the younger brother to hunt birds, the elder brother to hunt sea otters; having taken from everyone all the bird skins, after the men's wives, mothers, or sisters processed the skins and finished the parkas, the latter are issued to their men—and to others—against the sea otters they take. (Gedeon 1989:65)

> Besides beads, tobacco, and other European trifles, they are paid for their catch with parkas of birdskin, squirrel, and marmot. This trade is most profitable to the Company, because it costs it almost nothing. The material from which the women sew different items of clothing is procured by the inhabitants themselves on assignment and rendered to the store houses, from where they themselves then purchase it. For their labor the seamstresses only

Woman wearing waterproof gutskin *kamleika*, 1919. This woman from Kodiak Island is wearing a *kamleika* from seal intestines decorated with feathers much like those that Alutiiq women sewed for distribution by the RAC in the nineteenth century. *Photograph by Robert F. Griggs, courtesy of Archives and Special Collections, University of Alaska Anchorage, National Geographic Society Collection, hmc-0186-volume6-5210.*

receive the needles which are left with them after their work, and a toion's [chief's] wife sometimes gets a packet of tobacco. (Lisianskii 1947:191)

Sea lion skins for *baidarka* covers were procured and redistributed in a similar manner. The RAC had Alutiiq men hunt sea lions and then sold the skins to men who did not have covers for their own *baidarka*. These men paid for the skins by trapping foxes in the winter, together with those bird hunters who did not meet the quota required of them (Davydov 1977:195–196; Gedeon 1989:63–65).

Lisianskii—who, unlike some other Russian travelers who left accounts of the activities of the RAC, is generally not a particularly sharp critic of the company and excuses its exploitation of Natives with the argument that they are too lazy to provide for themselves—reports that all inhabitants of Kodiak Island were involved in some form of work for the RAC and often had no time left to gather enough provisions to feed themselves during the winter (Lisianskii 1994:163; 1947:191).

Even for food provisions, the needs of the RAC had to be satisfied first. Some Alutiiq men were sent out to hunt whales, of which they were allowed to keep less than half the meat. Women were required to provide dried fish and berries to RAC posts. This food, in addition to the dried fish produced by the *kaiury*, a special class of enslaved workers (see below), in turn became a source of the supplies with which the RAC could outfit their hunting parties or which it could advance to hunters over the winter, holding them in a state of debt. RAC employees also cohabited with Alutiiq women since there were very few Russian women in the colonies. Sometimes this may have happened by mutual consent, sometimes by coercion, but the absence of these women, not only as marriage partners for Alutiiq men but also as gatherers and processors of food, must have been felt in the villages (Davydov 1977:195; Gedeon 1989:66; Gibson 1996:38; Grinev 1999:26–27).

While the freedom with which the RAC drew on Alutiiq men and women for any task it needed done recalls the use feudal lords in Russia made of their serfs as a "natural resource" (Yaney 1973:129; cf. Sarafian 1970:154), Alutiiq were nominally free subjects and legally had to be paid for their work. Theoretically, they were paid in store credit, and it just so happened that most of the goods kept in the stores had actually been produced by Alutiiq women, whose unremunerated labor was likewise illegal. By 1818 Alutiiq hunters and workers were sometimes able to buy some "imported goods at an extraordinary and intolerable price" for their store credit in addition to the locally produced clothes, as the naval officer Vasilii Golovnin reports (Arndt 1985 [1861]:65).

There was another class of laborers, the *kaiury* (a Siberian term for slaves), who were completely bound to the RAC. Before the arrival of the Russians, the people of Kodiak had themselves held war captives as slaves, called *kalgi*. These were expropriated by the Russians after their conquest of Kodiak in 1784. Reinforced by formerly free men and women accused of crimes against the Russians, this class of people lived in the Russian posts. Male *kaiury* provided fish, meat, fox furs, timber, and hay and worked in construction, salt production, and brick making. Women processed fish and whale meat, gathered berries and roots, made nets, processed skins, and sewed. *Kaiury* were the first Alutiiq to be relocated by the Russians to new settlements away from Kodiak, on Ukamok Island, and at Sutkhum off the Alaska Peninsula coast. They were theoretically in service for life, unless they were bought out or replaced by their families (Davydov 1977:114, 190–191; Gedeon 1989:61–62; Lisianskii 1994:164).

As the anthropologist Claude Meillassoux (1998:89–91) points out, such a form of slavery, in which slaves are acquired as adults and can be replaced before the end of their productive life, is more profitable for the masters than serfdom, where each serf contributes to production only for part of his or her existence but still has to be supported by the serf community during childhood and old age, so that part of the labor power of the serfs of working age is taken up by providing for those unable to work. Even so, as Grinev notes, the RAC never made attempts to increase the number of *kaiury* beyond the level of about one tenth of the able-bodied Native population, apparently finding it more feasible or economical to use free hunters for the seasonal activity of the sea otter hunt (Grinev 1999:27). After 1820 those *kaiury* still in company service were released and replaced by seasonally hired workers (Sarafian 1970:174).[2]

Alutiiq Society and the Power of the RAC

Obviously, such extensive control over Alutiiq labor power in the absence of attractive outside trade goods could not have been established without what both Wolf and Grinev refer to as "extraeconomic coercion," that is, violence. But just how it was upheld over the long term is something of an enigma. Although the relations of the RAC to Aleut and Alutiiq hunters outwardly looked like capitalist hire of workers, they were actually obligatory labor that would have been impossible to establish without at least initial violent intimidation (Grinev 1997:177–178). Hieromonk Makarii, member of the first ecclesiastic mission sent to Kodiak in 1794, reports that Natives who brought in fewer fox pelts than required were beaten with sticks (Dmytryshyn, Crownhart-Vaughan, and Vaughan 1988:499). Gedeon, probably also relying on the testimony of the monks of this mission, describes how Russian *promyshlenniki* forced Alutiiq hunters to join the party of 1801 at gunpoint and with threats of putting them into chains. Still, the RAC had too few men at its disposal to govern the region by military force and violence alone. In all of Alaska there were about 400 Russians in 1805, which leaves no more than about 100–150 on Kodiak (Fedorova 1971:248; Gedeon 1989:69).

It is unlikely that the Alutiiq cooperated out of satisfaction with the system or loyalty to the Russians. Especially Davydov is quite clear about the fact that the Russians were deeply resented. In November 1802, only the arrival of his ship, the *Sv. Elizaveta*, disabused the Natives of the hope that they could kill all the Russians on Kodiak, since no ship had arrived from Okhotsk for five years and the Tlingit had been successful in their attack on Novoarkhangel'sk earlier that year.

Davydov gives examples of Kodiak and Chugach hunters allegedly killing individual Russians during hunting trips, blaming the death on an accident or an attack by enemy tribes. He also records more subdued expressions of hatred. When catching halibut for the Russians, Alutiiq fishermen smashed the heads, which, being the tastiest part, they were always careful to preserve for themselves. When a Russian came into a village, his guide would tell the people that he is a good friend who speaks their language, so that they were warned not to say anything they did not want him to hear. The safety of the Russians on the island, according to Davydov, was ensured only by the practice of taking hostages from the chief's family in every village near which the Russians founded a post (Davydov 1810:196–199, 1812:60–61, 67, 1977:156, 162–163).

Members of the Russian clergy represented the situation on Kodiak as equally violent, but for them the RAC was the aggressor, the Natives were helpless victims. The monks of the first mission had very difficult relations with Baranov from the start, and Gedeon joined them in protesting abuses of power and obstruction of missionary work (Dmytryshyn, Crownhart-Vaughan, and Vaughan 1988:465–475; Gedeon 1989:69–71).

While firearms and hostages made up in part for inferior numbers and gave the Russians a certain military advantage over Alutiiq opponents, this does not seem to be a satisfactory explanation for the RAC's success in upholding a system of forced labor that encompassed the entire Kodiak Archipelago. If Grinev is right and the economic dependency of the Alutiiq on the RAC as redistributor of important goods was a decisive factor, the question how the Company gained this position still remains. The available sources on the Russian conquest of Kodiak Island provide only partial answers. The first Russian hunters who reached Kodiak Island certainly did not find the inhabitants to be helpless but quite capable of defending themselves. The population of this densely settled island, experienced in warfare and probably warned of Russian conduct on the Aleutians through war captives and trading partners, prevented all Russian attempts to obtain furs from the island until 1784, when Grigorii Shelikhov managed to realize his plan to establish a permanent settlement as a base for hunting operations (Black 1991:165–168; Crowell 1997:33–34; Petrov and Troitskaia 1997:118–121; Shelikhov 1981 [1791]: 41–42).

Shelikhov, with 130 Russians and 12 Aleuts under his command, had great trouble overcoming the resistance of the islanders. His accounts of the conquest, juxtaposed with those of members of his crew and of Arsentii Aminak, an Alutiiq man interviewed by the naturalist Holmberg in 1851,[3] have been critically analyzed by Lydia Black (1991:169–173) and Aron Crowell (1997:40–46).

Having, after an initial failed attempt, defeated a significant force assembled on a fortified rock off Sitkalidak Island, presumably near the later site of Razbitovskoe village, Shelikhov took the survivors hostage and proceeded to construct a settlement at his place of landing, Three Saints Bay. He also sent out expeditions along the east coast of the island up to Afognak and Shuyak, where Russian firearms defeated small groups of adversaries. Most of the captives were eventually returned to their families; others were retained as hostages and settled near Three Saints Bay, a strategy that seems to have successfully prevented further attacks on the Russian settlement. The persisting memory of the defeat is shown by the Alutiiq place name, *Awa'uq*, to become numb, designating the bay on Sitkalidak Island (Partition Cove in English) where the refuge rock was located. Aminak reports that the stench of bodies made the place uninhabitable (Holmberg 1856:417; Knecht, Haakanson, and Dickson 2003).

Shelikhov claims that he had reason to suspect that reinforcements from "Kiliuda, Ugashin, Ugatak, Chinigak" were on their way (Shelikhov 1981:39; these may correspond to Kiliuda, Ugashek, and Ugatak on Map 1 and to Chiniak either on Woody Island or Chiniak Bay). Black concludes that Shelikhov's success lay in "breaking up or preventing an archipelago-wide alliance and manag[ing] to enlist some Kodiak Islanders from the western and Pacific Shores as his willing (or more likely unwilling) allies against other regions" (Black 1991:173). The place names given by Shelikhov suggest that the actual or projected alliance was not archipelago-wide but concentrated on the eastern (Pacific) shore. Differences in material culture and dialect indicate a division between southeastern and northwestern Kodiak Island. Whether this division sometimes led to armed conflict is uncertain, but Gedeon says that each side had its own traditional enemies on the mainland and the Aleutians, which would mean that each organized for war independently of the other (Black 1991:173; Davydov 1812:1–2; Gedeon 1989:43–44).

After the Russian victory, Shelikhov's alliances with the recently defeated neighbors of the Three Saints Bay *artel'*, as well as with the people at Karluk, the first Russian post on the west coast, may have prevented the villages along either coast from uniting against the Russians. Such strategic alliances were facilitated by the political organization of the islanders. Shelikhov's men encountered no permanent island-wide political or military institutions but found that elite families in the stratified village societies were already accustomed to establishing alliances with neighbors and rivals in order to enhance their own status (Davydov 1977:159; Gedeon 1989:42–43; Moss and Erlandson 1992:73; Townsend 1980:128–132).

Davydov had the following understanding of the islanders' political organization:

Their villages are situated on the coast all around the island and each has its own chief, called toion (a Yakut word) by the Russians. Some chiefs rule over many settlements which are descended from one tribe and named after the bay or cape near which they live. The power of the village chief is not great at all: often the Islanders show more respect and obedience to some rich person or good hunter. [. . .] In former times every Koniag considered himself a member of the village in which he lived, and as having equal rights with all the others in matters of general concern, which were always decided at assemblies of those Islanders who were most distinguished, by bravery or in other ways; in personal matters, everyone was subject to his own will only. (Davydov 1812:113, 115–116)[4]

According to Davydov, chiefdom was hereditary, usually passed on from uncle to nephew (Davydov 1812:114). Gedeon adds that the Alutiiq word for chief (whom he calls *khoziain* in Russian, "landlord" or "owner") was *ana-yugak*[5] and that he owned the *kazhim*, the large house in which communal events were held. An *anayugak* would designate "a son, a brother, an uncle, a son-in-law" as his successor by proclaiming his name at a feast for the male members of the community in the *kazhim*. Gedeon agrees that the powers of the *anayugak* were limited. He was accorded special respect in council, silence and quiet were observed in his presence, and whoever wanted to leave the village had to declare the reasons for doing so to him But the *anayugak* had no power to punish offenders except to redress a personal injury and "ruled solely over his own family, fosterlings, and *kalgi*." To persuade his followers to go to war he used "counsel and gifts," rather than being able to order them to go (Gedeon 1989:41; see also Ioasaf's description in Black 1977b:84).

The picture of Alutiiq political organization emerging from the Russian sources is that there were leaders who controlled powerful kin groups and held more limited influence over the general population of one or a number of villages, but not across larger regions. For the RAC, this system of ranks with local limits to chiefly power had the advantage that there was no unified resistance from the islanders, but an alliance with a village chief could help secure the cooperation of his followers. The Russians at Three Saints Bay noticed the political fragmentation of the island early on, and offered themselves to the chiefs of nearby villages as allies against old enemies.

Shelikhov reports that even though the presence of high-ranking hostages among the Russians did not cause Alutiiq attacks on exploring parties to stop immediately, Alutiiq resistance eventually ended because of his men's show of military prowess and superior weaponry—at the sight of a rock being blown up with gunpowder, "the Koniags of the island abandoned their efforts to force us out" (Shelikhov 1981:42). This demonstration made them realize the appeal of an alliance with the Russians for protection "from attacks by savages from other places" (1981:45). Davydov quotes the reflections of an Alutiiq chief who seems to assume the possibility of an island-wide alliance but also seems to expect that eliminating the Russians might cause new fighting among villages:

> In former times the Islanders still thought to rid themselves of the Russians at some point. In this matter they placed their hope in one of their chiefs who was a great terror to all the neighboring peoples. The Koniagas proposed to him the daring venture of destroying the Russians. Shelikhov, hearing of this, called the chief to him and reproached him for his evil intentions. The Savage gave him the following answer: You know that I am not afraid to die and that I can move the Islanders to destroy you; but if later the Russians come in greater numbers, what will happen to our wives and children? Besides, you have saved us from fighting amongst ourselves; and so, as long as I am alive the Koniagas will live in peace with the Russians. He kept his word, but of course only because it would have been impossible not to honor it. (Translation modified from Davydov 1977:168)[6]

Davydov's rendering of this chief's speech portrays his decision to keep peace with the Russians as decisive for the safety of Russians on Kodiak. It is doubtful that he alone had the authority to ensure that all islanders would keep peace. But Gedeon mentions that men from several villages sometimes assembled to go to war under one *anayugak* (Gedeon 1989:42–43), indicating that the decision of a respected, renowned leader not to attack the Russians may have had an impact beyond the boundaries of his village. The local traditions of concluding and cementing alliances were another part of Alutiiq politics that the Russians found quite compatible with their own practices.

Cooperation with Native leaders in order to facilitate the administration and exploitation of subject populations was established policy in Siberia. The word *toion*, part of the vocabulary for talking about Native societies that RAC employees brought to Alaska from Siberia, was a Yakut word used to designate persons identified as clan/tribal chiefs (*rodovye nachal'niki*). They were charged with *iasak*-collecting within their village or kin groups after the reform of Native administration in 1763 (Slezkine 1994:69–70).

Hostage-taking in particular was a practice familiar to both sides. In Siberia, Russians had adopted the Mongol practice of taking hostages from the relatives of subjugated leaders (at one time, the Russian princes were such vassals in the Mongol empire) to ensure the punctuality of tribute payments and the peaceful conduct of their relatives. Between warring villages of the Alaskan Pacific coast, high-ranking families exchanged children when peace was concluded. Alutiiq chiefs may have considered it to their own advantage to give hostages to the Russians as signs of alliance, even though the one-sided nature of the transaction—hostage-taking instead of hostage exchange—shows that Russians were in a position to disregard Alutiiq etiquette after their military victories (Crowell 1997:47; Forsyth 1992:41; Gedeon 1989:44).

Another practice at which both sides were adept was strategic gift-giving. In a society in which a chief's ability to entertain guests and provide them with gifts was a key to his power, even the limited supply of goods brought by the Russians may have made them attractive allies. Shelikhov mentions "small gifts" handed out to pacify the population near Three Saints Bay, and "some trade goods" given to a party sent to "Kinai Bay" (Cook Inlet) "to gather information" (1981 [1791]:42, 47). As mentioned above, beads and metal rings were found in the excavations at Three Saints Bay. The same scarcity of trade goods that made a fur trade in the strict sense of the word impossible must have made the beads and other small trifles valued prestige items. Exotic beads, those made of amber for instance, had been highly valued trade goods and objects of raids in the area before the arrival of the Russians, and jewelry had been an indicator of rank (Davydov 1977:149; Ivanov 1949:202). Given the importance of owning and distributing property evident from the Russian accounts of Alutiiq chiefdom, the strategic value of Russian trade goods in gaining ascendancy over rivals, rather than their utility in everyday life, may have made them attractive to chiefs. Shelikhov claims that the sheer admiration of the islanders for the technical inventions of the Russians (for example, a reflector lantern) and for the speed with which they built their houses brought them to "willingly put themselves under my authority" (1981:43). Although this statement is obviously self-serving, the display of objects, intended by Shelikhov as a demonstration of superior civilization, may have resonated with the role of owning and displaying prestigious goods in Pacific coast societies, showing Alutiiq leaders how an association with the newcomers could work to their own advantage.

Once the Russians were successfully settled on Kodiak, could a close relationship with chiefs have helped them establish the system of forced labor described above? The information on Alutiiq social institutions supplied by early Russian sources is fragmentary, but ethnohistorians have interpreted it in the light of similarities to better-described societies on the Pacific coast of North America (Lantis 1947:76–78; Townsend 1980). Joan Townsend finds that the importance of feasting and gift distribution for the determination of social status, alongside descent, is characteristic of all societies of the Alaskan Pacific

Rim. She defines them all as "ranked" societies, in which status depended not only on individual abilities but to a large degree on descent and wealth (cf. Fried 1967:109). There were slaves, some temporary, and some for life. Davydov's description of the council consisting only of those distinguished by bravery or "in other ways" indicates a hierarchy, or meritocracy, within the free class as well. Again referring to the classifications of different social systems proposed by Morton H. Fried, Townsend calls the distinction between slaves and free persons a class division, because the slaves did "not have equal access to the basic resources that sustain life," whereas the free class contained different ranks, distinguished not so much by access to resources but by social recognition. Chiefs in the area were what is known in anthropology as "big men" or "rich men," who maintained their status by redistributing the products that their kin groups accumulated. While all members of a kin group were able to use beaches, fishing and hunting sites, the chiefs managed to appropriate part of the product of their relatives' labor and to use it for feasting and gift-giving and to bind poorer people to their households to enhance both their own status and that of their kin group (Townsend 1980:134, 136–139; cf. Polanyi 1944:47–52).

Chiefs in Alaskan Pacific Rim societies had a more stable power base than big men in areas such as Melanesia, where descent played a much smaller role and status could be as easily lost as gained. But the redistribution of resources still did not reach the scale at which political anthropology speaks of chiefdoms, where networks of redistribution unite whole regions into one social network. In societies relying on collective agricultural projects such as large-scale irrigation or storage of grain in particular, certain high-ranking lineages can come to monopolize the roles of "coordinating specialized activities, planning and supervising public works, managing redistribution, and leading in war" (Wolf 1982:96–97), potentially transforming gradations of rank into class distinctions when certain families start to control vital economic goods (Sahlins 1972:132–148; Service 1962:148–149). In Alaskan Pacific Rim societies, redistribution remained at a more modest, local scale within coresidential or closely neighboring groups often related through kinship ties (Townsend 1980:149). The wider circles of redistribution built up by the RAC were a qualitatively new way of exerting control within Alutiiq society.

The extent to which the *anayugak* controlled the economy of an Alutiiq village is hard to infer from the sources. They say little about territoriality and resource ownership: were sites for fishing, gathering, and hunting open to all, restricted to inhabitants of a village, or to members of a kin group? Arsentii Aminak told Holmberg that his father "owned" Ukamok Island with its wealth of fur-bearing animals because it was given to him by a relative who had discovered it in the course of a perilous journey (Holmberg 1856:417–419). This story could be an appropriation of the Russian concept of the right of discovery but also recalls Northwest Coast custom, whereby resource ownership and other privileges were vested in the heads of families and accounts of how privileges were acquired often involved travel (Dauenhauer and Dauenhauer 1987:24–26; Drucker 1939:59–60).

Archaeological evidence indicates that Kodiak Island had a very high population density in the centuries before the arrival of the Russians, so that large, permanent villages existed close to one another, and the sharing of resources must have posed problems. Since subsistence opportunities varied with village location, it is possible that specific villages exchanged local products with other villages. The nineteenth-century pattern of seasonal movement between winter villages and various summer camps for fishing, sealing, and other activities would then be a consequence of population decline (Erlandson et al. 1992:46, 53).

Perhaps some of the neighboring villages with a common chief and common ancestry mentioned by Davydov were exploiting such different niches. In such cases, the chief may have organized the redistribution of the products of specialized resource harvesting. Chiefs may also have supervised the timing of hunting expeditions and organized groups of hunters into teams, analogous to the teams they dispatched to Russian posts to participate in sea otter hunts for the RAC. But even if this was so, there would be no direct correspondence to the RAC's role in organizing the procurement and redistribution of sea otter pelts, bird skin, and sea lion skin, for which contingents of people were combined from different villages and assigned to hunt in regions where none of them claimed any ownerships or use rights. Moreover, the RAC positioned itself as an intermediary in the exchange of men's and women's labor that would normally occur within one household. By binding the bulk of male labor power in the pursuit of sea otters, the RAC created for itself the task of coordinating groups of men who procured the raw materials for clothing and of women who made garments from them to clothe the men who had brought the materials as well as those whose products were removed to the outside market. When it appropriated the slaves, the RAC also took over one of the chiefs' sources of wealth and generosity, further consolidating its own monopoly on the accumulation and redistribution of wealth (cf. Ioasaf in Black 1977b:84).

The system of colonial labor set up by the RAC thus simultaneously relied on certain features of Alutiiq society and stretched their limits, placing heavy strains on Alutiiq social life. Based on Russia's claim to first discovery of Alaska north of the fifty-fifth parallel, and on its privileges granted by the tsar, the RAC considered itself entitled to the products of the whole country and the labor of its inhabitants, and also to the profits obtained from extracting one kind of product—the sea otter pelts—for sale on an external market. The sense of entitlement to land and people, combined with the exigencies of inefficient supply networks, led the company to set up the system I described above, in which the RAC was able to control the production of key goods and force Alutiiq hunters to buy items from their stores that Alutiiq women were producing, a process in which Alutiiq often accumulated debts to the company. Andrei Grinev refers to this system as "colonial politarism." In colonial politarism, the colonial administration—in this case a private company acting under imperial charter—holds a role analogous to the leading family of the chiefdoms described above: it exercises power through organizing key collective economic activities and controlling their products, some of which are important to the survival of the population, others (in this case, the procurement of sea otter skins) make the colonial enterprise profitable (Grinev 1996).[7]

Once established, the RAC could have maintained this central place in the system of redistribution of products within Alutiiq society without constant use of military force. This particular strategy of rule also explains the limits of Russian efforts to change Alutiiq society. Since the organization of collective activities would not have been possible without the cooperation of Alutiiq chiefs, the RAC had no interest in destroying the social order of ranks among the Alutiiq, although it worked to modify the chief's role in important ways. As in Siberia, the company called indigenous chiefs *toions*, but their role on the Aleutians and on Kodiak was more tightly integrated with colonial affairs than in Siberia. Rather than independently collecting pelts from their followers and handing them over to a tribute collector, *toions* consulted with RAC employees in planning the hunt and assigning men to the hunting parties, which were composed of men from different villages and which no single *toion* would have had the authority to organize by himself. The great distances to the remaining sea otter hunting grounds and the need for large groups of hunters capable of warding off Tlingit attacks may have been the reasons for this more complex form of organization compared to the collection of tribute in Siberia.

An aspect of the relationship between the RAC and the Alutiiq that was similar to the tributary system in Siberia was that the obligation to hunt for the company was separate from normal subsistence pursuits. Although the RAC made some efforts to accumulate stores of food for the hunting parties, ultimately Alutiiq hunters were expected to provide for themselves and their kin after they had satisfied the requirements of the RAC in pelts and provisions (Lisianskii 1947:191). Again, this meant that Russians had relatively little interest in changing the lives of their new subjects or assimilating them, beyond forcing them to accommodate the disruptions of their subsistence cycles described above. Except for a Christian mission, which arrived in 1794 and at first found its work obstructed rather than supported by the RAC, there was little effort to transform Alutiiq life until the further decline of the population made active measures seem necessary.

Similar patterns of minimal interference into Native community life and subsistence are typical of fur trading companies throughout the circumpolar north, especially during early periods of the fur trade (Kardulias 1990). What was distinctive about the RAC was that it managed to operate with a very small input of its own trade goods. Through a combination of military force over a population weakened by disease, diplomatic efforts attuned to the Alutiiq's own system of ranks, and the creation of a need for the redistribution of essential goods, the RAC kept the Alutiiq as the cheapest possible kind of labor—almost unpaid—for as long as the demographic and political situation allowed it.

Legal and Practical Changes

Most studies of the history of the RAC agree that the situation of Native and Russian employees improved after 1818, when Aleksandr Baranov, who had been manager of the company's Alaskan territories for twenty-eight years, was replaced by a succession of naval officers, most serving a term of five years. Russian employees were accorded a fixed (but insufficient) yearly salary instead of the (undervalued) equivalent of a share of the hunt, and acceptable and unacceptable uses of Native labor were more clearly defined when the company charter was renewed in 1821 (Alekseev 1975:177; Arndt 1985 [1861]; Black 1988:78–79; Gibson 1976:15; Sarafian 1970:33). The available sources on Kodiak Island suggest, however, that legal and administrative transitions were only one reason for eventual changes in Native policy. Concerns over disease and population decline added the needed sense of urgency.

The 1821 charter of the RAC (Dmytryshyn, Crownhart-Vaughan, and Vaughan 1989:353–366) is the first document establishing and regulating the RAC's right to conscript Native workers. The statement in paragraph 51, allowing half the male "islanders" between 18 and 50 to be drafted for company service for a maximum of three years, is probably a restriction of established practice but also the first legalization of the conscription of Alutiiq hunters (whose exemption from *iasak* and other taxes is confirmed in paragraph 45). Even with the restriction, complaints from villages that not enough men were left to hunt and fish for the winter continue, suggesting that the rule was not always kept. The decline of the Alutiiq population aggravated the shortage of labor for both the RAC and the villages. In the winter of 1829, the *toions* of several villages told the manager of the Kodiak office that they would have no men to send on the long-distance hunting parties in the spring, because no one would be left to hunt for food (RAC cs 7:187, May 26, 1830, to Main Office; also 42:152v, Aug 25, 1860, to Kodiak office).

Finding men and particularly women for special assignments such as the *artel'* on the Kurile Islands and Fort Ross in California was difficult. In 1840, the Chief Manager notes that no "Aleut" who returned from his term of six to eight years on the Kuriles had ever asked to go back, and all who were currently there wanted to leave at the first opportunity because pay was lower than on Kodiak and communication with Alaska difficult. Apparently it was not possible to send a ship every three years to make the required change of crews. In 1839, the Kodiak office was ordered to send six widows or orphan girls from among the smallpox survivors to the Kuriles, where women were badly needed to sew and cook for the hunters. During a visit to Fort Ross in the summer of 1838, Chief Manager Kupreianov decided that as many "Aleuts" as possible should be withdrawn and replaced by local Indians, since there was little sea otter hunting in California any more and the hunters were needed elsewhere (RAC cs 18:203–205v, May 2, 1840, to Main Office; 17:30–30v, Feb 20, 1839, to Kodiak office; 16:341, Aug 10, 1838, to Ft. Ross office).

The greater care for the diminished numbers of hunters is also evident from the fact that, by the 1830s, the perilous open-sea crossings by *baidarka* were given up, and hunters and *baidarkas* were transported in RAC ships. Fedor Litke, who visited Novoarkhangel'sk on a round-the-world expedition in 1828, writes that hunters were taken from Kodiak Island to Sitka on a sailing ship, whereas those remaining in the vicinity of Kodiak or the Peninsula traveled in *baidarkas*. By 1837, ships traveling between St. Paul Harbor and Novoarkhangel'sk were instructed to take hunters to Ukamok in the spring and pick them up at the end of the season (RAC cs 14: 6v–7, Jan 21, 1837, to Ensign Dingel'shtet, commander of the *Aleut*; 14:7v, Jan 21, 1837, to Ensign Kashevarov, commander of the *Kvikhpak*; 14:264v–265, May 10, 1837, to Ensign Kashevarov; Litke 1948:66).

Pay for hunting and services also seems to have become more fact than fiction during this period. According to Kirill Khlebnikov, manager of the Novoarkhangel'sk office in the early 1830s, parkas and *lavtaki* issued to hunters were no longer charged to their accounts from 1816, and those bringing their own *baidarka* complete with cover were credited 10 rubles, as reimbursement for their work or for the price of the skins at company stores (Khlebnikov 1994:85; Liapunova and Fedorova 1979:38). Each pelt delivered to the company brought credit at the company stores. Registered complaints in this period are no longer that hunters are not paid at all but that the pay is too low compared to the prices of goods in company stores. The prices paid to Alutiiq hunters and workers for furs and goods were increased repeatedly between 1818 and 1836, finally bringing prices for sea otter, fur seals, and fox up to 30 rubles, 75 kopecks, and 4 rubles, respectively. In comparison to the 350 rubles yearly salary for a Russian employee of the RAC, 30 rubles per sea otter does not seem bad, but the catch had been steadily decreasing since the beginning of the century (Arndt 1985 [1861]:65; Liapunova and Fedorova 1979:40; Sarafian 1970:37, 165, 171). In the early 1830s, Khlebnikov counted on 50–120 sea otter pelts per year from 50–70 *baidarkas* sent out by the Kodiak office (Liapunova and Fedorova 1979:37–38). A *baidarka* being generally manned by two hunters, this means that it was by no means certain that a man would have even one pelt to sell at the end of a hunting season.

In the face of the poverty suffered by smallpox survivors, the question whether pay should be increased again was raised around 1840, but the problem was that Kodiak hunters were already paid more than those from Prince William Sound and those employed on the Kuriles.[8] Chief Manager Kupreianov favored individual rewards to diligent *toions* and hunters over a general raise in pay (RAC cs 18:201–202, 203v–205, May 2, 1840, to Main Office; 19:50–50v, June 15, 1840, to Kodiak Office). Finally, a revised list of payments for goods and services in the Kodiak district was drawn up by the Kodiak office in 1840 and approved by Kupreianov's successor Etholen in 1841 (RAC cs 20:36v–45v, February 25, 1841, to Kodiak Office). Goods and services listed include food provisions such as whale meat and women's and men's work such as the sewing of different kinds of parkas and *kamleikas* and transportation by *baidara* or *baidarka* between St. Paul Harbor and outlying posts. Longer-term employment at different posts was remunerated with monthly salaries between 8 and 15 rubles (the most common being 12 rubles for men and 10 or 12 for women). Although the prices paid for pelts were not increased, hunting parties now had to be provisioned with tobacco, flint, powder, lead, needles, angling thread, flour, and other small things. These items were intended to enable hunters to provide food for themselves en route (Khlebnikov 1994:85). Hunters were not compensated for their time if the results of hunting were poor, and the labor that went into making a *baidarka* was paid only when it remained in the possession of the Company. For Native, Creole, and Russian employees alike, low pay and high store prices remained a source of discontent.

The ability of the RAC to offer manufactured goods for trade increased in 1839 through an agreement with the HBC. Since the transport of goods from Russia remained too expensive for large-scale trading, the British company would deliver goods and provisions to Novoarkhangel'sk in return for trading rights in the southern Alaska Panhandle (Gibson 1976:24). So while the new charter legally confirmed the service obligation of Alutiiq hunters, the RAC gradually became able to offer more economic rewards for service than in the first decades of its activities in the Alutiiq region. At the same time, the physical survival of the Native hunters became a stronger concern. In particular after the smallpox epidemic, it became clear that the RAC could not keep draining Alutiiq villages of their labor power without also showing some concern for the reproduction of these communities.

Managing Labor Resources, Reorganizing Settlements

From the first reports on the outbreak of smallpox in the Alutiiq region and the beginning of efforts taken to stem it, the emphasis on the preservation of the workforce is evident. Reporting to the Main Office in St. Petersburg in December of 1837, Chief Manager Kupreianov notes the quick spread of the disease, which had already claimed at least 265 victims, and comments on the poverty encountered in the Alutiiq villages by the medics sent for inoculation. In addition to medical care, his immediate concern is the effective use of the remaining people:

> Smallpox inoculation is being carried out there now; fortunately it was already started in the previous year, and done as far as possible, but even so, as reports tell me, they do not escape the disease, [but] at least they are spared from death. [. . .] In consequence of the decrease of the Aleuts owing to this unfortunate circumstance I find myself forced to release all those who are workers at the harbors in the districts, except for the indispensable baidarka rowers, using the rest for the hunt. (RAC cs 15:49v–50, Dec 7, 1837, to Main Office)

The dramatically diminished population not only endangered the sea otter hunt but also the production of "economic goods," that is, items of clothing, equipment, and food prepared by men and women in company service. Kupreianov also feared that winter trapping would suffer (RAC cs 15:50–50v, Dec 7, 1837, to Main Office). But the following spring the manager of the Kodiak office estimated that he could send out 40 *baidarkas* of sea otter hunters, almost as much as before the epidemic, still leaving enough people in the villages to feed the widows and orphans. Winter trapping brought good results again in the season of 1838/39 (RAC cs 15:313v, May 1, 1838, to Main Office; 17:20, Feb 20, 1839, to Kodiak office). Praise from the Chief Manager for this successful effort was followed by detailed instructions on how to gather an adequate number of hunters for this summer's party. Besides refraining from all dispensable work in the harbor during hunting season, women and children were to be employed to enable men to go hunting:

> Wherever possible according to their strength, employ adolescent boys and women for pay from the Company, and notify me of those who refuse. Announce this to them well in advance and how they will be rewarded for their services, (and the cases that have occurred: of women who refuse to prepare foodstuffs are not to be tolerated at the present time, such things especially cause suffering now.) By all means assign the tasks that are within the range of their capacities and strength to women in the District instead of to men wherever possible. Besides those tasks they have usually carried out up to now, I am sure that quite a few other assignments can be found for them on the cattle stations for cutting hay at level places. [. . .] It would be a shame to let men work in the vegetable patches or at other such tasks now. For women and boys employment of this kind should be for everyone's good. Let me emphasize that the Kodiak Office is to strive especially to put together as large sea otter parties as possible and to pay constant attention to this important matter. (RAC cs 17:50v–51, March 9, 1839, to Kodiak Office)

The death rate of about thirty percent from the smallpox epidemic on Kodiak Island matches the average in so-called virgin soil populations, where there are no individuals who have developed immunity from previous exposure to the virus (Fortuine 1989:230; Thornton, Warren, and Miller 1992:191–193). Although Dumond (1986:31–32) points out that diseases such as smallpox leave no skeletal evidence and it cannot be positively said that it had not reached Alaska via Siberia before the arrival of the Russians, we can thus assume that the disease was new to that generation of Alutiiq, and seeing so many relatives die rapidly from an unknown cause must have been traumatic for the survivors. In addition to the strain of reorganizing the lives of their much-diminished families and communities, these survivors were more intensively employed in the service of the Company, which put the continuation of the sea otter hunt above all else. The success of the RAC's measures is apparent from a report to the Main Office of May 1839, stating that this year's hunting party not only was no smaller than last year's but consisted of twenty-nine *baidarkas* more (RAC cs 17:294v–295v, May 10, 1839, to Main Office).

When women did work that had previously been assigned to males in accordance with the Russian conception of the sexual division of labor (see Chapter 5), this created the problem of how to relieve them of some of their other

Salmon drying on racks, Kodiak Island, 1915. Dried salmon continued to be a staple in the Alutiiq diet into the twentieth century. It had also been a staple for the Russians in Alaska, and RAC officials worried that the diminished Native population after the epidemic would no longer be able to accomplish the tasks of catching, gutting, splitting, and drying the salmon in sufficient quantities. *Photograph by Robert F. Griggs, courtesy of Archives and Special Collections, University of Alaska Anchorage, National Geographic Society Collection, hmc-0186-volume1-3604.*

tasks, such as the long hours of work that went into the preparation of clothing. In order to reduce the number of men tied up in birdskin hunting and women busy sewing birdskin parkas, plans were made to import woolen coats or Siberian parkas, so that every hunter would need only one bird skin parka per year for use in wet weather. An agreement was made with the Okhotsk office of the RAC in 1840 for the delivery of reindeer parkas and clothing made of the skin of deer calves (RAC cs 17:51v–52v, March 9, 1839; 19:49v, June 15, 1840, both to Kodiak office). I found no evidence to show if this practice continued in later years, but if it did, it also shows how the Russians, still suffering from a deficit of manufactured trade goods, took steps to widen the circle of redistribution controlled by them from goods produced within Alutiiq society to an exchange network between different regions across the Bering Strait.

Something similar happened with the sea lion skins and intestines provided to Alutiiq seamstresses for *baidarka* covers and *kamleikas*. They were delivered to Novoarkhangel'sk from the Pribilof Islands, where the RAC had resettled people from the Aleutians. From the colonial capital, company ships redistributed them to posts in the different districts (RAC cs 19:46v–47, June

15, 1840, to Kodiak office). Such North Pacific networks increased the power of the RAC over the Alutiiq, who became ever less self-sufficient owing to increased demands on their time but could not refuse to work for the Russians because their dependence on the RAC stores grew by the same process. Toward the end of RAC rule in Alaska, in 1863, former Chief Manager Etholen could argue that it was fair for the RAC to require "Aleuts" to turn over their sea otter catch to its officials, "since they could not engage in hunting without the assistance of the Company, which furnishes them with everything" (in Dmytryshyn, Crownhart-Vaughan, and Vaughan 1989:527). But frequent problems with production or delivery also made it dangerous to rely on this system. In the above-mentioned letter of June 15, 1840, the Chief Manager urged the manager of the Kodiak office to make greater efforts to organize sea lion or seal hunting in the Kodiak district, which consumed the greatest share of the supplies from the Pribilofs.

In the years after the epidemic, thanks to the 1839 agreement with the HBC, manufactured European items became available in unprecedented quantities. English earthenware is among the most common imported artifacts found in postrelocation *barabaras* at Karluk. Other items of European or Siberian origin include textiles, beads, parts of firearms, and Russian axe-heads. But the full range of Alutiiq lithic technology is still present at the Karluk site dating from this period (Knecht and Jordan 1985:24–30). Even though economic dependence on the RAC did not become complete, the increase in power over the diminished population of Kodiak Island enabled the RAC to make its first effort to interfere directly with Alutiiq social organization and subsistence by consolidating smallpox survivors into a few large villages, each under a single *toion*, and even trying to encourage horticulture there.

The idea seems to have occurred to Kupreianov on a visit to Amlia in the Aleutian Chain, where the Aleuts of neighboring islands had been gathered in a big village under the *toion* Nikolai Dediukhin in the early 1830s (Liapunova 1987:111). In February 1838, Kupreianov suggested to the manager of the Kodiak office that it would have been easier to send medical help to the Alutiiqs if they had been living in a few convenient locations, which would also facilitate the storage of food and mutual cooperation and make Alutiiq life as "worthy of emulation" as that of the Amlia Aleuts. Kupreianov's only worry was that the abandonment of presently inhabited sites might affect the hunt (RAC cs 15:151–152, February 26, 1838, to Kodiak office).

In some places, the voluntary movement of survivors from smaller villages to join relatives or seek aid from the Russians might have provided a starting point for a resettlement program ordered by the Russians. In an order to the

Kodiak office of April 1840, Kupreianov refers to smallpox orphans gathered at Three Saints Bay who are to be kept and raised there, receiving training in all the skills of the Natives. A communal dwelling (*kazhim*) for 100 people is to be built to house the additional arrivals expected in the near future. Now, he writes, it is important to find an "active *toion* who has grasped the whole benefit of communal living" and to make sure the people do not neglect their hunting (RAC cs 18:126–127, April 21, 1840, to Kodiak office). The construction of the first *kazhim* began at Three Saints Bay in the summer of 1840; by 1843 the Chief Manager reported that the resettlement to seven new villages was completed. During the planning stage, Kupreianov and Etholen express the hope that *toions* would convince their followers of the benefits of relocation, but later sources do not report how the population reacted to these measures (RAC cs 19:217–217v, Sep 27, 1840; 22:233, May 10, 1843, both to Main Office; 19:52v, June 15, 1840, to Kodiak office).

The RAC had appointed *toions* in Alutiiq villages from the beginning of the century (Davydov 1977:190). But the expectations placed on them now went beyond the general Russian practice of working with cooperative Native leaders. The role of the *toion* in selecting hunters and planning the parties together with RAC administrators was established practice, specified in paragraphs 47, 48, and 52 of the 1821 charter. In the relocation process, the selection of new *toions* suitable for governing the new villages was made the responsibility of the local RAC officials, who were asked to make sure that those appointed were respected among the Alutiiq and known "for their good conduct, modesty, sobriety and dedication to the hunt" (RAC cs 19:259, Oct 18, 1840, to Kodiak office). Apparently for the first time, *toions* on Kodiak Island were assigned a salary (up to 500 rubles per year, more than the salary of an ordinary Russian employee), following the example of the Atkha and Amlia *toions* on the Aleutians (RAC cs 19:52v, June 15, 1840, to Kodiak office). A set of rules defining the *toion*'s duties and position was elaborated in 1841 and submitted to the Main Office for confirmation, which was granted with minor corrections (RAC cs 20:73–81, March 22, 1841, to Main Office, English in Dmytryshyn, Crownhart-Vaughan, and Vaughan 1989:443–449; RAC cs 21:395–397, Sep 25, 1842, to Kodiak office).

The "Rules for *Toions* elected as elders over the common Aleut settlements in the Kodiak District" specified that the *starshina* (here referring not to a Russian official but to the leading *toion*) of a consolidated village would be elected by the Kodiak office from among the *toions* of the former villages, subject to confirmation by the Chief Manager. His responsibilities ranged from ensuring the punctual attendance of church services and the cleanliness of the village and keeping village statistics (with the assistance of a literate Creole if necessary) to organizing hunting parties, keeping communal stores, assigning orphans to reliable Alutiiq families, and taking care that no one left the village or settled there without authorization. His relationship to the Russian *baidarshchik* was defined as follows:

> The starshina of a common Aleut settlement, besides a complete dependence and subordination to the Kodiak office and its manager, is always to refer to the local baidarshchik as well as a person whom the higher colonial authorities have set over him. For disregard of the prescribed rules and for any disorder in his settlement or neglect of duty or injustice against the Aleuts entrusted to his care, the starshina will be subject to strict discipline and removal from his position. The baidarshchiki of arteli or odinochki are by no means to interfere with the domestic dispositions of the starshiny, but nonetheless they are not freed from responsibility to see that the rules pertaining to starshiny are carried out [. . .] and in case of neglect or abuse on the part of a starshina, the local baidarshchik must immediately report this to the Kodiak office, and the manager of that office is obliged without fail to investigate the reports himself on location, by no means relying on the word of the baidarshchik. (RAC cs 20:79–79v, March 22, 1841, to Main Office, translation modified from Dmytryshyn, Crownhart-Vaughan, and Vaughan 1989:447–448)

The *toion* thus, at least in theory, became an immediate part of the administrative structure of the RAC, which, though not interfering in "domestic arrangements," claimed the right to discipline the *toion* not only for neglect of his duties toward the RAC but also for abuses committed against his people.

But there is also evidence that the RAC had to take into account Alutiiq conventions when choosing *toions*. Under the Rules, the *toion* of a consolidated village was to be appointed from among those who held such a rank in the former villages. Holmberg (1856:358) confirms that the RAC always appointed *toions* from old chiefly families. The sources are silent on the question if there was competition among the former chiefs of abandoned villages for supremacy in the postepidemic villages. A comparison of the 1844 confessional records (which groups people together according to their new villages but notes which village each family came from and who was chief [*starshina*] in the former village) with the 1851 records (which list just one *starshina* for each new village) confirms that usually one of the former village chiefs became *starshina*, but the sample is too small and death seems to have interfered too often to be able to tell if the one already resident at the village site had an advantage over the new arrivals. In Karluk, the former chief of Uyak was *starshina* in 1851 but perhaps only because the chief of Karluk seems to have died during or shortly after the epidemic—only the *zakashchik* (second chief, probably a Russian-introduced institution) is listed in 1844. At Orlovskoe the chief of remote Ugak won dominance over the one from Igak, but all were newcomers to the site, since the *artel'* had only moved there in 1837 (ARCA D255/175:Kodiak parish confessional records, 1844, 1851). What happened to former chiefs who did not gain recognition as *toion* of the new village? Was their position recognized within the village? Did villagers experience conflicts of allegiance between their former chief and the chief of the new village? Davydov (1812:113) mentions that rich men and good hunters often had more influence in a village than the chief, so the presence of several leaders may not have been a new situation.

The election of Kodiak *toions* may have followed a similar protocol as in Prince William Sound, where the people of Kiniklik elected Ivan Anyky in 1860 to replace the deceased *toion* Ivan Shniagok, and the Chief Manager confirmed the election on a trip of inspection. This also indicates that the RAC could not disregard the wishes of Alutiiq communities. But the company became an institution for people to turn to when they were dissatisfied with their *toion*. On the same trip of inspection, the Chief Manager was approached by hunters from Chenega who complained about the bad conduct of their *toion* and asked for a replacement. Grigor'ev, the manager of Konstantinovskii redut, was asked to investigate the matter and nominate another *toion* if necessary (RAC cs 42:116v–117, June 15, 1860, to Kodiak office; 42:129, July 14, 1860, to Konstantinovskii redut).

The *toion*'s envisioned role as an agent of change promoting a more russianized lifestyle shows a new orientation toward a civilizing mission on the part of the RAC. Paragraph 11 of the Rules specifies that the *toion* should arrange for potatoes to be cultivated for common use and, if local conditions permitted, for a cow to be kept to provide milk for small children and the sick. He was also in charge of communal food stores (for which a special storehouse was built in the new villages according to an 1844 report, RAC cs 23:571v, July 28, 1844, to Main Office) and was advised to have his villagers donate a portion of their furs every year to create an account at the RAC office for the village to draw on in times of need. The admonition to keep the village and villagers clean has to do with the health concerns at the origin of the creation of these settlements. The task was to prevent another outbreak of disease through the replacement of "their low, stuffy and dirty *zhupans*" with "communal, spacious, light *kazhims*" built at "places elevated and dry" (RAC cs 23:571–571v, July 28, 1844, to Main Office). Concentrating the population at a few places was intended to facilitate the quick transportation of sick people to the hospital at St. Paul Harbor—another of the *toion*'s responsibilities specified in the Rules.

Not all *toions* appear to have lived up the Company's expectations in their commitment to reforming Alutiiq architecture and standards of hygiene. During Naval Captain Pavel Golovin's visit in 1861 only some *toions* had "spacious iurts," while "the rest live[d] as formerly in small little huts that are half underground" (in Dmytryshyn and Crownhart-Vaughan 1979:24).

In spite of these efforts to promote the introduction of gardening and health care, all efforts to introduce Russian ways of life remained subordinate to the RAC's commercial interests. Even if it had been feasible to turn the Alutiiq into a farming population—which climate and inclination prevented —it would not have been in the interest of the RAC, whose very reason for concerning itself with these people was that they were needed for the hunt. Chief Manager Etholen stressed repeatedly that relocation measures were to be taken only as far as they endangered neither the sea otter hunt and winter trapping nor subsistence hunting—for this reason, he supported the construction of several villages rather than a single large one for the whole island, and specified that the main criterion for the choice of locations should be "convenience for the gathering of sufficient food provisions and the uninterrupted continuation of trapping and hunting" (RAC cs 19:52, June 15, 1840, to Kodiak office). Etholen's predecessor Kupreianov had already stated that the advantage of consolidated settlements was that smallpox survivors there would not intermix with Russians nor be torn from their "natural pursuits" (RAC cs 18:201, May 2, 1840, to Main Office).

Separate Tasks for Separated People

A disintegration of Alutiiq communities was as little in the interest of the RAC as their full conversion to a Russian lifestyle. In the plans of company officials, the task of providing the colony with vegetables, beef, pork, and milk fell to Creoles and Russian retirees who chose to remain in the colony (so-called "colonial citizens," see Chapter 2). And they were supposed to do so in their own villages where they would neither be a burden on the Alutiiq nor be tempted to adopt their lifestyle. As I show in Chapter 5, the RAC administration repeatedly affirmed its policy to keep "Aleuts" and "Creoles" apart, and this made economic sense because each group had important tasks under conditions in which workers were generally scarce. Only by the end of Russian rule did the hope that settled Creoles would provision the colony seem to have foundered. By 1860 Creole parents were advised to send their children out with Alutiiq sea otter hunters to learn a skill that would enable them to earn money. Golovin reports that most Creole parents refused, evidently considering such work

Kayakers in a three-seat *baidarka* near Seldovia, early twentieth century. The middle man in this three-hatch *baidarka* has a harpoon ready to hand, indicating that these men were out hunting for the fur trade or for subsistence. *Courtesy of Alaska and Polar Regions Collections, Rasmuson Library, University of Alaska, Fairbanks, Charles E. Bunnell Collection, 1973-66-111.*

beneath their dignity (Dmytryshyn and Crownhart-Vaughan 1979:19). Still, the contrast to 1836 is striking, when the Kodiak office was ordered not to allow any Creole child of either sex to be raised an "Aleut" (RAC cs 13:395, July 22, 1836, to Kodiak office).

All endeavors to keep Alutiiq and Creole populations separate concern only men. In spite of the need for Alutiiq women as seamstresses and cooks there are no statements of concern over women leaving Alutiiq communities to marry Creoles and Russians. It can be assumed that the Alutiiq wives of Russians or Creoles living at RAC posts provided the same services as women from Alutiiq villages who were hired by the RAC, and even the Alutiiq wives of Creole settlers may have come to the posts to work and to supplement their families' generally insufficient farming and subsistence incomes. If they did not, the loss of these workers (and of prospective mothers of Alutiiq hunters) seems to have been accepted in the interest of increasing the Creole population. Only Russian men who married Creole women and took them back to Russia were treated as a more threatening scenario. Kirill Khlebnikov suggested forbidding the practice in order to prevent a potential drain on the Creole population (Khlebnikov 1994:83). Church statistics show that marriages among Creoles were common from at least the 1840s, although many Creole men also married Alutiiq women (see Chapter 5, note 9).

Although the RAC set for itself the most advantageous conditions for the exploitation of Native labor, its business became less and less profitable after 1840. Conservation measures, such as a rotation system by which the hunting party was sent to a different region each year, chosen by consultation with *toions* and experienced hunters, could not prevent the decline of hunting revenues. After 1846, the sale of Chinese tea in Russia brought more profit to the RAC than any income generated in Alaska. Efforts to diversify the economy through coal mining on the Kenai Peninsula and delivery of ice, dried fish, and lumber to San Francisco started in the 1850s but never created a source of revenue comparable to the sea otter trade (RAC cs 28:156v, June 22, 1847, to Kodiak office; Gibson 1976:37–42; Kushner 1975:7–10; Petrov 2006:171).

It is unclear whether the Alutiiq-Creole distinction still had significance in these new trades. In 1858, four "Aleut" men and one Chugach woman were working at the coal mine of Gornaia ekspeditsiia on Kenai Peninsula, which at least shows that Alutiiq labor was no longer exclusively reserved for hunting, unless mining was carried out outside the hunting season (ARCA D299/201: list of villages in the Kenai parish, 1858). But the RAC evidently did not think it would be able to recruit workers for all new enterprises from its own colonial population. In 1859, it inquired at an American labor contractor's office about possibilities of importing workers from China but received the answer that workers were hard to find owing to current upheavals, and that the Chinese would refuse to work for even twice the wage of ordinary workers in Novoarkhangel'sk (RAC cs 42:102v, May 19, 1860, to Main Office).

Before the sale of Alaska to the United States, members of the Russian imperial government discussed changes in the administration of Alaska, and the RAC monopoly was challenged by reformers, along with its right to force the Native population to work. After Russia abolished serfdom in 1861, labor obligations imposed on a subject population became harder to justify. Shortly before the expiration of the RAC's third charter, granted in 1844 for another twenty years, a committee of the imperial government submitted recommendations for the future administration of the colony. These included a gradual end of the RAC's monopolistic position and the replacement of obligatory labor by free hire (Dmytryshyn, Crownhart-Vaughan, and Vaughan 1989:537–539). But these debates were cut short by the government's decision to sell Alaska to the U.S.A. The RAC shifted its activities to the Russian Far East and was liquidated in 1881 (Gibson 1976:29).

ENDNOTES

1. In a common method of hunting, a group of hunters in *baidarkas* surrounded the otters, killing the animals with darts launched from throwing-boards (Lisianskii 1814:203–205).

2. As far as the RAC employees who came to Alaska from the Russian Empire are concerned, they were never serfs of the Company but free subjects (that is, state peasants or members of the burgher or other city-dwelling estates) given a seven-year-passport to leave the Empire and paid at first with a share of the sea otter catch, then, from 1818, with a yearly salary. Eighteenth-century legislation had formalized the monopoly of the nobility on serf labor, and the RAC was a bourgeois enterprise, although a few of its shareholders were from the nobility. So it was excluded from the right to own serfs. But in spite of their nominal freedom, low salaries and high food prices brought many employees into debt servitude to the RAC (LeDonne 1991:6; Sarafian 1970:29–33).

3. The 1844 confessional records of Kodiak parish (ARCA D255/175) list Arsentii Aminak, aged 77, as chief of Aiakhtalik. This would mean that he was about 17 years old in 1784.

4. Colin Bearne's translation in the edition of Davydov's account, published by Limestone Press (Davydov 1977:190–191), differs from my version in several instances. Most notably, the second sentence reads: "Some of the chiefs rule over many settlements and are all descended from one tribe, and named after the bays or capes near which they live." In the last sentence, the phrase "and as having equal rights . . . by bravery or in other ways" is translated: "and as having an equal share in matters of general concern with all the others, when they were decided at public assemblies, by bravery or some other means." Grammatically the Russian original is quite clear that the villages, not the chiefs, are descended from a common tribe and named after bays and capes, and that not bravery decided matters at public assemblies but people who had distinguished themselves by bravery. In the original, the first excerpt reads: "Nekotorye Nachal'niki upravliali mnogimi seleniiami, proiskhodiashchimi ot odnogo roda i nazyvaiushchimisia po imeni gubi ili mysa, u koego oni zhivut" (Davydov 1812:113). And the second: "V prezhnee vremena vsiakoi Koniaga schital sebia chlenom togo seleniia, gde zhil, imeiushchim ravnoe so vsiakim pravo v obshchestvennykh delakh, kotorye reshalis' vsegda na sobraniiakh vazhneishikh, po khrabrosti ili inomu, Ostrovitian" (Davydov 1812:115–116).

5. This term is probably derived from Alutiiq *angyak*, open skin-boat. It would then have the same connotations as Inupiaq *umialik* and Russian *baidarshchik*, all of which associate political power with ownership or command over a boat that needs a team of rowers. I thank Richard Knecht for pointing this out to me.

6. Bearne renders the last sentence: "He kept his word, which was only broken when he was unable to prevent it." Again this is inconsistent with the Russian original: "On sderzhal svoe slovo, no konechno ot nevozmozhnosti tol'ko neustoiat' v onom" (Davydov 1812:56).

7. The term "politarism" (from Greek politea, state) comes from the work of the Soviet anthropologist IUrii Ivanovich Semenov, who coined it as a more neutral designation for Karl Marx's Asiatic mode of production. The basic idea of the Asiatic mode of production—that is, that there are societies in which the state administrative apparatus holds the position of a ruling class—was disputed among Marxist political economists and considered provocative when Semenov developed his theories in the Soviet Union of the 1970s, because it had been used by critics of the Soviet Union to describe the Soviet system itself. I provide a more in-depth discussion of Grinev's conceptualization of Alaskan colonial history and its background in Soviet revisionist Marxism in Luehrmann 2005.

8. The power of the RAC to conscript workers remained limited to the Aleuts and Alutiiq. In economic relations with northern regions along the Nushagak, Yukon, and Kuskokwim Rivers, which were much promoted during the post-1818 period, pure mercantile trade comparable to the Canadian fur trade prevailed, with free hunters bringing as many pelts to the posts as they needed to obtain the metal goods, tobacco, and decorative items offered there. Alutiiq and Aleut hunters could also hunt independently but were prohibited from selling their catch to foreign ships (Gibson 1976:16–17; Khlebnikov 1994:85; Michael 1967:102).

4

From Mainstay to Auxiliary: Alutiiq Labor after the Sale of Alaska

The ACC and Its Rivals: Competitive Fur Trade

In 1862, Navy Captain Pavel Nikolaevich Golovin, sent by the Naval Ministry to inspect the American colony, predicted what would happen if the "Aleuts" were freed from the obligation to hunt for the RAC:

> [T]he Aleuts will go hungry at first because they will not agree to work and thus will have no means to buy all the things they need. Later, however, when they realize that they cannot expect help from anyone, they will gradually learn to rely on themselves alone to earn their food. Thus by granting them full freedom it will be better than constantly supervising them, as the Company has had to do in the past. (Dmytryshyn and Crownhart-Vaughan 1979:23)

The dependence on the company for *baidarka* covers, clothing and "certain luxuries," said Golovin, had become so great that the "Aleuts" would return to work of their own accord even if they were no longer forced to (Dmytryshyn and Crownhart-Vaughan 1979:23). The development of the sea otter trade after 1867, when several U.S.-based companies were operating in Alaska, none of which had the authority to force Natives to work for them, proves him right to a certain extent, even though it is not clear if hunger was really a problem. The sea and rivers of the region still provided an ample supply of fish, meat, and blubber, and the spreading out from the consolidated Russian-era villages to old and new village sites during the first decades under U.S. administration shows that people were willing and able to take advantage of such resources. Sea otter hunting was not a primary livelihood but provided the means to buy such commodities as tea, tobacco, flour, and clothing. The trader Vladimir Stafeev, one of the Russians who stayed behind in Alaska and worked for American trading companies, mentions boots, pants, vests, and hats as popular items at Nuchek and Kodiak. Sugar was another coveted item of trade, which the ACC rationed because its agents suspected customers of using it to brew alcohol (Stafeev ms. Aug 3, 1880, Jan 4, 1883, Jan 7, 1884).

American companies fitted out hunting parties on credit from their stores in the spring and hoped for a return in furs that would exceed their expenses. This is very similar to the practices of the RAC, except that parties now were small and locally organized instead of gathering at a few central places. The agents of the ACC and other companies also continued to cooperate with local *toions* and to support those leaders who favored their company. During his time as trader for the Western Fur & Trading Company at Nuchek, Stafeev sided with the *toion* in a split between followers of the *toion* and the *zakashchik* (second chief), noting one day that the *zakashchik* was out hunting for the rival ACC although he was in debt at Stafeev's store (Stafeev ms., Aug 1 and 2, 1880). When working for the ACC at Douglas, he was outraged when the people of "Kuk." (Kukak?) elected a new *toion* without consulting either him or the priest. On his reprimand, they promised to keep the old one (Stafeev ms., Feb 1 and 2, 1893). The continuity in the relationship between companies and local leaders must have been facilitated by the fact that many of the traders were, like Stafeev, Russians and Creoles who had formerly worked for the RAC (Woldt 1884:324, 341, 362).

Like the RAC, the American traders, especially the ACC as the company with the tightest network of stores in the Alutiiq region and a wide range of connections to other parts of Alaska, took over wider social functions than those normally associated with keeping a store. In addition to importing manufactured goods from the United States, they continued to sell *lavtaks* and purchased *iukola* from local producers to provision their hunters. Agent Petr Chechenev at Afognak sometimes arranged for the sewing of *kamleikas* by local women for sale on Afognak and in Kodiak, sometimes purchased them elsewhere (ACC, April 1883, Ivan Pestriakov to Agent McIntyre; April 20, 1900, Petr Chechenev to Agent White; June 20, 1901, Peter Chichenoff to Agent Goss).[1]

With the advent of steam boats, the ACC also took on the role of transporting goods, mail, and people: hunters and their *baidarkas*, priests making the rounds of their parish, teachers on the way to their posts, letters and mail-ordered goods, and ethnographica collected by traders or by travelers such as the Norwegian sailor Johan Adrian Jacobsen, who made a collection for the Berlin

View of Karluk, 1900–1901. This photograph shows the distinct worlds within the village as described by Shalamov (see p. 109) and other observers: an Anglo-American house in the foreground, Alutiiq *barabaras* in the center, the Orthodox church and government schoolhouse on the hill in the background, and the cannery buildings down by the waterfront, all set apart by different architecture styles and spatial arrangement. *Photograph by W. C. Fitchie, courtesy of Anchorage Museum of History and Art, Anchorage, b90-13-1.*

Museum of Ethnography in 1882/1883 (ACC, April 20, 1899, Pavel Chechenev to Agent White; Harvey 1991:47; Jacobs 1997:6–8; Lee 1996:34–35; Morseth 1998:58; Woldt 1884:224, 320, 397). In the absence of government and social services during the first decades of U.S. rule in Alaska, the ACC handled the U.S. mail, provided banking services to the church and to travelers, and occasionally distributed medicine free of charge among the Natives (ARCA D271/185:report from Father Ioann Bortnovskii to the Sitka Consistory, Kenai, Jan 29, 1900; Fisher 1880:3; Lee 1996:34; Sloss 1977:128).

The greatest change in the relationship between the trading companies and the Alutiiq after 1867 was not so much the abolition of forced labor—the persistent willingness of Alutiiq to hunt for trading companies suggests that that system may not have been necessary for the RAC anymore. Rather, the presence of competition between companies gave Alutiiq new choices and leverage to manipulate trading partners even as it precipitated the end of the fur trade in Alaska. Even before the sale, some Alutiiq hunters had other trading partners besides the RAC. Golovin notes that the Chugach were selling some of their furs to foreign ships, but the RAC at least tried to protect its monopoly through negotiations with the United States and Britain and prohibitions and sanctions directed at Russian subjects (Dmytryshyn and Crownhart-Vaughan 1979:25; Kushner 1987:307–309). The American companies and individuals operating trading posts in Alaska after 1867 had to compete with one another for customers,[2] one consequence of which, as I pointed out in Chapter 2, may have been the creation of small trading posts in numerous old and new villages, simultaneously following the dispersal of the population and promoting it.

Another consequence was a more rapid decline of the sea otter population, because the conservation measures—alternate hunting in different areas—practiced by the RAC in its final decades no longer made sense in the context of unregulated competition for the quickest exploitation of a given area. Federal legislation starting in 1879 reserved the right to take pelts in Alaska to Natives or residents with Native wives but did not regulate the activities of trading companies (Cook and Norris 1998:66). So, in the new situation, Natives were at once rapidly losing the source of their income and gaining a certain power because, as long as the business lasted, several competitors coveted their furs. To retain their business, traders were forced to give more credit and equip more hunters than they would otherwise have done and to maintain even small stores beyond the point of profitability in order to keep the competition from moving in. When Vladimir Stafeev was trader at Nuchek, he was in direct competition with the ACC store there. He repeatedly records his frustration over having to take more hunters than he needed in order not to lose business to the competition, although he expected only meager hunting results. In spite of an agreement with the ACC trader to pay no more than $35 per pelt, attempts of one store to outbid the other continued, and prices were at $40–60 in 1880. A few years later at Douglas, where Stafeev worked for the ACC, a hunting trip of one and a half months already yielded only two sea otters in 1889, but the post was kept open for at least another decade (Stafeev ms. May 21, 1880, Aug 2, 1880, June 22, 1889; Oswalt 1967b).

Gradually, mergers between competing companies shifted the advantage toward the traders. The ACC bought the Western Fur & Trading Company in 1883, causing fur prices to fall in the Kenai/Prince William Sound area. In the late 1890s, a merger between the ACC and the North American Commercial Company had a similar effect on Kodiak (ARCA D261/180:report from Father Nikolai Kashevarov to Hieromonk Antonii, Afognak 1899; Cook and Norris 1998:73). In this situation especially, Orthodox priests stress the ways in which the credit system, often seen by traders as a pitfall they would be happy to avoid, worked to the advantage of traders and to the detriment of their parishioners. In 1899, Father Tikhon Shalamov, priest in the Kodiak parish, reports that the merger allowed the ACC to raise prices and to deduct the better part of each catch for the payment of old debts. Debt and lack of economic alternatives had turned into a system of oppression that Shalamov describes with great passion:

> The enslaved people, suffering from the terrible oppression of the trading companies, entangled in nets of debt, see the evil, but, with their own weakened, worn-out strength, cannot throw off the heavy yoke of the companies without outside help. [. . .] The question of the oppression of the Aleuts by the trading companies is not just a local question, but a question concerning all of Alaska, because the robbers' nets and the system of robbery are the same all over Alaska, all the way to the Yukon: A[laska] Co[mpany] and N[orthern] C[ommercial]. (ARCA D259/179:report from Father Tikhon Shalamov to Sitka Consistory, Kodiak, April 10, 1899)

Even after the mergers, competition from private traders operating individual stores as well as from other companies continued to determine the order of business. Pavel Chechenev, trader at Eagle Harbor, sent an urgent request for more goods to Kodiak in October of 1899, because hunters from Kiliuda and Old Harbor had bought up all his provisions before the Eagle Harbor party returned, and he was afraid of losing their pelts to another store (ACC, Pavel Chechenev to Agent White, Oct 26, 1899). If the RAC had operated in a similar situation of competition and depended on its ability to furnish supplies on demand, it would not have stayed in business very long.

The developments after 1867 confirm that the difference between the Russian and American methods of fur extraction from Alaska cannot simply be described as one between a tributary and a mercantile system. I have shown that the relationship between the RAC and the Alutiiq was never strictly tributary and that it developed toward a more conventional arrangement of mercantile trade during the time of Russian rule, because the supply of trade goods for the colony improved and the self-sufficiency of Alutiiq communities decreased, making unusual methods of labor recruitment less necessary. The relative ease by which manufactured goods could be procured by Russian and American companies seems to constitute the main difference, along with the different legal bases of a monopolistic charter company in the Russian period and unregulated competition after the sale to the United States.

Changes between competitive situations and a monopoly or near-monopoly of one company also occurred during the history of the Canadian fur trade.

Examples show that it is hard to say which situation is more advantageous for the fur hunters, and that different phases of the fur trade should not be seen in isolation from one another. As in Alaska, competition enabled hunters to drive up prices and to get credit from one store in the spring, then bring their catch to another one in the fall. However, periods of competition between different companies or colonial powers sometimes led to a rapid depletion of the fur-bearing animals and violent attempts to coerce or intimidate hunters into trading at one particular post. In a situation of monopoly, as it existed in large areas of the Canadian north after the merger of the Northwest Company and the Hudson's Bay Company in 1821, the credit system turned into a mixed blessing for traders and hunters. Hunters could hope to receive more credit now that the trader was sure all furs would go to him, but traders could also try to curtail favors such as credit or gifts that were formerly needed to create a bond between trader and hunters (Francis and Morantz 1983:38, 123–124; Ray and Freeman 1978:27–36; Yerbury 1986:69, 117).

In Alaska itself, particularly on the Aleutians, the competitive phase in the late eighteenth century generated a great deal of violence against Natives, when rival Russian entrepreneurs tried to get hunters to provide as many furs as quickly as possible. Some of this ceased after 1799, when the RAC received its monopoly, which gave it both a future-oriented, paternalistic interest in preserving its labor force and the power to create an administrative-redistributive system that did not rely on violence alone (Metropolitan Innokentii 1888 [1840]:397–402). After 1867, the isolation of individual traders at their posts precluded the use of force to make hunters work for a specific company.[3] All American companies in South Alaska benefited from the dependence on store-bought goods created by several decades of Russian rule. The transition from subsistence hunting to part-time fur hunting for trade, which took some time in most parts of Canada, was already completed in Alaska by the time U.S. companies took over (Kardulias 1990:29; Yerbury 1986:130–131). Theoretically Alutiiq hunters, made indispensable by their skills and their legal status giving them the exclusive right to hunt sea otters, could also have benefited from the end of the RAC monopoly, playing the traders of different companies against one another. But the steady decline of the sea otters made it increasingly difficult for hunters to earn their living except by incurring ever greater debts, changing their position from one of skilled, sought-after laborers to dependents of companies that were already looking for alternatives to a business that was doomed to end soon.

Even if it had not been for their debts to the companies, Alutiiq hunters had little choice but to persist in their specialization on sea otter hunting. Until it was completely prohibited in 1911, it was the one area of the cash economy that their skills and the law reserved for them alone. Even the Creoles of Little Afognak and Mitrofania became sea otter hunters during this period, taking up an occupation they had scorned during the Russian era (ACC, Petr Chechenev to Agent White, April 26, 1899; Partnow 2001:157). The alternatives—fox farming and winter trapping—which were developed both by individuals and by the trading companies around the turn of the century, were open to competition from the increasing number of resident whites. In the canneries, the expanding business of the time, quite different labor requirements and strategies of hiring and production marginalized Native labor.

Canneries: A New Ethnic Division of Labor

When salmon canning was introduced to South-Central Alaska in the 1880s, an established system of hiring and division of labor was transferred from more southerly regions along the Pacific coast. Asian contract workers processed and canned the fish, while white crews did the fishing. Chinese labor contractors either arranged for the immigration of young workers from China or acted as intermediaries between American employers and immigrant communities in California or Washington State. Contractors received a specific sum per case packed and were responsible for paying and feeding the workers. The crews were recruited each spring in San Francisco or Seattle and taken north to Alaska for the salmon season, where they often spent most of their wages on the meals for which the contractor charged them or on additional food bought in overpriced company stores. With the 1882 Chinese Exclusion Act, the immigration of Chinese laborers all but stopped, and although experienced Chinese workers were still considered the best for the high level of skill, precision and speed required in butchering the salmon, contractors hired more and more Japanese men to fill the gap. Japanese immigration was in turn restricted in 1908, when the Japanese government, in order to spare itself the humiliation of having an exclusion law passed against its citizens, signed the so-called "Gentlemen's agreement" pledging not to allow laborers to emigrate to the United States. The 1924 National Origins Act totally stopped Japanese immigration. So from the 1920s onward, Filipinos (the only Asian group whose status as U.S. nationals permitted them to immigrate in unrestricted numbers since the Philippines were a U.S. possession since 1898), Mexicans, Puerto Ricans, and African Americans formed the new cheap labor pool (Friday 1994:42–43, 98; Immigration Commission 1911:406; Liljeblad 1979; Masson and Guimary 1981; Norris 1984:30–45; Takaki 1989).

Uyak cannery, late nineteenth or early twentieth century. A cannery was founded in Larsen Bay in 1881 but had its heyday after the Karluk cannery was moved there in 1911. As with most Alaskan canneries, the processing sheds are built on stilts as close to the water as possible to enable easy transfer of the salmon catch from the pier to the canning line. *Courtesy of Alaska and Polar Regions Collections, Rasmuson Library, University of Alaska, Fairbanks, Amelia Elkinton Collection, 1974-175-122.*

While Asian and later Latin American immigrants staffed the processing plants on shore, fishermen employed by Alaskan canneries were mainly Scandinavian and southern European (Italian and Greek) immigrants who were also taken to Alaska on a seasonal basis and often worked in crews segregated by national origin. They were paid a fixed monthly salary as well as a certain amount per fish caught or case of canned salmon. During the first decades of the Alaskan salmon industry, the only canneries that employed a large number of Native on-shore workers were those at Klawock and Metlakatla in the Panhandle area. The importation of Chinese workers caused riots and strikes among the Tlingit at Sitka and Chilkat, and Natives were hired as fishermen from the start of canning operations in 1878. In the Alutiiq region the situation was different. Natives were rarely hired for canning, and when they fished, they usually sold their catch to the canneries on a piece-by-piece basis rather than being employed for the whole season (Mitchell 1997:106; Moser 1898:23; Norris 1984:45–51; Roppel 1986:18, 191, 201).

There were several reasons why it was more attractive for packing companies to hire immigrants than local Natives. Jefferson Moser, who inspected

Alaskan fisheries for the U.S. Fish Commission in 1898, reports on the attitude of cannery managers toward Native labor:

> The complaint is made everywhere that Indian labor—that is, the labor of the men—is uncertain. After making sufficient wages to supply their personal wants and getting a few dollars ahead, the desire for hunting and fishing seizes them and they are apt to leave when they are most wanted. [. . .] The Indians are doubtless improvident, knowing that nature has provided for them without much labor. Their frequent boast is that white men and Chinese must work to get something to eat, while the waters and the forests furnish the Indian with all they want. (Moser 1898:25)

Decades of participation in the fur trade had accustomed the Natives of South Alaska to certain commodities, which, with the decline of fur hunting, they needed cash to acquire. While they were evidently willing to take up wage labor at canneries, mining camps, and sawmills, their still-functioning subsistence lifestyle gave them a bargaining power not available to the Chinese workers who, once in Alaska, had no choice but to stay there the whole summer even if they were dissatisfied with their pay and living conditions. Native workers could leave in mid-season when they had made enough money, or go on strike for higher wages. In 1898, the Tlingit packers at the Klawock cannery were paid 51 cents per case as a result of several strikes, whereas Chinese packers would have done the same work for 45 cents (Moser 1898:24).

The possible financial advantage of hiring local crews rather than transporting workers to Alaska and back was offset by the fact that ships had to go back and forth anyway to take provisions, tin sheets, and other canning equipment up north and bring down filled cans. And, different from the Panhandle, South-Central Alaska had such a small Native population by the late nineteenth century that there would not have been enough people to keep up canning operations even if the whole adult population had been interested in doing wage work the entire summer, which was probably not the case. The 1890 census lists 1,433 "Mongolian" males in the Kadiak District, ranging from Odiak on Prince William Sound to Mitrofania on the Pacific side of the Alaska Peninsula. Since immigration laws made it very difficult for Chinese women to come to the United States and establish families, all these men must have been working adults, the overwhelming majority employed in the canneries. Of the 1,056 white males, many were probably cannery fishermen. The "Indian" population, in contrast, consisted of 1,494 males and 1,288 females of all ages, to which 784 "Mixed" people can be added (Porter 1893:4). Although this census was compiled from hearsay and various estimates more than personal counts, and the Native population is the most likely to be underestimated under such circumstances, church statistics for these years do not add up to significantly higher figures (Pravoslavnyi Amerikanskii Vestnik 1897). This means that the labor needs of the canneries significantly exceeded the number of working-age Natives.

In regions where the Native population was larger, as in the Alaska Panhandle, British Columbia, and Puget Sound, packing companies did use them as an additional source of cheap labor besides Chinese, other racialized groups, and wives and children of fishermen. The subsistence economy that made Natives dangerously independent also made it possible to pay them wages below the cost of their survival needs, and a diverse workforce decreased a company's dependence on Asian workers, whose employment created other problems, such as labor shortages caused by exclusion laws, workers signing on and disappearing with their advances rather than boarding the steamer to Alaska, and, from the early twentieth century onward, unionization (Boxberger 1988:169–172; Friday 1994:42–43, 85; Muszynski 1988:109–113). In the Alutiiq region, Natives looking for wage work presented a convenient local pool of extra hands who could be hired as the need arose during the peak periods of salmon runs. In 1906, some of the ships bound for Alaska were destroyed by the San Francisco earthquake, and the cannery at Alitak was forced to employ people from Akhiok and other Alutiiq villages instead—for the first time according to the parish priest (Kashevarov 1907:209; Roppel 1986:170).

Given the declining importance of the fur hunt, even such casual opportunities could make canneries an increasingly worthwhile part of the yearly round for Alutiiq families. Dumond and VanStone (1995:10) reason that the cannery at Naknek attracted Alutiiq and Yup'ik people to live nearby in the late nineteenth century because those few Natives who were employed there would share the food they received with their relatives, and leftover fish could be harvested from cannery fish traps. A stay at the fisheries, whether for wage work or independent fishing, was easily integrated into the yearly subsistence round, and Native employment at the canneries gradually increased and became widespread in the second decade of the twentieth century, after the ban on sea otter hunting (Partnow 2001:237). Larry Matfay, born in Akhiok in 1907, remembers the yearly migration of villagers to Alitak and Karluk to work in fishing and processing as a fixed part of his childhood. As a young man, he joined one of the Native fishing crews at the Alitak cannery. These crews were distinct from the white crews brought up from San Francisco and caught less fish with their smaller nets and less modern equipment (Rostad 1988:45, 79–80).

Dispossessed Politics

Although cannery work as a seasonal activity was quite easily integrated with those elements of the yearly round that focused on hunting and fishing for subsistence and trade, it brought significant changes to the region. Outside commercial interests had already dominated the terms of exchange in the fur trade, but canning was the first widespread commercial venture in the region in which non-Alutiiqs also owned the means of production. The transition from conscripted hunting and trade to wage labor brought with it a political disempowerment of Alutiiq village communities. The anthropologist Gerald Sider characterizes trade in natural products such as furs as "domination at the point of exchange, not production" (Sider 1986:34), because it leaves producing communities in control of the organization of the work process. I have already noted that the RAC interfered in the organization of the sea otter hunt to a degree unusual for fur trading companies. Its officials organized hunting parties, assigned special tasks, attempted to increase the size of a group under one leader, and influenced the internal affairs of the communities through such measures as relocation. Sider himself also recognizes that communities of commodity producers undergo social transformation—social hierarchies may shift as the authority of those leaders who direct production and trade simultaneously grows and is undermined by their lack of power to control the market forces, "creating a situation where the apparently traditional social forms are largely 'about' production for merchant capital" (Sider 1986:38). But even the transformed Alutiiq communities participated in the fur trade *as communities* and were recognized as such by Russian officials. This changed after the sale of Alaska to the United States, and especially with the decline of the fur trade and rise of the canneries.

To transform Alutiiq social forms to make them "about" sea otter fur production, the RAC had to compensate for its own tenuous connections to the supply routes of the world market by creating an intraregional circle of redistribution and keeping its workers at once too busy to produce everything they needed and self-sufficient enough to survive. For this end, the RAC found support in the legal system of the Russian empire, in which the members of lower estates had collective obligations to render service to the state or to nobles. Within Russia, leaders of subjugated peoples had a recognized role in organizing such collective service, as the Siberian institution of the *toion* shows. Alutiiq leadership under the RAC was simultaneously stronger and weaker than before the arrival of the Russians. Individual households lost autonomy in the new division of labor, strengthening the position of the village chief, but the RAC claimed the right to confirm and depose chiefs and to organize ventures involving several villages, while no indigenous political institution above the village level emerged. The children of mixed marriages formed a separate class as Creoles, standing outside a chief's authority.

American fur traders had little reason to change the social institutions left over from the Russian era. They recognized the chiefs as important partners, retained Russian as lingua franca and continued to offer privileged positions for Creoles as traders and interpreters (ACC correspondence, Afognak Station; Woldt 1884:173). Still, although the ACC took over some quasi-governmental functions, political responsibility for Alutiiq life grew more diffuse. Trading companies as well as canneries sometimes offered health care or supported the construction of schools or chapels (ARCA D262/181: travel journal of Father Nikolai Kashevarov, July 24, 1916; Agnot 1987:31; Friday 1994:90; Lee 1996:34–35). But they had no clear mandate to do so and shared such responsibilities with other companies as well as with teachers, clergy, and agents of various government commissions. While in some fields, such as education, several agencies competed, other aspects of public life were neglected. For instance, there was no resident physician in Kodiak from 1867 until after 1919 (Chaffin, Krieger, and Rostad 1983:56).

Shifting alliances between institutions were possible. Although Orthodox priests sometimes denounced the exploitation of Natives by the trading companies, psalmist Andrei Kashevarov, exasperated by his parishioners' refusal to contribute to the building of a school house at Nuchek, found ready support from the ACC agent Washburn, who, for his part, hoped that in exchange for building material, Kashevarov would stop the villagers from drinking and "get the settlement back to work as they ought to do" (quote from ARCA D303/203: letter from M. L. Washburn to Andrei Kashevarov, Kodiak, Aug 27, 1894; see also ARCA D303/203:letter from Andrei Kashevarov to Father Vladimir Donskoi, Nuchek, March 27, 1895).

But different from its Russian predecessor, the U.S. government did not officially recognize any indigenous political entities or institutions in Alaska. From 1871, the U.S. Congress no longer recognized Indian tribes as treaty partners, but assumed the power to regulate their lives unilaterally through legislation. For Alaska, this meant that no treaties were ever made, and hence the government had no interest in identifying Native leaders who would have the authority to sign such treaties. While chiefs continued to be recognized by Alutiiq communities and also took action toward the outside world in writing petitions or, after World War II, becoming active in the statewide land claims movement, there was no form of Native self-government recognized by territorial or federal law until some villages formed tribal councils under the 1934 Indian Reorganization Act (Case 1984:6; Davis 1986:167; Harvey 1991:55; Kodiak Area Native Association 1987; Mitchell 1997:277).

It was under these political conditions that the transition between the fur trade and the era of the canneries occurred. The fur trade had brought Russians and white Americans in relatively small numbers, presenting no significant competition for food resources. Canneries not only made the Alutiiq a minority in their homeland but also challenged Native rights to resources they had always used—and salmon was more crucial to survival than were the sea otter pelts the Russians had prohibited the Alutiiq from using. Conflict erupted especially at those places where fisheries were situated directly next to Native villages, as was the case at Karluk. But there was no institutionally recognized way for the villagers of Karluk to represent themselves. The Russian priest Father Tikhon once again made himself their spokesman in the *Orthodox Messenger* and in reports to his superiors:

> From the strait, one does not notice the Aleut barabaras at all—only the beautiful houses of the company, canneries, store houses. Many million cans of fish are produced every year at the canneries here; they have already made many tens of millions of dollars out of the Karluk River. Only the Aleuts are poorer here than at other places, only they, the rightful owners of the river and the wealth of fish, are made homeless by robbery and the already too insatiable exploiting instinct of the factory owners, as well as by the destructive influence of the transient cannery workforce, more than 300 strong, without home or family, of mixed origin and tribes. They, poor people, do not even have houses, but live in barabaras, and in dirty and low ones at that. (ARCA D262/181:travel report of Father Tikhon Shalamov for 1895, Kodiak, March 4, 1896)

Communication with the federal government occurred through an investigation by the U.S. Fish Commission, not through political representation of any local residents. Special Agent Murray, who visited the fisheries in 1894, reported on violent conflict between employees of the several big companies operating canneries on the spit at the mouth of the river. He recorded complaints of Alutiiq villagers that they were being denied employment as fishermen for the canneries, while their own fishing was ruined by seine nets stretching across the mouth of the river and preventing salmon from reaching Native fishing sites upstream. As a result of Murray's and other reports, the river and lagoon were closed to commercial fishing in 1898, but fishing continued on the seaward side of the spit. This arrangement also made it illegal for villagers to sell their catch to the cannery and again provoked their protest, but it remained in effect for the next decades. Villagers started fishing in other rivers for the same canneries (Pracht, Luttrell, and Murray 1898:409; Roppel 1986:41–43).

The canneries themselves, where overseers and managers organized the process of production, created no need for the kind of tight interaction with indigenous institutions that existed in the fur trade. However, there was room for old and new social groupings to form within Native fishing crews, in the sharing of wages and food with relatives, and in the movement between summer camps or cabins near the cannery (at Chignik and Alitak, for example) and winter trapping and hunting sites. Independent commercial fishing, where fishermen used their own boats and sold the catch to the cannery, required large amounts of capital to purchase equipment and thus created a new kind of social stratification. In a study of late twentieth-century commercial fishing at Old Harbor, the anthropologists Craig Mishler and Rachel Mason found that many successful fishermen were descendants of Scandinavian men who married Alutiiq women and that crews were largely composed of kin groups (Mishler and Mason 1996:264–265).

The diversification of the regional economy in the early twentieth century—adding fox farming, mining, saw mills, railroad construction to canning, fishing, and hunting—gave the Alutiiq some alternative opportunities for wage labor. In Chapter 2, I pointed to some regional differences, for instance the importance of copper mining near Tatitlek, the opportunities for work as carrier in Valdez on the way to the Klondike gold fields, and the brief oil boom at Kanatak. But in all these fields, Natives were marginal, supplementary laborers, who were excluded from any real profits by such laws as the 1884 Organic Act, which extended a mining law to Alaska that limited the right to stake claims to U.S. citizens and immigrants intending to become such. Since Alaska Natives did not have general citizenship until 1924, they, as well as Asians who were "aliens ineligible for citizenship," could not participate in the Alaskan gold rushes (Mitchell 1997:125–126).

This chapter and the previous one have focused on comparing the place of Alutiiq labor in the colonial economies of the Russian and early U.S. periods. From this perspective, a major difference between the Russian and U.S. colonial periods lies in the intertwining of politics and economics during the Russian period, when the RAC, itself combining economic and administrative functions, was obliged to engage with Alutiiq political institutions in order to achieve its aims. Another difference is the ethnically and economically increasingly diverse society of U.S.-owned Alaska, where a new division of labor and new economic pursuits made Alutiiq labor superfluous to the cash economy. The RAC needed Alutiiq labor and had little to offer in return; hence it needed to combine cooptation of Native leaders, control over the production and distribution of local goods, and violence to obtain its aims. The American canneries could do without Alutiiq labor but profited from its cheap availability, and American trading companies had no difficulty supplying those goods for which the Russians had created a need.

Politically, the RAC took the village as administrative unit, attempting to shape it to fit into the structures developed for governing the peasants of the Russian empire. Supporting the *toion*'s position as mediator, executor of orders, and source of hunting knowledge was a familiar as well as economically useful strategy for the Russian administration. The United States, by contrast, had no concept of Native communities within its body politic, and either treated them as separate tribes and "domestic dependent nations" or as culturally alien people to be assimilated individually. Representing a country that expanded through white settlement and brought its cheap labor from Africa and Asia, the U.S. government had more interest in Native land than Native labor power (Spicer 1962:345, 348; Takaki 1990:64).

But the changes in the political role of Alutiiq villages and village leaders do not stand in a purely economic context. The different social, legal, and political traditions within which Russian and U.S. administrators operated deserve more detailed attention and are the subject of the next chapter.

ENDNOTES

1. Documents from the Alaska Commercial Company records, Manuscripts Department, Elmer E. Rasmuson Library, University of Alaska Fairbanks. I have not done research in this collection and am grateful to Gordon Pullar and Shauna Lukin, Afognak Native Corporation, for allowing me to review copies of documents pertaining to the Kodiak Archipelago. Petr Chechenev and Peter Chichenoff are the same person, once writing in Russian, then in English and spelling his name accordingly.

2. The fur-seal harvest on the Pribilofs was an exception. First the ACC, then the Northern Commercial Company held a monopoly on this most profitable source of Alaskan furs from 1870 to 1910, when the U.S. Department of Labor and Commerce took charge of operations. The Aleuts who carried out the sealing lived much like wards of these companies and agencies (Lee 1996; Orbach and Holmes 1986).

3. This does not mean that the conditions of the trade and of debts to the trader could not be experienced as coercive by Alutiiq hunters and their families. The stories Patricia Partnow recorded about the Kodiak ACC agent McIntyre, murdered under unclear circumstances in 1886, certainly attest to a memory of having been forced to go out to sea under dangerous circumstances by the tyrannical demands of a trader (Partnow 2001:117–125).

5

Paper Villages: Statistical Categories and Social Life

One of the most compelling images of Russia's Alaskan colonies is that of a crossroads between worlds, where Yakut and Aleut men hunted together, Finnish sailors waltzed with Creole women in elegant Russian dress, scholarly administrators wrote treatises in German, Siberian-born priests translated into local languages liturgical texts passed down to them from Byzantium, and American shipbuilders got drunk with Russian merchants. Alaska's indigenous people were "put in touch with world culture," as the standard phrase in Soviet literature goes. Some Anglophone scholars even place them at the helm of colonial society:

> By that time [toward the end of Russian rule in Alaska], Aleuts were running the operation. Aleuts were sailing the ships, writing the books, keeping the accounts, engraving the maps, translating the Bible, exploring the coasts, navigating the seven seas, and populating Alaska's cities. At the time of the sale of Alaska to the United States, in 1867, Sitka, the capital, was 60 percent Aleut, and Kodiak, the second city, was 90 percent. The Russians did not stay. In fact, they were forbidden by law to remain. Unless they had married an Alaskan and had personal/family ties that forced them to remain permanently, Russian employees were legally obliged to return home. Alaska was becoming an Aleut province. (Oleksa 1987:17)

Contrast this with the disillusionment with which Nuchek parents, by 1898, told their children that they would neither be captains at sea nor surveyors of the land and thus were wasting their time studying geography, and the transition from Russian to U.S. rule appears as a change from tolerance and free development to confinement and racist domination; from participation in administrating one's country or sailing the seven seas to being stuck at the bottom rung of a ruthless, exploitative frontier society; from life at a crossroads to life at the world's dead end during fifty years of Cold War.

There are certainly ways in which idealizations of past times can be useful. Since there is nothing to be done about the past anyway, using it as a positive contrast to the present may serve as a kind of alternative vision of reality, a lens through which present problems appear at once starker and more amenable to change. However, one must always ask what that vision helps to see and what it obscures. Oleksa's passage celebrates the achievements of "Aleuts" in Russian America, without asking for whom exactly they were possible and under what conditions. If Sitka and Kodiak had large indigenous populations, this makes them no different from colonial cities the world over, which is certainly a contrast to the demographics of North American settler colonies—but it is also well known that numerical preponderance in colonial situations rarely translated into political power or social prestige. This is not to deny that the Russian period offered certain opportunities for advancement no longer available to Alaska Natives after their incorporation into the United States of the post-Civil War era. But a more rewarding question to ask of Alutiiq history may be not which colonial period was best for them but how this history can help us understand differences between Russia and the United States in their relationships with the indigenous populations of the land they claimed during colonial expansion.

In her work on the Creole class, Lydia Black observes that although race was not as much a factor in determining a person's place in Russian-American society as it became after 1867, the estate system of the Russian empire constituted an equally formalized hierarchy. However, she stresses the relative flexibility of this system and the possibilities of rising from one rank to another, arguing that it was less arbitrary and constraining than the ascriptions based on "percentages of blood" for which she criticizes U.S. statistics (Black 1990:153). Richard Dauenhauer favorably contrasts the Russian use of Native languages and lack of racial segregation in education and worship with the simultaneously assimilationist and segregating practices of Protestant missionaries and teachers. To explain this difference, he cites the Orthodox belief in each person's potential divinity, leading to "respect for the language and culture of the individual" (Dauenhauer 1996:80; see also Mousalimas 1995). As I discuss later, the sources in the RAC and Russian Orthodox Church correspondence do not unequivocally bear out all of Black's and Dauenhauer's statements concerning social and religious life under Russian rule. But both authors point to important aspects of society and culture that need to be taken into account in comparing the Russian and U.S. periods in Alaska.

In the previous two chapters I showed that Alutiiq men and women were assigned to social and legal categories by each colonial administration, categories that structured the division of labor, settlement patterns, and access to social and economic advancement. Differences and similarities among the categories used in each period can be interpreted in light of different demands on Alutiiq labor, as I did when discussing the division between Creoles and Alutiiq in Chapter 3. But the political, religious, and ideological traditions of the Russian empire and the United States should also be taken into account, as well as the specific historical moment at which Alaska was part of each country's sphere of influence. Furthermore, administrators and other members of the elite in each setting may have had very different ideas about social distinction and propriety than did members lower down on the hierarchical ladder, be they Siberian-born RAC employees or Scandinavian or Japanese immigrants of the 1890s. And even members of each colonial elite differed among themselves concerning schemes for governance and changed their minds about the best strategies for social transformation.

For understanding the social dynamics during each colonial period, villages once again provide a good focus of discussion, this time not so much in their shape as dots on a map but as they appear in population statistics: lists of people living together, identified as Russians of various estates, Creoles, or Aleuts in Orthodox Church records; as individuals of various races and as citizens or noncitizens in the U.S. census; and always as people of either male or female sex. We will see that generating the necessary statistical information was a gradual and difficult achievement for colonial officials, so that an orderly census list neatly dividing the population into categories was in itself a claim to administrative control. It will come as no surprise to readers familiar with colonial histories the world over that population statistics may say more about the kinds of societies Russians and Americans hoped to create in Alaska than about lived reality. But the sources also show that the categories to which an individual was assigned could have real consequences for her or his life.

Feudal and Racial Hierarchies: The Life of Legal Categories

To understand some of the differences between the social systems brought to Alaska by Russian and U.S. expansion, it is instructive to look at what happened to the Creoles after 1867. The reliance of the RAC on local Alaskan populations for a variety of tasks made it necessary to assign each group a place within the framework of Russian imperial society. Those inhabitants of Alaska who were known to the Russians as "Aleuts" were considered to be subjects of the tsar by virtue of their submission by the RAC and its eighteenth-century predecessors. The 1821 and 1844 charters of the RAC treated them as a category of people comparable to a feudal estate in Russia. Like other Russian subjects, they had service obligations specific to their rank (specifically, to hunt sea otters for the RAC), but individuals had the possibility to rise to higher categories "by virtue of their service or other opportunities" (in Dmytryshyn et al. 1989:361 [quote from charter text], 470).

Creoles, the descendants of Russian men who had married Native women, constituted a separate category unique to Alaska. In the Russian empire, children generally belonged to their father's estate (peasant, burgher, merchant, clergy, different ranks of nobility, and so on), children born out of wedlock to their mother's. Socially or ethnically mixed marriages thus caused no problems for the classification of offspring. Marriages between Russian men and Siberian women were common during Russia's eastward expansion. In the nineteenth century, many groups of "Old Settlers," such as the Kamchadal, saw themselves as being of mixed Russian-Native heritage and were recognized as such by outsiders, without anyone seeing a need to create separate estates for them (Forsyth 1992:78, 143, 198–199; Slezkine 1994:97–98).

The situation in Alaska was different in part because it was not legally part of the administrative divisions of the Russian Empire. The RAC's employees were there only on seven-year passports and remained registered in the tax rolls of their city of origin. Children born in Alaska to Russian fathers had to be registered in their father's city in order to become members of a Russian estate. Head taxes for male children were then deducted from the father's pay.

As explained in Chapter 2, this arrangement was inconvenient for the Russian men, for their Alaskan wives and children, who might be unable or unwilling to move to Russia and resented being forced to pay taxes there, and also for the RAC, which needed a self-sustaining population in Alaska to alleviate the difficulty of hiring employees from Siberia and European Russia. Thanks to the lobbying efforts of the RAC main office in St. Petersburg, the Creole estate was created in 1821, followed by the colonial citizens' estate in 1844, for those Russian employees who chose to settle permanently in Alaska after they retired from company service. Creoles generally had the right to live in Alaska; Russians had to petition to be released from the rosters of their home town when family attachments, infirmity, or lack of relatives in Russia prevented them from leaving Alaska. Whether company servants or settlers, Creoles were free from taxation as long as they stayed in Alaska. Those born out of wedlock had the right to an education at company expense. Other Creoles also studied in company schools, in order to fulfill the RAC's need for skilled craftsmen, clerks, navigators, and medics (1844 charter, Article 228, in Dmytryshyn, Crownhart-Vaughan, and Vaughan 1989:467; see also Black 1990:143–145; Sarafian 1970:135–149).

The designation "Creole" itself suggests that the estate was created less out of the idea that the children of mixed marriages were inherently different from "Russian" citizens than out of the need to reconcile a legal system based on patrilinearity, patrilocal residence, and restriction of a subject's freedom to move with the wish to create a population available for service at their mother's place of residence. "Creole" was a term applied to people born of European parents in the Spanish, Portuguese, and French colonies. According to Ilya Vinkovetsky (2001), the first on record to apply the term to Alaska was, in 1805, Nikolai Rezanov, special envoy of the imperial government and member of the round-the-world expedition under Krusenstern and Lisianskii. Rezanov had been exposed to Iberian colonial culture during stopovers on the Canaries and in Brazil, as were the officers of subsequent round-the-world expeditions. That the term came to be formally used in Alaska—apparently from around 1816 (Black 1990:143)—seems to indicate that Russians thought of the offspring of Alaskan marriages as distinguished by extraterritorial birth rather than racial descent.

Even after the introduction of the legal category of Creole, population statistics maintain the Russian principle of patrilinearity by listing women and children under the father's estate. An Alutiiq woman married to a Russian of the peasant estate would be counted as a Russian peasant, as would her children until they established their own households. Then the sons would be listed as Creoles, the daughters under their husband's estate. This does not mean that a married woman's ethnicity was forgotten or thought irrelevant—when an Alutiiq woman married to a Russian appears in baptismal records as a godmother, she is identified as, for instance, "the wife of Vasilii Zykov, the Aleut woman Anna" (VS E27, Kodiak, baptisms 1826). But it means that when church statistics break down their figures into "Russians," "Creoles," and "Aleuts,"[1] members of families are counted under the estate of the (usually male) head of household. This system of counting members of status groups rather than individuals is quite different from the numbers of the U.S. census, which were intended to differentiate among individuals according to each person's biological ancestry, thought of in terms of blood quanta.[2]

In part because of this understanding of social categories as representing individual descent rather than social status, Creole status not only ceased to afford privileges but even became highly problematic after 1867. In the legal system of the United States, an individual's status as "white" or "colored" made a decisive difference, especially in the time after the Civil War. "Mixed bloods" had no clear place in this distinction, and the idea of "miscegenation" raised deep anxieties in the popular and scientific thought of the time, where there was much speculation about its degenerating effects (Pascoe 1997:70; Takaki 1990:209–210, *passim*).

The uncertainty of Creole status started with the question of citizenship. The Treaty of Purchase gave all Russian subjects who chose to remain in Alaska the right to become U.S. citizens, "with the exception of uncivilized native tribes," who would be "subject to such laws and regulations as the United States may from time to time adopt in regard to aboriginal tribes of that country" (Article 3, quoted in Dmytryshyn, Crownhart-Vaughan, and Vaughan 1989:546–547). The treaty left undefined whether Creoles were eligible for U.S. citizenship or excluded as members of "uncivilized tribes," and the question seems to have been handled differently at different locations. The 1875 confessional register for Sitka distinguishes 90 "American citizens," most of them with Russian names, from 173 "Creoles," seeming to indicate that only the Russians obtained citizenship (ARCA D414/265:Sitka parish confessional records, 1875). This may reflect the priest's interpretation of the treaty rather than any official distinction, since Alaska had no civil government at the time and very few public institutions, which means that it must have been of little practical relevance whether or not one was a citizen. Sitka church records of later decades no longer make the citizen/noncitizen distinction, so that information on long-term developments is lacking in this source.

The historian David Case (1984:59) cites a Navy report to the effect that only 229 residents of Alaska were "citizens by treaty" in 1880, a number that would include those Russians who chose to remain and any Creoles who gained citizenship. Hannah Breece, schoolteacher at Afognak and Woody Island from 1904 to 1909, noted that the population of Kadiak City, "part native Alaskans and part Russian, with inclusions of other Caucasians deriving from every part of Europe," was equal to white citizens both "in appearance, dress, and manners" and in legal standing (Jacobs 1997:50). By contrast, Mitchell cites cases in which the citizenship requirement for staking mining claims under the 1884 Organic Act was used to exclude Nulato Creoles, and states that by the 1890s, most "half-breeds" were not considered citizens. The difference may lie in the fact that the Creoles of Kadiak resided in an incorporated town rather than in a Native village. In the *Elk v. Wilkins* case of 1884, the U.S. Supreme Court had decided that American Indians were not citizens, because they were subject to the jurisdiction of their tribe. In Alaska, where no tribes had been officially recognized, members of the state legislature interpreted this ruling as excluding anyone from citizenship who lived in a Native community (Mitchell 1997:125–126, 212).

For Creole communities, it may have been advantageous to get themselves recognized as white to avoid such confusion about citizenship and other legal rights. Ninilchik, the Russian retirement settlement on the Kenai Peninsula, is a telling case for the ambiguities of the racial ascriptions in U.S. statistics. The village was established by Russian retirees with Creole or Denaina wives, whose children were considered Creoles under Russian law (Arndt 1996:246). The U.S. census for 1890 lists 16 "Indian" residents, 53 "Mixed," and 12 (all of them male) "Whites." The 1900 census lists the entire population (51) as "White," although surnames such as Oskulkoff, Darin, Kumkoff, Californski, and Astrogin indicate that the village was still a predominantly Creole community, as does the fact that all residents but two were born in Alaska. These two are a Finn (probably a later immigrant) and a 68-year-old man, Alexa Oskulkoff, born in California (Fort Ross, no doubt) of a Finnish father and an Alaskan mother. In 1910, 80 residents are counted, all of them designated white, except for the "Aleut" family of storekeeper Wasillis Bayou (who did not appear ten years before) and a "mixed" woman of "unknown tribe" married to one Gerasim Oskolkof, another Russian/Creole name. In 1920, the whiteness of the community is cast into doubt, and 84 of 87 residents are designated "mixed," including someone with two parents born in Russia. The only three "white" residents are a Canadian married into one of the families, a widowed schoolteacher and a widowed merchant (1900 census, Nenilchik; 1910 census, Nenilchuk; 1920 census, Ninilchik).

In these early census reports, racial ascriptions were made by the census taker and may not reflect the perception of that community in the eyes of other agents of the government or of their neighbors. But given the legal and social stigmatization of Natives and the uncertain status of—and racism directed at— "mixed bloods," the people of Ninilchik may have made a conscious effort to be recognized as whites. For that end, being relatively free of associations with the local Native population (some Denaina had married into the village, but most families had originated from Kodiak) must have been of help. At Afognak, where a large Creole community lived in direct vicinity of an Alutiiq village, only post-1867 immigrants tended to be listed as "white," the rest of the population as "mixed" or "Aleut." Even Little Afognak, a former retirement settlement with a similar history as Ninilchik, officially had only one "white" resident in 1900; all the others were counted as "mixed" (1900 census, Afognak Settlement,

Little Afognak village). As long as Ninilchik was considered "white," its residents escaped having to furnish further proof of their civilized life in order to maintain rights as U.S. citizens; but, if it is permissible to generalize from the shifts in the census classifications, such ascriptions were highly unstable.

Social Distinction and Biology: Evolving Ideas

Although the transition from the Russian to the U.S. system of social classification had far-reaching implications, there were also developments during the Russian period that seem to foreshadow the shift toward a greater emphasis on biological descent. From Siberia, Russians brought with them two kinds of meaningful distinctions between different Native groups. The first was the distinction between baptized and unbaptized populations, the second between sedentary and nonsedentary groups. A change from heathen to Christian lay within the range of possibility of any group or individual within one lifetime. But the second distinction, which gained significance over the course of the eighteenth and nineteenth centuries and is more relevant to understanding the Russian administration of Alaska, had connotations of a slow movement up the evolutionary ladder toward civilization that sometimes came very close to racialized thinking.

In seventeenth-century Russia, the distinction between Christians and non-Christians was connected to different tax obligations: the latter paid *iasak*, the former head tax, unless they were members of an estate not subject to it. The standard term for Siberia's indigenous people at the time was *inovertsy*, people of another faith, and an *inoverets* who accepted baptism in the Russian Orthodox Church ceased to pay *iasak* and assumed the same status as a Russian state peasant. This changed in the eighteenth century, when mass conversions became more common and christianized tribes continued to pay *iasak*, at the same time as the Russian state became more secularized under Peter I and Catherine II. Russian elites, influenced by the efforts of Enlightenment philosophers to classify mankind, began to see the distinction between themselves and indigenous Siberians as one between civilization and savagery, not to be overcome by the mere act of baptism (Slezkine 1994:18, 43, 53–55).

In Alaska, which came under Russian administration when this secularizing trend was well under way, conversion never meant freedom from work obligations —the monks of the first mission wondered why RAC officials at Kodiak seemed opposed to their missionary efforts, although baptism changed nothing in a hunter's status (Gedeon 1994:89–90). Instead of making a distinction between baptized and nonbaptized, the RAC distinguished between "settled" or "dependent" Natives, who were subjects of the tsar and under obligation to hunt for the RAC, and "independent" people who traded with the RAC at will. In the 1844 charter, the first category comprises all those known as Aleuts and also Chugach and Kenaitsy (Denaina); in other sources the latter two groups are designated "semidependent" (Dmytryshyn and Crownhart-Vaughan 1979:25; Dmytryshyn, Crownhart-Vaughan, and Vaughan 1989:470–474). The Tlingit and all Natives of interior and northern Alaska were considered independent— in fact, the Russians had to be very cautious of Tlingit military strength and often depended on them for supplies of meat and potatoes (Gibson 1996:31). These distinctions in some ways recall those made for Siberia in the Statute of Alien Administration (*Ustav po upravleniiu inorodtsev*), adopted in 1822 and providing for different forms of governance for various peoples depending on their lifestyle and mode of subsistence.

Called *inorodtsy*, people of a different tribe or descent, the non-Russian peoples of the eastern parts of the Empire were divided into settled, nomadic, and wandering categories under the statute. The first paid the same taxes as Russian peasants; the second and third continued to pay *iasak* and were only partially under the jurisdiction of Russian courts and officials (Forsyth 1992:156–157; Slezkine 1994:83–84). The distinctions among Native groups with varying degrees of closeness to the Russians in the 1844 charter of the RAC may present an Alaskan adaptation of this scheme of classification.[3] More generally, RAC regulations and the 1822 statute shared the assumption that there is a permanent boundary between "Russians" and "Natives." The statute explicitly envisioned that all "alien" peoples would eventually develop a settled lifestyle, but there were no provisions for moving from the settled alien category to that of Russian peasant. Slezkine speculates that such a move was possible only for the individual who left the Native community (Slezkine 1994:85). In the same spirit, the RAC regulations of 1821 define personal service for the RAC as the only way for an "Aleut" to move into any of the Russian estates (Dmytryshyn, Crownhart-Vaughan, and Vaughan 1989:361).

So the trend in the Russian empire through the eighteenth and nineteenth centuries was to conceptualize and govern Native communities as different and separate from Russians and to make legal standing as a Russian dependent on individual rather than communal lifestyle changes, quite similar to the equation of "civilized life" with "life outside an Indian community" as a requirement for U.S. citizenship. Such similarities notwithstanding, I have pointed out in the previous chapter that a crucial difference for Alaska was that the RAC, in accordance with Russian imperial practices, recognized Native villages as political entities and village chiefs as links between the Russian administration and the Native population, whereas the U.S. administration of Alaska denied Native communities political status for a long time. The majority of Alutiiq who did not rise to the status of Russian company employees under the RAC remained part of communities whose leaders provided a political linkage to the Russian administrators. In U.S.-administered Alaska, Natives who did not have citizenship had no alternative institutions to represent them.

Most of the dealings of the U.S. government with Alaska Natives fell in the period after it had stopped recognizing Indian tribes as independent po-litical entities. The Russian-era distinction between dependent and indepen-dent peoples lost its significance, because all Native peoples of Alaska were thought to have come under U.S. sovereignty through the Treaty of Purchase, no matter if they had previously recognized Russian authority over them in any way. Although chiefs continued to exercise authority over their communi-ties and also spoke out on behalf of them, U.S. Indian policy during the period between 1870 and 1930 was directed toward breaking up Native communities and assimilating individuals rather than interacting with Native political in-stitutions (Berkhofer 1979:170–175; Hoxie 1984:10–11). Lacking reservations, Alaska Natives did not even have Indian agents via whom to connect to the government. Since Sheldon Jackson, a Presbyterian missionary convinced that the status of reservation Indians under Bureau of Indian Affairs tutelage only hindered progress and individual assimilation, had persuaded Congress to put the Bureau of Education rather than the BIA in charge of Alaska Natives, for a long time the Native-federal relationship in Alaska remained largely limited to the funding and administration of schools by the federal government.

In 1906, the Dawes Allotment Act was amended to apply to Alaska. Al-though its effect there was more beneficial than in the Lower 48—instead of breaking up reservations, it enabled Natives to obtain legal title to land for the first time—the intention of getting Natives accustomed to private property and the pursuit of profit was the same. Political organizations that sprang up to rep-resent the interests of Alaska Natives—most notably the Alaska Native Brotherhood (ANB), founded in 1912 and taking position against reservations and for Native citizenship and land rights—had most of their membership in the Southeast, among the Tlingit, Haida, and Tsimshian, with little effect among the Alutiiq before World War II (Case 1984:137–138; Mitchell 1997:78, 195–197).

Of course, Alutiiq conceptions of their communities were not and are not necessarily restricted by the legal framework of the Russian or the U.S. admin-istration. A discussion of legal categories always begs the question of how they contribute to the construction of collective or individual identities, and what consequences they have in lived experience. To look at such categories in action, education is a fitting subject. With its promise of a chance to rise above the circumstances one was born into, it calls to question any static conception of social reality and of distinctions between colonizers and colonized. But at the same time, with the restrictions apparent in law and practice, it demonstrates the practical relevance of legal categories for personal biographies.

Education: Bone of Contention

When Michael Oleksa claims that "Aleuts" were translating the Bible and exploring the coasts, he is mainly referring to Creoles who had taken advantage of the educational opportunities offered by the RAC. Creoles who had been educated at the schools maintained at St. Paul Harbor, Unalaska, and Novoarkhangel'sk were obliged to serve in Alaska for fifteen years, those who had been sent to Russia for ten years. Some were also trained as clergymen in Irkutsk or at the ecclesiastical school established by Bishop Innokentii (Ioann Veniaminov) at Novoarkhangel'sk in 1841 (Black 1990; Black and Arndt 1997:22; Okladnikova 1987).

People born into the Aleut category were also among those who received training at such schools, and there were cases of men rising from classification as Aleut to Creole and Russian during their lifetime, thanks to their education and service to the Company—a possibility that the second and third charters explicitly provided for (Black 1990:152). That said, the RAC set up its educational system to serve its own economic needs. Given the functional role of the ethnic division of labor in the Russian-American economy (see Chapter 3), it was not in the interest of the RAC to have people change categories at will.[4] Statements on education in the Chief Managers' correspondence show their concern with separating children of various origin in order to prepare them for different functions in colonial society.

The first school on Kodiak Island was founded by Shelikhov for hostage boys at Three Saints Bay. He described it as part of his measures to impress the people of Kodiak with the benefits and superiority of Russian civilization and persuade them to keep peace (Shelikhov 1981 [1791]:45). When Hieromonk Gedeon reorganized the school in 1805, it still taught students "of different tribes," among them orphans and Tlingit hostages. Besides reading, writing, catechism, history, arithmetics, and geography, subjects included agriculture, fishing, and the gathering of herbs and roots—a remarkable combination of local and Russian-introduced knowledge in the area of practical skills (Gedeon 1994:88, 105). Already at this early stage, the aim seems to have been to equip

the students to be self-sufficient under Alaskan conditions (albeit slightly mod-
ified through the practice of horticulture) rather than having them adopt the
lifestyle of the Russian elite. In later years, when the Alutiiq population no longer posed a military threat but rather presented cause for concern because of
the high mortality rate, determining who should be educated for what end became part of the strategy of managing the shrinking labor force. In 1836, Chief
Manager Kupreianov warned that going to school should not keep an Alutiiq
boy from learning traditional skills "useful to him and the Company" (RAC cs
13:28v, March 3, 1836, to Kodiak office). The following year, he expresses his
displeasure at seeing the names of three Alutiiq boys on the lists of students at
the Kodiak school:

> The occupation of these three boys must not be primarily at school, for the
> future I ask the Office to make sure that the children of Aleuts are not in any
> way drawn away from their natural life style and thus not to deprive the Com-
> pany of hunters, whose number has suffered a significant decline in recent
> times owing to the mortality among the Aleuts. (RAC cs 14:280v–281, May
> 16, 1837, to Kodiak office)

With the same rationale of preventing the loss of potential hunters, both
Kupreianov and his successor Etholen were adamant that the smallpox orphans should be raised in Alutiiq communities. Etholen gave order that Rus-
sian or Creole families were under no circumstances to take in Alutiiq orphans.
Specifically, the Alutiiq boy Roman Lavrent'ev had to leave the household of
Kondratii Burtsov in St. Paul Harbor (notwithstanding the fact that Burtsov
seems to have been born an "Aleut" himself) and was assigned to the care of
the *toion* at Three Saints Bay (RAC cs 20:49–50, Feb 25, 1841, to Kodiak office).
Creole children, for their part, had to be kept from living the life of an Aleut.
In 1836 the manager of the Kodiak office was asked to keep a list of all Creole
children of both sexes and make sure they received useful training according to
their capacities from age eight (RAC cs 13:395, July 22, 1836, to Kodiak office).

It seems that as RAC control over the Alutiiq region strengthened, schools
increasingly concentrated on educating Creoles rather than high-ranking
Alutiiq children. The education of the growing Creole population was a responsibility of the RAC mandated by its charter, and the shrinking numbers
of Alutiiq men were needed for their hunting skills rather than for anything
a Russian school could teach them. A school for girls was founded at St. Paul
Harbor in 1839 and attended mainly by daughters of Creoles and of Russian
officials (Okladnikova 1987:238). Khlebnikov mentions an earlier girls' orphanage established under Chief Manager Murav'ev (1820–1825). He claims that

it was the refusal of Alutiiq parents to part with their children that forced the Russians to concentrate on orphans in their educational work, an important reminder that, if Russian officials had doubts about the wisdom of educating Alutiiq children, the children's parents may have had their own objections as well (Liapunova and Fedorova 1979:35, 37).

Although such educational institutions offered instruction to Creoles from poor families or those whose fathers had abandoned them, there remained many children of simple Company employees who had no schooling, were illiterate, and also lacked the skill or motivation to work as sea otter hunters—these were the people for whom the Creole settlements founded in the 1830s and 1840s were intended (Black 1990:153; Fedorova 1971:192).

U.S. educational policy in Alaska reversed the priorities in some ways. Government effort now concentrated mainly on schooling for Native children, which was a responsibility of the federal government. White communities had to organize and fund their own schools. Creoles found themselves in an in-between position in this respect as well, especially since education in the late nineteenth-century United States, with its Jim Crow laws and the infamous "separate but equal" decision in *Plessy v. Ferguson*, was becoming more and more segregated along the lines of "white" and "colored." When Hannah Breece was teaching at Afognak, she was in the service of the Alaska division of the Bureau of Education in the Department of the Interior, the office in charge of Alaska Native affairs until 1931, when responsibility was transferred to the Bureau of Indian Affairs. Breece was hired specifically to teach the "Aleut" children and instructed to take on the "Russians" only temporarily because there was no way of organizing an independent school for them. In the fall of 1905, she was told to dismiss all "Russian" children from school because of a newly passed law, the Nelson Act. This act provided for federal funding for schools in unincorporated towns with fifteen or more white children, or children of "mixed blood who lead a civilized life" (law text quoted in Cole 1996:317). Breece managed to obtain permission to continue teaching the "Russian" children until a Nelson school could be organized in Afognak (Jacobs 1997:32).

Father Pavel Shadura, Orthodox priest from Kenai, also writes that Creole children in his parish qualified as white in the racially segregated educational system set up under the Nelson Act, but this time it was to their advantage and to the detriment of the "black" Denaina children:

> My parishioners of Kenai village have been divided into two parties—into whites-creoles and blacks-Kenaitsy [Denaina Athabaskans]—by the opening this year of an American Territorial Public school for whites in Kenai. For

five years an American school administered by a different office existed here
for Indians, of course everybody used it, and I had no trouble at all in church
or school matters, but worked hand in hand [*shel ruka ob ruku*]. (ARCA
D266/183:letter from Father Pavel Shadura to Bishop Evdokim, Kenai, Dec
18, 1915)

But Creole children were not always so easily recognized as white. In
some Alaskan communities, white settlers objected to having their children
taught together with "mixed bloods," and since the meaning of the phrase "a
civilized life" was ill-defined, it was relatively easy for a court to exclude a child
on grounds of the parents being uncivilized (Cole 1996:317; Mitchell 1997:90).
According to Hannah Breece's memoir, children of white fathers on Kodiak and
Afognak generally qualified for the white schools (Jacobs 1997:32). At least in
the period before the Nelson Act, children of U.S.-American men and Alaska Native women were also accepted at Chemawa Indian School in Oregon.
In 1902, Hieromonk Mefodii reported from Nuchek that eight American fathers had taken their children to Chemawa to be trained in "various American
trades and crafts." Most of the children's mothers were dead, and the fathers
were voluntarily sending their children to this boarding school, partly, as Father Mefodii hinted, to keep them out of the local Orthodox parish school. No
Chugach children had been sent to Chemawa at that time (ARCA D303/203:
report from Hieromonk Mefodii to the North American Consistory, Nuchek,
Oct 15, 1902).

The link between educational and religious concerns evident in Hieromonk Mefodii's report was typical of debates about Native education in Alaska.
The Orthodox Church remained active in Alaska after the sale, even with renewed vigor through the founding of the Alaskan diocese in 1870. The Russian-
era educational system persisted in the form of parish schools, many of them
the only school in a village until the early twentieth century (Antonii 1900;
Kan 1999). The Orthodox tradition of creating alphabets for Alaskan languages,
translating liturgical texts, and training bilingual Creoles as priests and readers
provided a potential for a different pedagogical practice than did the assimilationist stance of Sheldon Jackson and the Bureau of Education. The Bureau
ignored the Orthodox Church when it contracted schools to Protestant missionary organizations. The official policy at these Protestant schools was that
students should speak only English, and school regulations often prescribed
physical punishment for children who spoke their Native language. They were
expected to become Protestant Christians in faith and lifestyle.

The chapel and girls' dormitory of the Baptist orphanage on Woody Island, 1915. Ash from the Katmai volcano is still visible on the field in the foreground of this picture, taken three years after the Katmai eruption. The Baptist orphanage, founded in 1893, was much criticized by Orthodox priests for taking children out of Orthodox families. Along with the Baptist school in Kodiak City, it also laid the foundation for a sizable Baptist community among Kodiak Island Alutiiq today. *Photograph by Robert F. Griggs, courtesy of Archives and Special Collections, University of Alaska Anchorage, National Geographic Society collection, hmc-0186-volume1-3609.*

The Kodiak archipelago came under the tutelage of Baptist missionaries, who paid little attention to the fact that virtually all children in the region were baptized in the Russian Orthodox Church, and some of them were literate in Russian. A bitter rivalry between the churches resulted, similar to the tensions between Orthodox and Presbyterians in Sitka and Tlingit villages of the Alaska Panhandle described by Sergei Kan (1999:240–244, 266–273). The Baptists founded an orphanage on Woody Island in 1893, and a year later there was an Orthodox orphanage at Kadiak, in spite of the general lack of funds in the diocese and the repeated protest of parishioners that they were unwilling and unable to finance it themselves. There were disputes over the custody of individual children as well as over the question of allowing Orthodox children living at the Baptist orphanage to attend Orthodox services, which the Baptist missionaries refused. Father Tikhon Shalamov claimed that the Baptists were concentrating on work with orphans and children taken from their families by force, some of them brought from as far away as the Aleutians and Sitka, because they could not convert any adults away from Orthodoxy.[5] Ten years later Hannah Breece claimed that more Alutiiq families were trying to enroll their children as day students at the Baptist school than could be admitted (Jacobs

Priest, students, and teachers at the Kodiak Orthodox orphanage. The Orthodox orphanage was founded in 1894, one year after the Baptist orphanage, as part of the rivalry between the two Christian confessions over the upbringing of Alutiiq children. *Courtesy of Alaska State Library, Michael Z. Vinokouroff Collection, p243-1-018.*

1997:72). Both sides accused each other of physically abusing students (A. K. D. 1899:602; Pullar 1992:186–188; Roscoe 1992:69).

The Orthodox Church had generally a weaker position in these disputes, given that the Baptists had been officially entrusted with Native education by the U.S. government, whereas the Orthodox schools and churches were suspected of teaching allegiance to the tsar. Where a Bureau of Education school was opened, the priests gave up their all-day parish schools and concentrated on teaching religious subjects and Russian in the afternoons. Spending all day in two different schools was exhausting for the children, and several Russian priests and teachers complained of low or irregular attendance in the church schools (ARCA D249/172:report from Kodiak clergy to Father Vladimir Donskoi, Kodiak, July 6, 1893).

As far as the use of Native languages is concerned, differences between the Russian and U.S. schools are less obvious than some writers claim. The example of Saint Innocent (Ioann Veniaminov), who taught writing in Aleut at his school in Unalaska and instituted classes in various Alaskan languages at the Novoarkhangel'sk seminary (Dauenhauer 1996:78–79), does not seem to be representative of Orthodox education in the Alutiiq region after 1867.

When priests and teachers at Kadiak, Afognak, Nuchek, and Tatitlek list the subjects taught at their schools,[6] Alutiiq appears, if at all, as the language in which some prayers are taught, but the main language of instruction is Russian, occasionally supplemented by English lessons. Many priests themselves relied on interpreters to communicate with those parishioners who did not speak Russian (Morseth 1998:83; ARCA D305/204:report from Andrei Kashevarov to Father Vladimir Donskoi, Nuchek, July 8, 1894). Although there are no indications that Alutiiq was prohibited in the schools, Russian was the medium that enabled communication between students and teachers and gave students access to knowledge.

The historian of Russian missions Andrei Znamenski (1999:64–66) remarks that although it was not an official position of the Russian Orthodox Church that christianization required russianization, there were influential voices among nineteenth-century missionaries who advocated this idea. While American Protestant churches and Bureau of Indian Affairs officials were more explicitly assimilationist in their policies, differences to Orthodoxy seem less clear-cut in the practice of Protestant day schools as documented in teachers' memoirs. Anglo-American teachers also had to make linguistic compromises, especially in the beginning, to enable the children to understand them at all. Ernest Roscoe at Kodiak hired Ivan Petroff as a Russian interpreter both for regular day school and evening classes for adults, and Hannah Breece, arriving later, already found English-speaking residents to translate into Alutiiq for her. Evidently these teachers at local day schools could not enforce language policies as strictly as boarding schools in Sitka or the continental United States, where many students entirely forgot their native language (Jacobs 1997:34; Pullar 1992:185; Roscoe 1992:4–5, 24).

As far as the exclusive claim to the right way to heaven is concerned, the Baptists and the Orthodox were equally uncompromising. And neither side seemed to think that Alutiiq parents should have a say in their children's education, as exemplified by psalmist Andrei Kashevarov's dispute with parents at Nuchek over the teaching of geography, quoted in Chapter 1 (ARCA D305/204: report from Andrei Kashevarov to Church Consistory, Oct 14, 1897).

While the degree of indigenization of nineteenth-century Orthodox education should thus not be exaggerated, it is safe to say that Alutiiq conversion to Orthodoxy generated an amount of autonomous teaching and religious activity unmatched by the Baptist church. In the outlying villages of the Orthodox parishes, where the priest visited only once or twice a year, Alutiiq lay psalmists were in charge of the chapel and also of teaching the children prayers, reading, and writing. Father Vladimir Donskoi from Sitka, after an inspection tour of the Kodiak parish in 1892, reports on the work of such men, not without suspicion of their independent authority. Psalmists had in the past even performed sacred acts reserved to ordained priests, such as processions with the gospel during services or the blessing of holy water, and an ACC agent told Father Vladimir that the people of Aiaktalik had repeatedly expressed their intention to "live an independent religious life."

The Kodiak priest Aleksandr Martysh had tried to discourage such strivings for autonomy by making more frequent, longer visits to every village and choosing men loyal to the church as psalmists and teachers. Father Vladimir recognized that better discipline was kept now, but in observing the work of Stefan Kaliaudok at Kaguyak, IUvenalii Aminak at Aiaktalik, and Andrei IAkusha at Akhiok, he noted that they themselves needed additional schooling in order to understand the texts of the prayers and the religious concepts behind them. Aminak was the one who spoke the best Russian and otherwise made the most positive impression:

> According to the priest Martysh, Aminak is quite a bright person and respected among the Aleuts. He has been serving as a psalmist for thirty-six years and always taught reading and writing to the children. The psalmists of the villages adjacent to Aiakhtalek are all his students. Young Aleuts even come up to him for the blessing [which only a priest is allowed to dispense], and even though he does not bless, he allows them to kiss his hand. The singing in the Aiakhtalek chapel is better than in the other Aleut villages. Even the children participate in reading. (ARCA D259/179:report from Father Vladimir Donskoi, Sitka, Nov 14, 1892)

In such settings, where religious knowledge was passed on within the Alutiiq community, reading and writing Alutiiq may also have been taught. A report of 1891 mentions that although few Alutiiq speak Russian, many know the Cyrillic alphabet and use it to write one another in their own language (ARCA D259/179:report from Father Aleksandr Martysh to Church Consistory, Kodiak, Oct 4, 1891). The Alutiiq prayers and catechisms used in the Orthodox Church must have provided the major opportunity for people to become familiar with reading and writing their language in the Cyrillic alphabet. Copies of an Alutiiq primer and catechism, as well as a translation of the Gospel according to Matthew, prepared by Il'ia Tyzhnov and published in the 1840s, are preserved in the archives of St. Herman's Seminary, Kodiak (Black 2001).

Under U.S. administration, by contrast, the decline of literacy in Cyrillic did not lead to the use of the Roman alphabet to write Alutiiq. The Baptist church did not publish and use Alutiiq translations of liturgical texts, aiming to teach Alutiiq converts English instead. Added to that was the diminishing role of both written and spoken Alutiiq in public life, owing to the combined effects of teachers' efforts to make students identify the English language with getting ahead in the world, and of the demographic and economic changes that brought in more and more English-speaking employers, foremen, traders, husbands, and in-laws.

In religious as well as secular life, Russian colonial society offered graduates of its schools greater chances to apply their acquired skills in practical life than existed for graduates of U.S. Indian education. For instance, the Orthodox Church actively trained Native clergy. An imperial decree from the year 1841 permitted the training of Native and Creole clergy from Kamchatka, the Kuriles, and Alaska, and several priests active in the Alutiiq region in the late nineteenth century—Petr Kashevarov and several of his sons, Aleksandr Petelin and others—were Creoles, although there were no Alutiiq priests, strictly speaking. The Protestant churches active in Alaska at the time at most allowed Natives to become lay readers, catechizers, and interpreters (ARCA D259/179: report from Father Vladimir Donskoi, Sitka, Nov 14, 1892; D259/179:report from Father Tikhon Shalamov for 1896, Kodiak; D261/180:report by Father Vasilii Martysh for 1901, Afognak, March 15, 1902; Dmytryshyn, Crownhart-Vaughan, and Vaughan 1989:430; Kan 1985:199–202; Rathburn 1981:15).

As far as secular occupations are concerned, the RAC's educational program was tailored to the company's needs for trained personnel, and educated Creole and Alutiiq men were actually entrusted with responsible posts. The reverse side of this was that access to education was dependent on the administration's calculations of its needs, resulting in the warnings against educating Alutiiq boys needed as hunters, as quoted above. The education offered in U.S. day and boarding schools, by contrast, was of little use to people who could most realistically hope to make a living by a combination of hunting, trapping, and fishing and/or cannery labor. Educational and economic planning was no longer carried out by a single institution, although there was a widespread idea among white educators that it served Native children best when they were educated for humble occupations—hired hands, domestic servants, and craftsmen (Littlefield 1993:49–50; Mitchell 1997:118, 203; Schmeckebier 1927:217–218). In Alaska there was no more demand for skilled Native workers after the end of the fur trade, and as unskilled wage laborers they faced competition from Asian and other immigrant groups. Educated Alutiiq children no longer had even the limited chances of rising up in colonial society that had been open to them before 1867.

Students and parents, teachers and administrators thus constantly confronted the legal categories that determined who was educated where, what was taught, where the funding came from, and who had the right to decide these matters. But these categories also met their own practical limitations as teachers had to compromise with a view to local conditions. In the following section, I show that even keeping population statistics, seemingly the area in which administrative categories could exist in their purest form, required practical compromises. For Russian as well as U.S. administrators, setting up a system of population records involved many acts of redefining, reordering and reexplaining, and the difficulties of creating statistics according to predefined ideas of social order sometimes point to the limits of colonial rule.

Statistics, Family, and Gender

Both Russians and Americans made efforts to name, count, and categorize the people of their Alaskan territories, and statistics served many purposes. Shelikhov used them as proof of the great numbers of new subjects he had brought under the authority of the tsar, enemies of the RAC as evidence of population decline through its abusive practices, Sheldon Jackson to show the destitute condition of Alaska Natives and the success of his relief measures. The division of the population into different, countable categories made it possible to manage the work force and plan for the allocation of resources and school funds. In addition, extending familiar forms of record keeping to Alaska was a gesture of incorporating and domesticating that region. Not only in architecture, dress, and food did administrators and settlers try to maintain home standards but also in generating the statistical information that was deemed necessary by the national government or other institutions. Confessional records, vital statistics, and U.S. census records were often based on inadequate information and difficult to compile with any degree of precision, but considerable energy went into making them nonetheless. Russian and U.S. government and church hierarchies asserted their control over subordinate agencies and individuals in Alaska by requiring them to present statistical reports (cf. Appadurai 1993:324).

Confessional records are a good example of statistics that function to control both a population and the institution required to compile them. In 1722 the Ecclesiastical Regulations, recently introduced as part of Peter the Great's effort to bring the church administration under his immediate control after the example of the Protestant German states, were amended to require all parish priests to record who came to confession at least once a year and who did not. The purpose of these records was to catch schismatics (Old Believers who rejected liturgical reforms introduced in the late seventeenth century) and people disloyal to the throne. Priests were required to report parishioners to state authorities when they absented themselves from confession without excuse or confessed subversive plans (Cracraft 1971:238–240; Smolitsch 1964:125, 464).

Stemming from a particular set of conflicts between church and secular authority, between the imperial government and segments of the population, and within the church hierarchy, the law remained in effect in Russia until the revolution of 1917. In the Alutiiq region, confessional records were kept for Russians and baptized Natives, ideally arranged by village, estate, and patriarchal family units, listing every individual's name and age and noting who participated in confession and communion, who was excused for reasons of young age or necessary absence, and who was absent without excuse. While the presence of Old Believers among recently converted Alutiiq was unlikely, the compliance of an individual with church requirements may have been read as an indicator of submission to Russian authorities in general. Besides, by sending duplicates of the confessional records and clerical register to his superiors in the church hierarchy each year, the parish priest documented that he was carrying out his duties as required.[7]

The RAC published its own statistics in yearly reports, and it is not clear if it consulted church records in compiling them. One of the duties of *toions* in the postepidemic villages was assisting the clerk at the Kodiak office in making a list of the population each year, which suggests two separate systems of record keeping, although the priests may have relied on the same source of information (RAC cs 21:395–397, Sep 25, 1842, to Kodiak office; Fedorova 1971:248–251). Conflicts between church and secular authorities on the local Alaskan level could also crystallize around issues of statistics. Under Baranov, the priests complained that they were not given the necessary information for recording births and deaths, and they accused the RAC of trying to hide the decline of the Alutiiq population (Arndt 1985 [1861]:64).

The development of the confessional records over time shows that even without mutual obstruction by different Russian authorities, it was difficult enough to gather information and fit it into the required form. The earliest confessional records from Kodiak parish preserved in the Library of Congress, dating from the 1830s (ARCA D255/175), list only the population of St. Paul Harbor and other Russian posts, mainly Russian and Creole families and a few "Aleuts." The 1841 records are the first to list greater numbers of "Aleuts," but they do not arrange names by village (perhaps all individuals are from the vicinity of St. Paul Harbor) and only rarely by family. The records consist mainly of blocks of names without any indications of residence or kinship connections. In 1843, the priest seems to have traveled around the island to hold services at Orlovskoe, Three Saints Bay, and Karluk. While the Alutiiq population of St.

Paul Harbor is listed mainly as families (and those who are not may be small-pox survivors without immediate kin), in the other villages most names are simply arranged into alternating blocks of women and men. The following year, people in all villages are listed in family groups for the first time.

The slow growth of the church records in coherence and completeness speaks, among other things, of the changes brought by the smallpox epidemic, both to the situation of the Alutiiq and to the interests of the RAC. Under Chief Manager Baranov at least, the RAC had looked at missionary efforts with suspicion, but after the epidemic the slow progress of the mission on Kodiak became a cause for concern. In 1839, Kupreianov noticed with displeasure that there were still unbaptized people on Kodiak Island although priests had been present for over forty years. He asked the manager of the Kodiak office to do what he could to encourage Father Aleksei Sokolov's missionary efforts. Father Aleksei had arrived on Kodiak in 1833 to replace Kodiak's first "white" (secular and married, as opposed to the "black" or monastic clergy) priest, Father Frumentii Mordovskii, who was sent back to Russia for immoral behavior (Pierce 1990:363).

Father Aleksei was also soon criticized for drunkenness, and that his mis-sionary zeal was not very great is indicated by the vital statistics for the 1830s. In June/July 1832, a trip by Father Frumentii around the island is documented, with baptisms and marriages in each village, but in Father Aleksei's time, all re-corded ceremonies seem to have been performed in St. Paul Harbor, and many of the Alutiiq involved were in company service. Of close to 1,000 smallpox deaths in 1837, only eight are recorded. When Sokolov's successor, Father Petr Litvintsev, traveled around the island in 1843, the majority of villagers are list-ed as taking communion for the first time in their lives (RAC cs 19:185–185v, Sep 27, 1840, to Main Office; 17:14v–15, Feb 20, 1839, to Kodiak office; VS E27, Kodiak 1832–1840; ARCA D255/175:Kodiak parish confessional records, 1843). Although there was popular affection for the monk German, a member of the first mission who lived in a hermitage on Spruce Island until his death in 1836 and was remembered among the Alutiiq for sheltering orphans and heal-ing the sick, Ioann Veniaminov described the Kodiak archipelago in 1840 as a place where "shamanism" continued to be widely practiced and where people showed little inclination toward the Christian faith (Black 1997:275–276; Met-ropolitan Innokentii 1888:371).

Kupreianov blamed the lack of Christian faith among the Alutiiq for the high death toll on Kodiak Island and for the suspicion of inoculation that Rus-sian medics had encountered. If Kodiak had a priest like Father IAkov Netsve-tov on Atkha or Father Ioann Veniaminov on Unalaska, the Alutiiq would develop a better understanding of religion and morality and give up such harmful practices as segregating their sick relatives in abandoned huts instead of tending to them or taking them to the Russian hospital (RAC cs 15:248v-253, May 1, 1838, 18:333v, May 25, 1840, both to Main Office). RAC officials also seem to have hoped that faith in the Christian God might make smallpox survivors less likely to blame diseases on the Russians and revolt against them. In 1840 the Creole Afanasii Klimovskii was sent out to the northern Alaska Peninsula to convince people that "this disease was not from the Russians, but from God" (RAC cs 19:220v, Sep 6, 1840).

Alutiiq suspicions that the Russians were bringing them the disease were of course not unfounded, especially since they observed that the Russians were not dying from it. Isolating sick people in abandoned houses may have served to avoid the obligation to destroy the family's house, as, according to Davydov, was required after someone had died in it (Davydov 1977:179). The inoculation with infected human lymph did indeed make symptoms of the disease appear and was not without risks. In Europe the introduction of smallpox vaccination also often led to a struggle over the bodies of children and ideas of health and disease between medics and administrators and rural or working-class parents. Where vaccination was made obligatory, vaccination records became a proof of civil obedience (and important source for historians) comparable to confessional records in Petrine Russia (Wolff 1995).

Smallpox survivors may have been more willing to accept Christianity after their own religious specialists had proven incapable of healing the disease. But the development of church statistics after 1840 reflects not necessarily a boost in Christian conversion but the fact that the inhabitants of the new villages were easier to oversee, count, and monitor for their fulfillment of church obligations—and easier to represent in the required form. As I noted above, the 1844 confessional records arrange the whole population in family groups for the first time. But these families, neatly numbered within each village and assembled into subgroups according to their pre-epidemic village of origin, are far bigger than the units of later records. For instance, the fourth family at Aiakhtalik consists of thirteen people: Terentii Naikok, three of his nephews, the wife, daughter, and two brothers-in-law of one of the nephews, another nephew's wife and his two children, niece, and brother (that is, a fourth nephew of Terentii Naikok?). Other families are much smaller and show the gaps left by the epidemic, such as the second one from the same village: Safron Kuchup, his wife Anna Panali, an adopted son, two nieces, and a grandson (ARCA D255/175: Kodiak parish confessional records, 1844). It is not clear if these are people who lived together in one house or if they came to confession together and identified one another as relatives. By 1851, such complex relationships have disappeared, and the records appear as a succession of nuclear family groups, where the only kinship connections indicated are between husband, wife, and children (ARCA D255/176:Kodiak parish confessional records, 1851).

With this, Alutiiq families as portrayed in church records finally took on the form of the patriarchal household that determined the legal status of an individual in the Russian system of estates. Actual Alutiiq kinship, marriage, and gender practices had long confused and irritated Russian observers. Davydov claims that sons sometimes married their mothers, and that priests who baptized and married couples often unknowingly joined together close relatives. Conflicting ideas about kinship continued to make life difficult for priests who tried to enforce the prohibitions of the Orthodox Church against marriage with one's parent, child, sibling, first cousin, or with the child of one's godparent (Davydov 1977:181; Taylor 1966:213). In 1899, Father Konstantin Pavlov from Nuchek complained that many people married two or three times, leaving the children of previous marriages to be raised by relatives. This often made it impossible for him to determine who the biological parents of prospective marriage partners were and what rules against incest applied (ARCA D305/204: report from Father Konstantin Pavlov to Hieromonk Antonii, Nuchek, 1899).

The position of women and female sexuality among the Alutiiq also struck Russian observers as unusual. Shelikhov already reports that one woman may "keep" two or three husbands and that one man also may have two wives (Shelikhov 1981:56). Polyandry, along with the accepting attitude toward sexual relations out of wedlock and frequent divorce, is repeatedly commented on (Gedeon 1994:61; Holmberg 1856:399). The recognition given to "dexterous and skillful women" (Gedeon 1994:70)—to the extent that they might gain the power to "keep" two husbands—was at odds with the ideas about women's status held by Russian travelers. Usually the women of "savage peoples," writes Davydov, "are more slaves than companions to the men," but among the Alutiiq "they wield a lot of power, and the girls are not chosen by the men but they choose their husbands," although women cannot sit in council and are excluded from certain feasts (Davydov 1977:165–166).

Even more disconcerting were the cases of gender shifting. There were men who wore women's dress, performed women's work, and were sought-after marriage partners for men. Many were said to have shamanic power. A girl, by contrast, might be given a man's name and be introduced to sit in council along with the men, but her father had to distribute a greater number of presents to legitimize the occasion than was customary for a boy (Davydov 1977:166, 184; Gedeon 1994:61, 78).

These examples show that gender divisions were salient for Alutiiq as well as for Russians, but that each group drew distinctions differently. The fascination with which such instances are related by Russian observers shows their deep investment in unambiguous gender divisions. Church statistics have separate columns for men's and women's ages, and count men and women separately. Priests insisted that every man and woman should have only one marriage partner, and of the opposite sex. If other forms of marriage continued, they must have grown harder to sustain in the consolidated settlements, where people were more constantly under Russian observation and Russian priests and administrators had more leverage in influencing Alutiiq behavior. Holmberg's translator pointed out a "man-woman" (*Mannweib*) during a visit to Woody Island in 1851, leading him to speculate that the practice might be quietly carried on. Holmberg does not make clear whether the person he saw was in male or female dress, but the words of his translator, "this guy is a woman" (*dieser Kerl ist ein Weib*), suggest that s/he was dressed as a man, concealing any transgender role (Holmberg 1856:401).

As Black (1990:149–151) points out, efforts to enforce official standards of sexuality and morality were not only aimed at the Alutiiq but also at lower-class Russians. Marriage as a temporary union sanctioned only by the community was practiced in the northern Russian and Siberian communities where most of the RAC employees originated, but in the course of the eighteenth century the government and the church increased their efforts to have all marriages performed by a priest and to shun frequent divorce. One of the reasons for bringing resident clergy to Kodiak, Black suggests, was to formalize the marriages of Company employees and legalize the status of their offspring. Some of the record-keeping efforts of the Russian administration may also have been driven by a concern to maintain class distinctions between Russians while distinguishing them from Natives, in accordance with the RAC's general efforts to maintain a range of social groups to fulfill different tasks in the colonies (cf. Stoler 1989:138).

When it comes to assuming fixed gender divisions and a patriarchal family structure, the U.S. census operated no differently from Russian records. The census forms listed people in households, starting usually with a male "head," then enumerating other members designated according to their relationship to him: "his wife," "his son," "his daughter," "lodger," "servant," and so on. As under the Russians, only widows could be female heads of households.

Russians and Americans also promoted similar ideas of the sexual division of labor. The RAC employed men and boys for vegetable gardening and hay-cutting (at least before the epidemic), although working with plants could have been considered closer to the gathering of roots, berries, and grasses that was traditionally part of women's work. There is an echo here of the surprise with which Russian travelers reacted to the notion that it might depend on a woman's productivity whether she had one or two husbands. The production of Russian staples (cultivated grains and fodder for cattle) was identified as a male provider's job—even though peasant women in Russia did their share of the sowing and reaping, and the berries and roots whose gathering the RAC considered women's work must also have contributed significantly to the colonial diet.

Not surprisingly, the idea of the male provider resurfaces in the form of lower wages for women and children. According to the RAC's 1841 regulations, daily wages for women in the Kodiak district were lower than men's at some posts, but not everywhere. In the canneries, women were generally paid less—a report on the 1892 season in Alaska shows that where Natives were employed, men were paid $1.50–1.75 per day, women $1.00 (RAC cs 20:36v–45v, February 25, 1841, to Kodiak Office; Pracht, Luttrell, and Murray 1898:393).

Like teachers in Indian schools elsewhere in North America (Wall 1997), Baptists in the Alutiiq region taught women gender-specific, domestic skills. Ida Roscoe, whose husband was the first Baptist teacher appointed to Kodiak, taught a class for adult women, where they learned reading and writing in English but also baking with Ida's recipes and sewing on her new sewing machines. Hannah Breece taught a class in breadmaking and sewing for Afognak girls on Saturdays (Jacobs 1997:21; Roscoe 1992:62–63). What is interesting is that sewing and food preparation were now seen as domestic skills, enabling women to provide for their families and households. During the days of sea otter hunting, female work such as sewing *kamleikas* and *baidarka* covers and preparing dried fish had been part of the commodity production organized by the fur companies, not of a purely domestic sphere.

It is hard to tell if the nuclear families recorded in postepidemic Russian and U.S. census records corresponded to actual changes in marriage and residential patterns. Rules of postmarital residence are not clearly described in the early sources. After a period of bride service during which the husband lived in his wife's house and worked for his parents-in-law, the couple moved to their own residence, but neither Davydov nor Gedeon specifies where that lay, nor do they say whether or not marriages were usually contracted between partners from one village (Davydov 1977:182; Gedeon 1994:69). Vital statistics from the postepidemic villages suggest a rather self-contained world, where marriage partners as well as godparents for children mainly come from the same village. In 1855, of 40 Alutiiq weddings, 37 were between people from the same village. The three intervillage couples were all listed at the husband's village two years later (VS E30, Kodiak, weddings 1855; ARCA D255/176:Kodiak parish confessional records, 1857). Part of the reason for this may be that the seven consolidated settlements created after the smallpox epidemic lay quite far apart from one another, and may have united villages that had maintained regional kinship ties before. Before the epidemic, the picture seems more heterogeneous, with more intervillage marriages and godparenthoods, often between neighboring villages, many of which were later relocated to the same consolidated settlement.

While it is uncertain what the precolonial Alutiiq way of reckoning descent was,[8] the naming practices of Russian and U.S. records make the place of women in the descent line increasingly invisible. In the 1840s and 1850s, confessional records in the Kodiak parish list every person with two personal names, one Russian (received at baptism) and one Alutiiq. By 1873, only adults are listed with two names, their children with one Russian name. After that year, only a male head of household's Alutiiq name still appears, as if it was the family name. The effect is that a woman's life, or an individual's female line of ancestry, becomes almost impossible to trace: listed first in her father's, then her husband's family, a woman is identified only by her Russian first name, except during periods of widowhood, when she appears with a personal Alutiiq name as a head of household. On Prince William Sound, where Russian influence was weaker, personal Alutiiq names were still listed for everyone in 1894. Russian surnames were mainly limited to Creoles, although some Alutiiq men also acquired them from Russian godparents or other close associations (ARCA D256/177:Kodiak parish confessional records, 1873; D305/204: census of Nuchek, 1894; D306/205:census of Tatitlek, 1894).

In U.S. census records, every family has a surname. Those who have no Russian or Anglo/Scandinavian name often get an Alutiiq surname, possibly the name of the father. These Russian, Scandinavian, English, and Alutiiq surnames continue to be used today, reflecting a family's history in terms of the males who married into it. But in Creole families and in families with immigrant fathers, kin connections on the mother's side must have been of far greater practical importance, because the father's relatives were often far away, as Mishler and Mason (1996:265) point out.

When a mixed family with a Euro-American father lived in a predominantly Native or Creole community, the female line was also important for passing on religious allegiance to the Orthodox Church. Understandably, although Russian and U.S. traditions generally agreed about patrilinearity, the Orthodox Church insisted that the children of Orthodox mothers should be raised Orthodox. Outside of Kadiak and Woody Island, it was not uncommon for Euro-Americans and European immigrants to attend Orthodox services, because there was no other church, but there were also instances when Scandinavians tried to prevent their wives from teaching Orthodox religion to their children (ARCA D261/180:report by Father Vasilii Martysh for 1901, Afognak, March 15, 1902; D262/181:travel report by Father Tikhon Shalamov for 1895, Kodiak, March 4, 1896; D305/204:report by Father Konstantin Pavlov to Bishop Tikhon, Nuchek, May 6, 1899; Jacobs 1997:23; Shalamov 1898).

Official patrilinearity and the erasure of female kin connections, along with the quest for unambiguous racial classification, combine into special quandaries in the case of marriages between Alutiiq women and Japanese men, of which there were quite a few during the heyday of the canneries. In the 1920 census, Irina, the Alutiiq wife of the Japanese cook Joe Yoshida, living at Kodiak, as well as the wives of Frank Kugunu and Charlie Ugroka at Tatitlek, are designated "Al"[ien] under the column "naturalization," which is usually filled out only for immigrants. Someone in the census bureau may have filled in the column post factum with reference to the 1922 Cable Act, which specified that any American woman who married an "alien ineligible for citizenship" (that is, a nonwhite immigrant) would cease to be a citizen of the United States (Takaki 1989:14–15).

Like some of the Russian-period records, classifications in the U.S. census turn out to be a work in progress reflecting the difficulty of making the marriage choices and kin relationships of real people conform to established categories. The race of Irina's and Joe's sons was originally indicated as "Mxd," but this is crossed out and changed to "Jap" with another pen. Evidently somebody thought that "mixed" referred only to persons with some white ancestry, although the same census also lists other children of Japanese-Alutiiq parentage (mainly girls) as mixed. During the Second World War, it was definitely decided that men such as the Yoshida brothers were to be considered "Jap": in 1942 males with one Japanese parent over the age of sixteen were sent to internment camps together with Alaska's Japanese and Japanese-American residents (Naske 1983; ten Broek, Barnhart, and Matson 1968:134–135).

Multiracial Society and Its Loose Endings

With the last examples, the concept of race has come up again as a defining element of U.S. society that was not present in the same way under the Russians, in spite of other continuities between Russian and American categorizing efforts. So to conclude this chapter, I return to the issue it started with: the gradual loss of status, function, and conceptual recognition of the mixed families who had been one of the main supports of Russian colonial society. This is not an issue that is unique to Alaska—multiracial communities providing a special role for the descendants of mixed marriages existed in all regions of the North American fur trade, and all eventually came under pressure and sometimes disappeared from popular memory as the white settler frontier reached them (Barman and Watson 1999; Peterson and Brown 1985; Van Kirk 1980). In Alaska as elsewhere, it is difficult to answer the question how the relationships among groups, and the concepts people held of their own and other's identities, changed over time. But various sources afford anecdotal glimpses, whose interpretation will take up the remainder of this chapter.

First of all, I have been arguing throughout this chapter against a view of Russian colonial society as all too integrated and equal, even though it is hard to gauge how close or distant ties among different groups might have been. The residential segregation between Creole and Russian males on the one hand and most Alutiiq men on the other should not make one forget that Alutiiq villagers worked and camped with Russian and Creole employees on hunting and work parties, and that there were many kinship connections through women. For those Alutiiq company servants living at or near St. Paul Harbor, Creoles often became ritual kin by serving as godparents of their children (cf. Kan 1996:624). Distinctions in lifestyle were nonetheless maintained by Creole settlers, who, as naval officer Golovin reports, were proud of their independence and freedom from the work obligations of "Aleuts" (Dmytryshyn and Crownhart-Vaughan 1979:15). After 1867 several American observers comment on the contempt in which Creoles hold "Aleuts." Lieutenant Huggins, stationed on Kodiak and Afognak from 1868 to 1870, during the period of military rule in Alaska, claims that the two groups hardly even intermarried:

> One thing which struck me as rather strange was that, although the natives and creoles often live in villages very near together and are so nearly related, there is very little intercourse between them, and one of the latter with a native wife is rarely seen, so that at present nearly all the creoles are the children of creoles on both sides, or of Russians and creoles. (Huggins 1981:9)

I have not systematically analyzed marriage statistics, but a small sample from the 1830s to the 1860s shows that marriages between Creoles and Alutiiq were quite common, although the data may suggest that there was a tendency away from intermarriage in the last two decades of Russian rule.[9] Hannah Breece writes that in spite of the many kinship connections between the Russian village and the Aleut village at Afognak, Creoles "were regarded by themselves and seemingly by the Aleuts as a higher social class," and the Creole students chased away the Aleut children during the first week of school, refusing to accept such "ragged and dirty" classmates. She could only reestablish peace by engaging the Creole children in a civilizing mission "to train the Aleuts" (Jacobs 1997:16, 18).

Differences increased when the Alutiiq came from more remote regions. Katie Ellanack, who moved with her family from Katmai to Afognak sometime before the 1912 eruption, remembers being made to suffer by classmates and teachers for not speaking English:

> We didn't know how to talk English, not a bit. So, we start going to school. [. . .] We didn't know what to do. We didn't understand English. We can't talk English. They used to make fun of us in school even. They talk lies about us. Getting spanks. Before, teachers was no good. They used to spank kids. (Ellanack 1987:35)

When the refugees from the Katmai eruption were sheltered at Afognak for about a month before being taken to the Perryville site, they also stood out as different from Afognak people in dress and complexion (Partnow 1993:201).

If Creoles regarded themselves as superior to Alutiiq, Russian statements about Creoles cast doubt on the argument that there is a clear difference between the social distinctions drawn in Russia and the racial distinctions salient in the United States. The writings of members of the Russia-born, educated upper class show a clear preoccupation with the physical and moral qualities of the offspring of interethnic unions in the colonies. In their combination of social, environmental, and hereditary explanations they are very much in line with the history of western thought about colonized populations, in which concepts of race as biological heredity competed against other theories well into the second half of the nineteenth century (Bitterli 1991 [1976]:214–215, 325–366). The similarities are not surprising, given the influence of western European scholars and western education on the development of eighteenth- and nineteenth-century Russian science (Knight 1998:109–111; Slezkine 1994:54–56).

In 1840, Chief Manager Kupreianov wrote to physicians Volynskii and Blaschke to inquire if during their work in Alaska they had observed any differences in the process of puberty between Aleuts, Creoles, and Russians (RAC cs 18:109–109v, March 23, 1840, to physician Volynskii, to physician Blaschke). Kirill Khlebnikov, manager of the Novoarkhangel'sk office of the RAC from 1818 to 1832, describes Creole behavior as governed by milieu and education rather than inborn characteristics but also finds it necessary to stress the need for strict discipline if they are to achieve moral and practical improvement:

> It is unfortunate that because they lack basic education, they do not have maturity and firmness of character, and while understanding Russian rules for good behavior, they do fall to the temptation of vices: above all, the use of strong drink, which for many has resulted in death. [. . .] There are many examples of persons who studied shipbuilding {in St. Petersburg} and returned without understanding either theory or the practical application of the science, and because of that they are of no use. Several of them understand navigational skills quite well, but while in the capital they developed a taste for luxurious things and acquired bad habits. Young people everywhere always follow examples: in a small society they are subject to one person along with the watchful eye of the father; in such a small society there can be no such vices as in a large city. [. . .] Based on examples, we have noticed that the Creoles who studied here in the local schools and ships, have worked out quite well. Some who are apprentice seafarers command small vessels; some are accountants and prikazchiks {clerks}, who know their jobs; there are coppersmiths who have great skill and who are not inferior to their teachers. Soon, we hope to have students who will study medicine, surgery and navigation. (Khlebnikov 1994:82–83, comments in brackets mine)

Pavel Golovin, the agent of the Naval Ministry sent to inspect the colonies in 1860/61, has an even more pessimistic view of Creoles when he portrays them as inclined "toward hooliganism, primitivism, dishonesty, and laziness," all because of their "mothers' blood" (Dmytryshyn and Crownhart-Vaughan 1979:17). Drawing connections between physical and moral qualities and between inborn factors and those that develop over an individual's lifetime in a fashion quite typical of early racialist thought in western Europe as well, Golovin notes that "creoles are all likely to be sensitive, proud, and quick to take offense," although they also have "good qualities, notably an aptitude in mechanical crafts." Being "well-proportioned and very good looking, especially the second and third generations," their problem is "an inclination toward a carefree life," which soon causes them to "become weak":

> Between the ages of 30 and 35 nearly all suffer from a chest disorder, which often develops into consumption. The result is that very few creoles live to an advanced age. Drink, especially, is their ruination. [. . .] Under strict supervision they behave acceptably, but when left to their own devices they revert to their natural behavior and become embittered drunkards. (Dmytryshyn and Crownhart-Vaughan 1979:17–18)

Golovin claims that his negative view of Creoles is shared by Alaskan society in general, mainly because Creole families are considered to be descendants of illegitimate unions:

> The Russians who live in the colonies have not lost sight of the illegitimate origin of the creoles. They look at the reprehensible conduct of the creole women and the careless attitude of the men, most of whom are willing to hand over their wives to anyone in exchange for a few bottles of rum. Consequently not only [do the Russians] look on them with great contempt, but the word "creole" is used as a pejorative. Even the Aleuts have no respect for the creoles, and say that they are lower than Aleuts because their mothers were immoral women. This contempt, this constant oppression, is very destructive to the sensitive nature of the creoles. They are ashamed of being called creoles. (Dmytryshyn and Crownhart-Vaughan 1979:17–18, brackets added by the translators)

The views of these men are clearly informed by their upper-class perspective—Golovin's disdain for the idleness and dishonesty of the Creoles is hardly different from his opinion of the lower-class Russian colonial citizens, whom he calls "nothing more than moral parasites" (Dmytryshyn and Crownhart-Vaughan 1979:15). Lower-class Russians, many of them Siberian-born and probably less influenced by racialized thinking than were the western-oriented St. Petersburg elites, may have intermingled more closely with Creoles but also envied them for their tax and educational privileges (Black 1990:147; Vinkovetsky 2001). Somewhat contradicting his own claims about the shame of being called Creole, Golovin says that Creoles considered themselves the legitimate owners of the land and resented having to "submit to Russian influence" (Dmytryshyn and Crownhart-Vaughan 1979:18). In 1862, Aleksandr Kashevarov, a Creole navigator born on Kodiak and uncle of the psalmist-teacher Andrei Kashevarov, intervenes in the debate on the future of Alaska and argues for local management of the furbearing animals and an end to the RAC's monopoly:

> [I]t would be strange to deprive the inhabitants of the coastal colonies of the right to the free use of the resources of their native sea, which God has given them for their own good! [. . .] Do we need government supervision to carry this out, using local inhabitants of the Russian American colonies, through legally instituted regulations for the development of their well-being and the prosperity of the country? (We cannot) compare private hunting with the terrible period of the past, carried on by unbridled foreign opportunists and crude intruders into our lands, with potential future hunting undertaken by local people. [. . .] We yearn for the rights of property in our country. (Dmy-

tryshyn, Crownhart-Vaughan, and Vaughan 1989:523, parentheses added by
the translators)

Although Kashevarov identifies with the Aleut population robbed by
"crude intruders into *our* lands" (emphasis added) and later speaks of the benefits of continued hunting specifically for Aleuts, his discourse also recalls what
Benedict Anderson, in a South American context, calls "creole nationalism," as
well as the concern of the North American revolutionaries with property and
representation (Anderson 1983:50–51, 62). In those two cases, the self-asser-
tion of the overseas-born colonial population as true owners of the land and
resources soon came to be at odds not only with the European colonial powers
but also with the claims of the indigenous population. Even though the color
line ran somewhat differently in Russian America (Anderson's creole national-
ists are whites born in the colonies), Kashevarov would clearly not have considered himself an Alutiiq in the way that some contemporary scholars treat
Creoles as "Native leaders." This more recent identification of Creoles and Natives probably originated with the gradual loss of separate Creole status in the
American period that I outlined at the beginning of this chapter.

The softening of earlier barriers between Creoles and Alutiiq after 1867
occurred at a time when the question of who was a local and who was an out-
sider became ever more complex. The unregulated fur trade and the canneries brought great numbers of new immigrants, still predominantly male. The
multiracial fur trade society persisted for a while, but the relevant distinctions
shifted. Patricia Partnow argues that Creoles in this period came to be seen
less as outsiders in Native villagers than before, and that the appellation "Russian" or "Russian Aleut" came to denote "culture, intelligence, and nonforeign-
ness" as new kinds of outsiders entered the region (Partnow 2001:144). But the
new immigrants did not remain total strangers for long either and formed an
alternative group to which Creoles could develop social proximity. In terms of
fur-hunting regulations, marriage to a Creole or Native woman made a man
into a "resident." On Kodiak Island, many of the first Scandinavian immigrants
married Creole women. The reason for this was possibly the more Europeanized lifestyle of Creole families—they lived in houses instead of *barabaras*, kept
gardens and cows—but also the fact that the same places that had appealed to
the Russian and Creole settlers were also attractive to the Scandinavians: Afognak and the wooded northeast side of Kodiak Island (Jacobs 1997:23; Lethcoe
and Lethcoe 1994:41; Martysh 1902; Mishler and Mason 1996:263–264).

Although these Protestant settlers and husbands seem to have fit into the
Creole communities without too much friction, Orthodox priests looked at
them with suspicion. This suspicion was even stronger when it came to those

cannery workers who remained transient. Father Tikhon Shalamov blamed the
Chinese for bringing liquor to Alaska and selling it to Natives illegally, and the
European workers for entering into illicit sexual relations with Alutiiq women
(ARCA D262/181:travel report by Father Tikhon Shalamov for 1895, Kodiak,
March 4, 1896). Singling out those workers who were not of Anglo-Saxon ori-
gin as a particular problem, U.S. Government agent Murray lamented the fate
of the "unfortunate Aleuts," who were "hustled out of the way of these Medi-
terranean fishermen" without a chance to appeal to any higher agency (Pracht,
Luttrell, and Murray 1898:409).

The idea of danger brought by cannery workers is also expressed in Larry
Matfay's recollection of the Alutiiq saying "When spring comes and the ships
come up from down below, they bring disease" (Rostad 1988:67). This is of course
quite an apt conclusion about the origins of contagion, as when nineteenth-century Alutiiq identified the Russians as source of the smallpox. Matfay, born in
Akhiok in 1907, remembers the interaction of ethnic groups at the canneries as a
peaceful but distanced coexistence. In the words of his biographer:

> People from the various ethnic groups worked side by side during the day,
> but when it came time to eat and sleep, they gravitated toward their own
> kind. They ate in separate mess halls and slept in separate cabins. Larry and
> his peers were warned to stay away from those strangers, who spoke, dressed
> and acted differently than the villagers. "Just mind your own business," was
> the rule. But there were rare occasions when the segregated people social-
> ized. On weekends when the fishing ceased, the workers gathered in an empty
> warehouse for a dance. Cannery musicians from the different ethnic groups
> provided the music. (Rostad 1988:47–48)

But for the Alutiiq too some workers were stranger than others, or easier
to reject. Father Tikhon Shalamov tells the following story about a mass he
celebrated at Karluk:

> Many Americans attended the service, only the Chinese were not there, whom,
> by the way, the Aleuts not only bar from the chapel as unbaptized heathens,
> but do not even allow to come near, they have even painted the lower parts
> of the window glass white, so that they, as the toion explained, could not look
> in even when all the Aleuts were gathered for prayer. (ARCA D262/181:travel
> report by Father Tikhon Shalamov for 1895, Kodiak, March 4, 1896)

The reason for this strict exclusion of Chinese workers may have been religion rather than racism: Karluk's Alutiiq residents recognized white Americans as
fellow Christians, whereas the Chinese were "unbaptized heathens" and could not

Father Vasilii Kashevarov leads icon procession near Afognak, early twentieth century. Judging from the snow on the ground and the location outside the village, this is probably a procession to bless the waters on Epiphany, or the Day of the Baptism of Our Lord and Savior Jesus Christ (January 19), popularly known as "Jordan Day." The Scandinavian surname of the photographer shows that processions such as this one made Alutiiq Orthodoxy visible to newcomers in the villages and presented opportunities for them to participate on the fringes of Orthodox parish life. *Photograph by E. Christensen, courtesy of Alaska State Library, Michael Z. Vinokouroff Collection, p243-2-024.*

be allowed inside the church during mass according to church canons. Although the gulf between Chinese workers and Alutiiq rarely seems to have been bridged, I mentioned in the previous section that some Japanese workers, who came to Alaska in rising numbers around the turn of the century, stayed and married into Creole and Alutiiq families.[10] The reason the Japanese seem to have formed closer relationships to Alutiiq communities than did the Chinese may lie in the age of the workers. Because of the Chinese Exclusion Act of 1882, most Chinese cannery workers in the 1890s and 1900s were already older men, while many Japanese were young, recent immigrants. The Orthodox priests required them to be baptized before marriage to an Orthodox woman but otherwise seemed less suspicious of Japanese husbands than of Protestant whites, who had to swear an oath that they were not already married (ARCA D252/174:report from Hieromonk Nikita to Bishop Nestor, Kenai, Aug 4, 1880; D303/202:report from Father Konstantin Pavlov to Archimandrite Anatolii, Nuchek, Oct 12, 1898; D248/172, baptism certificate of Genrikh Mai, Kodiak, March 25, 1896; Jacobs 1997:24).

There are no records of Alutiiq families objecting to unions with Japanese men, but the dean of the Sitka district of the Alaska diocese, Father Vladimir

Donskoi, was confronted with a dramatic case of a white in-law's protest during a trip through Prince William Sound in 1895. Traveling on the boat from Nuchek with the by now familiar psalmist Andrei Kashevarov, Father Vladimir had an argument with an American by the name of T(h)orstonson, whom he had married a few days before in Nuchek to a Creole woman with the last name Grigor'eva. The sister of this woman was engaged to a Japanese man by the name of Tom Fudi (or Fuji), who had been preparing for baptism for three years. Torstonson evidently learned of this plan after his own marriage and was furious:

> Torstonson, having learned of the intention of the Japanese to marry his wife's sister, became determined to prevent this marriage and appeared in Nuchek with this aim. There he came storming into the bride's house and wanted to bind her by force and take her away to Odiak, but since she together with her mother resisted this violence, he, taking from the bride a box of her possessions, took it on the steamer and threw it into the sea from there. Having done enough mischief in Nuchek, Torstonson went to find me, and we met on the steamer "Pacific," which was taking us from Odiak to Tatitlak. Appearing in the captain's quarters, where I was staying with Kashevarov, he bluntly and insolently demanded that I should not marry the above Japanese, threatening to throw out his wife in case I did not comply with this request, and then to gather white people from Odiak at Nuchek who would cause me and Kashevarov much troubles and discomfort. (ARCA D305/204:report by Father Vladimir Donskoi on an inspection of the Nuchek and Juneau parishes, Sitka, 1895)

When Father Vladimir refused to yield to these threats, Torstonson shook his fists at the two clergymen and predicted trouble for Kashevarov. The captain's intervention ended the incident. Tom Fudi was chrismated on August 6, 1895 and married Aleksandra Grigor'eva the same day. In 1900, the couple was living at Valdez, where Tom worked as a cook (VS E58, Nuchek 1895; 1900 census, Valdez). I have found no evidence to show if Torstonson really left his wife or realized his other threats, but his story exemplifies the complexity of intergroup marriage in Alaska. Torstonson and the "white people from Odiak," the cannery town, seem to be concerned mainly with property rights over women. They see no dishonor in marrying into a racially and religiously different community, but the idea of an Asian man doing the same and becoming an in-law, and of the community making its own choice to admit him, provokes violent rage and fantasies of mob terror. In Russian as well as U.S. Alaska, "miscegenation signaled neither the presence nor absence of racial discrimination; hierarchies of privilege and power were written into the *condoning* of interracial unions, as well as into their condemnation," as

Ann Stoler (1991:86, emphasis in the original) puts it with reference to other colonial societies.

This story affords a glimpse at the intricacies of the multiracial Alaskan fur trade society in the last decades of its existence. First, it draws attention to the variety of social distinctions that were important to different people. The Russian priest was concerned about maintaining Orthodox church membership and was thus more welcoming of a Japanese bridegroom who was willing to convert to Orthodoxy than of the interconfessional marriages that resulted when Protestant men married Orthodox women. In the absence of a large Japanese community, the Japanese man also had far less opportunity to exert cultural or religious influence on his children, while the increasing predominance of Anglophone and Protestant American culture in their parishes worried the Orthodox clergy, who often found themselves in a rather weak position in a confrontation with white residents. Creole families seem to have been accepting of new in-laws of various origins. From this story it is hard to say what the concerns or motivations of the Grigor'evs were, except that they obviously rejected their son-in-law Torstonson's attempt to interfere with the choice of a marriage partner for their other daughter, suggesting that they expected outsiders who married into the family to respect its autonomy and its ways of making decisions.

Torstonson is the only character in the story for whom racial distinctions appear to be the most important, as he violently defends himself against the possibility of becoming related to a Japanese man and is enraged by the refusal of his Creole in-laws to defer to his wishes. But in his threats against Kashevarov, he also alludes to religious and national distinctions, more specifically the difficult position of Orthodoxy in Alaska thirty years after the Treaty of Purchase. Orthodoxy was coming to be seen as a foreign religion, at the mercy of the willingness of "the white men" to tolerate its institutions.

What Tom Fudi thought of the whole situation also remains unknown. Nor is it clear whether he wanted to be baptized in order to be allowed to marry or whether he met his future bride during the three years of preparation for baptism. But the fact that he spent such a long time in association with Nuchek's Orthodox congregation, presumably studying with Andrei Kashevarov or with Donskoi on his occasional visits, or perhaps with future in-laws knowledgeable about Orthodoxy, is evidence that he was able to forge long-term relationships in this foreign community.

The second point to take away from the story is that many of these intricacies easily get lost in historical memory—the idea, for instance, that different social distinctions may matter to different people or in different situations, or that close contact can mean intense antagonism at the same time as it affords opportunities for unlikely affinities. In Alaska as in other parts of North America, the pressure on mixed families to identify as either white or Native caused them to be left out of historical narratives, only recently to be rediscovered and celebrated. However, some processes of erasure still seem to continue. Whereas Russian or Scandinavian ancestry was always remembered on Kodiak Island and became a point of identification for many who were made to feel ashamed of their nativeness (Mishler and Mason 1996:264; Pullar 1992:184), Japanese ancestors rarely receive public recognition, and they seldom find entry into literature on Alutiiq history (but see Partnow 2001:13).[11]

One reason for this silence is probably the small number of Japanese men who married into Alutiiq villages, isolated from the Japanese immigrant communities that existed in North American cities. Even more so than in the case of Scandinavians, ties to the maternal, Alutiiq or Creole, side of the family must have been much stronger for children of such couples than was the influence of their father. Two daughters of mixed Japanese-Alaska Native marriages interviewed for an oral history project, Hana Yasuda Kangas, born in Beaver in 1914 of an Inupiaq mother, and Marie Matsuno Nash, born in Ugashik of an Aleut mother, remembered living no differently from other village children and not feeling particularly Japanese (Kangas 1990; Nash 1991). Japanese family names may have disappeared as daughters married. However, war and internment would also have given families reasons to keep quiet about Japanese fathers or grandfathers. And today, when Japanese factory trawlers are in competition with Alaskan fisheries, Japanese ancestry may still not be a popular thing to celebrate.

The memories of such people as Marie Matsuno Nash and Vera Kie Angasan (Partnow 2001:13) indicate that some of these grandfathers and great-grandfathers are quietly remembered in their families. If others are not, many Swedes, Norwegians, and Russians may be forgotten as well. The point of uncovering traces of old family histories is certainly not to prove that Japanese *kokeshi* dolls would be as authentic an Alaskan souvenir as Russian *matrioshki*. But such traces can bring up the question how laws, labor migration, religion, family values, and lynch mobs interact to shape the boundaries between what is socially possible and what is impossible, what is remembered and what is forgotten. Learning to tell such stories in their complexity and ambivalence may be more stimulating for the present social imagination than creating images of an ideal past.

ENDNOTES

1. Within the general category of "Russian," the clerical registers of Kodiak parish often distinguish officials (*chinovniki*) and clergy (*dukhovnye*) from (ordinary) Russians (*russkie/rossiiane*). Confessional registers further break down the latter into the various estates: merchants (*kuptsy*), burghers (*meshchane*), a mixed class of craftsmen and laborers (*raznochintsy*), and peasants (*krest'iane*).

2. For Alaska in 1890, the census categories were "White," "Mixed," "Indian," "Mongolian," and "all others." The 1880 census, conducted by the Russian-born Ivan Petroff under consultation of Russian documents, still uses "creole" as a category besides "Indian" or "Eskimo" and "white" (Petroff 1884; Porter 1893).

3. Although greater closeness was understood to mean greater degree of civilization in both cases, the status of "wandering" or "independent" also implied a greater degree of self-governance. For instance, friendly Tlingit chiefs in Alaska, part of the independent category, were eligible for the medal *Allies of Russia* (*Soiuznye Rossii*), customarily given to friendly Tlingit chiefs, but Alutiiq chiefs were not, because they were considered "subjects" (*vernopoddannye*) rather than allies (RAC cs 19:258v, Oct 18, 1840, to Kodiak office). Alutiiq *toions* were elected subject to approval of the Chief Manager, while the RAC had only a limited degree of influence on questions of succession in high-ranking Tlingit families.

4. To my knowledge, no historian of Russian Alaska has done a study of the records to check how many "Aleuts" actually rose to other categories. But not every change in the classification of an individual necessarily reflects a permanent rise to another category. Filipp Kotel'nikov, listed as a Creole company employee at Fort Ross in 1820/21, appears as an Aleut in the 1843 confessional records for Kodiak, then again as a Creole in the vital statistics recording his death in 1862. His son Stepan is always designated Creole, although Filipp seems to have been Alutiiq by birth, and Stepan's mother was a Californian woman, probably Pomo (ARCA D255/175:Kodiak parish confessional records, 1843; VS E72:Sitka, marriages 1836; E29:Kodiak, marriages 1851; E30:Kodiak, deaths 1862; Istomin 1992:20–21; Osborn 1997:386–387). Another example is Kondratii Burtsov, a carpenter educated at St. Petersburg, who is variously referred to as an Aleut or a Creole (RAC cs 20:49–50, Feb 25, 1841, to Kodiak office; ARCA D255/175: Kodiak parish confessional records, 1830, 1840; VS E27:Kodiak, baptisms 1832; Pierce 1990:77). Both cases indicate that the categories of Creole and Aleut were flexibly applied and could reflect a man's closeness to the RAC at a given moment in his life rather than either his ancestry or a permanently achieved social status.

5. On custody disputes, see: ARCA D248/172:report from Father Tikhon Shalamov to the Alaska Consistory, Kodiak, June 4, 1894; D249/172:statement signed by Simeon Dobrovol'skii and Paraskeva Rod, Kodiak, Apr 18, 1898; D249/172:

report from Father Tikhon Shalamov to Archimandrite Anatolii, Kodiak, May 10, 1898; D249/172:report from Hieromonk Anatolii to Bishop Nikolai, Sitka, Oct 26, 1898. On the founding of the Kodiak orphanage: ARCA D249/172:report from Father Tikhon Shalamov to the Alaska Consistory, Kodiak, April 28, 1894; D249/172:letter from Vladimir Stafeev to Bishop Nikolai, Kodiak, March 9, 1898; D249/172:letter from Father Tikhon Shalamov to Alaska Consistory, Sep 5, 1898. On accusations against the Baptists: ARCA D259/179:letters from Father Tikhon Shalamov to Bishop Nikolai, Apr 29, 1894; D259/179:report from Father Tikhon Shalamov for 1894, April 20, 1895; D259/179:letter from Father Tikhon Shalamov to Bishop Nikolai, Aug 1, 1895.

6. The following subjects are reported in archival sources:

Kodiak 1872: Reading, morals for the basic level, arithmetic, grammar and catechism (zakon bozhii) for four more advanced boys (ARCA D249/172:report from Father Petr Kashevarov to Church Consistory, 1872).

Kodiak 1881: Sacred history, catechism, arithmetic, writing, English, secular history, reading from the Scriptures (ARCA D249/172:list of enrollment in the Kodiak school, prepared by Nikolai Rysev, July 22, 1881).

Afognak 1899: English, arithmetic and other subjects at the American school; catechism, Russian, and Slavonic reading at the parish school (ARCA D260/180:report from Father Nikolai Kashevarov to Hieromonk Antonii, Afognak, Oct 7, 1899).

Nuchek 1894: Russian, English, catechism, prayers in Slavonic and Alutiiq, arithmetics, singing (ARCA D303/203:report from Andrei Kashevarov to Father Vladimir Donskoi, Nuchek, Oct 18, 1894).

7. Today, the copies sent to the diocese are part of the collections held by the Library of Congress; those which remained in Kodiak and Afognak parish are in the archives of St. Herman's Seminary, Kodiak.

8. No early Russian observer explicitly asks how the Alutiiq reckoned descent. In the 1844 confessional records family groups are ambilineal, composed of individuals related in the mother's or father's line or by marriage. But it may be that kinship connections that would not normally have had much importance were used pragmatically to make sure that no one was left alone after the death of one third of the population in the smallpox epidemic. Davydov's observation that the title of chief was often inherited by a nephew may indicate matrilineal descent, as existed among the Tlingit and probably on the Aleutians, but he does not specify whether nephew means sister's or brother's son. Gedeon says that sons, brothers, uncles, nephews or sons-in-law were all potential successors for a chief (Davydov 1977:190; Gedeon 1994:61). Among the Chugach of the 1930s, chieftainships nor-

mally passed from father to son, but a brother or a brother's or sister's son could also be heir (Birket-Smith 1953:92).

9. Weddings in the Kodiak parish, the status of the partners given in the order bride/ groom (VS E27-E30): 1832 (St. Paul Harbor):

   Russian/Creole 3, Creole/Creole 3, Creole/Aleut 1, Aleut/Aleut 2.

   1842: Creole/Creole 5, Creole/Aleut 3, Aleut/Creole 3, Aleut/Aleut 11.

   1845: Creole/Creole 1, Creole/Aleut 4, Aleut/Creole 3, Aleut/Aleut 35.

   1855: creole/creole 6, creole/Aleut 1, Aleut/creole 1, Aleut/Aleut 40.

   1865: creole/creole 4, creole/Aleut 2, Aleut/creole 2, Aleut/Aleut unknown number.

10. Russian sources and U.S. census records record a total of twelve or thirteen Alutiiq-Japanese couples. Among residents of Kodiak parish in 1912, these were Mikhail Fushida (43 years) and Irina (30); Nikolai Chusoki (50) and Aleksandra (30); Feofan Kasarada (34) and Mavra (17); Anastasiia Lohr (60) and IAkov Aleksandrov (ARCA D258/178:Kodiak parish confessional records, 1912). Mikhail Yamoda, Kodiak (32), and Irina Chakli, Eagle Harbor (19), were married Sep 5, 1901 (VS E36, Kodiak). Judging from their ages and allowing for misunderstandings of last names, this is possibly the same couple recorded as Mikhail and Irina Fushida in 1912. The same couple, judging from their children's names, seems to appear as Joseph Yoshida and Irina in the 1910 census, Joe Yoshida and Irene in 1920. Henry/Pavel Mai (33) and Aleksandra (15), married at Kaguyak Aug 31, 1896 (VS E35, Kodiak), were also listed in the 1900 census in Eagle Harbor and in Aiaktalik in the 1920 census. Tom Fudi (22) and Aleksandra Grigor'eva (16) married at Nuchek 1895.

    The 1910 census records Paul Morris and Donia, Beatson's Mine, Latouche Island (Prince William Sound); Charles Nakmra and Alexandra, Kodiak; Harry Wata and "Aleut" wife, Alitak cannery. The 1920 census adds Joseph Ota and Sophia, Pilot Station; Frank Kugunu and Charlie Ugroka, both with Native wives, Tatitlek.

11. Japanese have been absent from the surge of new representations of Kodiak's heritage that appeared at the turn of the twentieth and twenty-first centuries. During cursory inquiries among Alutiiq living in Anchorage and people I met on a short visit to Kodiak in 1998 I encountered no one who had heard of Japanese-Alutiiq intermarriage. According to Lydia Black (personal communication, summer 1998), there were no families who remembered such Japanese roots on Kodiak anymore, only on the Shumagin Islands. Ronald Inouye of the Alaska Japanese Pioneers Project, Fairbanks, also knew of such marriages from census records but explained that descendants on Kodiak Island and in Prince William Sound had married back into the Native community (personal communication, summer 1998).

Conclusion

Contrast or Sequence?

The guiding question of this book has concerned the differences and similarities between the Russian and U.S.-American periods of colonial rule in Alaska, as they affected the lives of Alutiiq people. Steering away from attempts to decide which period was more harmful or benign than the other, I have argued that both brought drastic and sometimes catastrophic changes to Alutiiq communities, but that the point of comparison should be to understand the different dynamics of political, economic, social, and religious interactions made possible by each colonial system. I have also emphasized the need to take into account that the two colonial periods followed each other. Any comparison between the two must be mindful of this historical sequence and also of the particular political and social developments in the metropole with which each colonization coincided. In other words, neither Russians nor Americans brought a fixed system of colonial relations to South-Central Alaska, but each group of administrators and entrepreneurs worked with the conditions it found there and was influenced by changes in policy and in scientific and public opinion back home.

To take colonial economies as an example, one can certainly contrast the Russian use of conscripted Native labor in sea otter hunting with the American marginalization of Natives in salmon canning. The different positions occupied by Alutiiq men and women in each economic system can be linked to the tradition of imposing communal work obligations on Russian peasants on the one hand and to the use of immigrant and slave labor, rather than Native workers, during the Anglo-American expansion across North America on the other. But we can also consider the conscription of Unangan and Alutiiq hunters as a contingent decision born of the restrictions imposed by the Russians' inability to hunt from kayaks and the lack of trade goods. The marginalization of Native labor after 1867 was predetermined in part by the decline of the fur trade owing to dwindling sea otter populations, which in turn was a consequence of Russian overhunting. If the RAC had remained in Alaska, it may have further diversified its economy to pursuits in which Natives (though perhaps not Creoles) would have played a less central role.

Similarly, when pointing to the contrast between the RAC's willingness to approach Native groups as communities represented by their leaders and the lack of officially recognized communal institutions for Native Alaskans during the first half-century or more of U.S. administration, juxtaposing the political philosophies of Russia and the United States can be helpful. In the dynastic Russian empire that saw itself as a confessionally, ethnically, and regionally "clustered society" (Burbank 2006:409), principles of collective rights and obligations were applied to Russian populations of various estates as well as to non-Russian subjects, making it necessary to identify and work with indigenous groups and their leaders. By contrast, attempts in U.S. Indian policy to break up communities and make individual farmers and craftsmen out of the male heads of nuclear family households can be linked to the liberal individualism and the myth of the yeoman farmer that have shaped the United States since its founding.

At the same time, Russian policies and proposals for Alaska also evolved in response to changing political ideas in St. Petersburg. In the aborted negotiations about the renewal of the RAC's charter in the early 1860s, there were a fair number of voices advocating the end of communal labor obligations for Alutiiq and Creoles and a change toward individual contracts for hunters and workers in company service. This was the era of Russia's Great Reforms that led to the abolishment of serfdom, and the Naval Ministry, centrally involved in governing Alaska through the naval officers who served as RAC Chief Managers, was one of the most liberal institutions in the imperial government (Bolkhovitinov 1999). As I explained in Chapter 3, the improved supply of manufactured goods through the 1839 agreement with the HBC and the establishment of posts among unsubjugated peoples in interior Alaska had also changed the RAC's economic operations to increasingly resemble conventional mercantile trade, creating favorable conditions for a reform of the labor conscription system. The acquisition of Alaska by the United States, for its part, coincided with the short period of reconstruction after the Civil War, soon to be replaced by increasing legalization of racism and the infamous Jim Crow laws. It was also a time when Congress was refashioning its relationship with Native tribes, based on the assumption that Native resistance to settlement in what would become the lower forty-eight states had largely been overcome. The end of treaty-making in 1870 meant that this way of establishing relationships with Native communities as "tribes" was no longer practiced in Alaska. If the U.S. had acquired Alaska during an earlier time, or if Russia had kept it long enough to implement some of the envisioned reforms, the contrast between Russian communalism and U.S. individualism in Native policy might have seemed less pronounced.

The point is that contrasts between two colonial periods can appear starkest when they are compared as if they were two unrelated and unchanging systems, whereas in actual historical processes, the practices of each colonial power undergo internal changes and stand in relationship to each other. People who come to govern and exploit unfamiliar lands do bring certain techniques and patterns of legitimization with them but also work with what they find (sometimes including infrastructure set up by previous colonial agents) and make up rules as they go along. Furthermore, they both influence and are influenced by political and scientific views emanating from their homeland and other colonial regimes.

Colonies can also become spaces of social experimentation, where techniques of governing that are not possible at home can be tried out. The governing of Alaska by a merchant-run company, unique in tsarist Russia, is a case in point, as is the creation of the equally unique Creole estate, breaking the rule that children are part of the estate of their father. During the U.S. period, examples of such social experimentation include the contracting of Native education to Protestant missionary organizations, in spite of the constitutional principle of the division of church and state, as well as malleable attitudes toward restriction on movement and forced resettlement of populations. I noted in Chapter 1 that Russian records treat villagers as people who are tied to their place of residence, whereas for the U.S. census they may always be on the way to somewhere else, and that these bureaucratic practices correspond to the different value placed on personal mobility in each country's image of itself. The many small new villages that appear in the Alutiiq region after 1867, in contrast to the RAC's attempts at restricting the population to a few consolidated villages, may testify to the practical effects of these different attitudes. But where U.S. companies held a monopoly, as was the case in the fur seal harvest on the Pribilof Islands from 1870 to the 1950s, they had no qualms about restricting the freedom of travel of the Unangan Aleuts who constituted their workforce—and had the support of government agents in this (Orbach and Holmes 1986:76–78). And during World War II, Unangan, like Alaska's residents of Japanese ancestry, were forced to leave their homes and live in camps in the Alaska Panhandle while the Aleutian Islands were occupied by army bases (Naske 1983). Part of the benefit of comparing how states with very different political systems behave in a colonial setting is to see both the practical consequences of their political principles and the pragmatic limits of these same principles.

In addition to the many contrasts that can be drawn between Russia and the United States as colonial powers, an important similarity lies in the overall continental character of their expansion, contrasting with the overseas empires of Spain, Britain, and France. In the United States, where expansion across the continent plays a crucial role in mythologized national history, the imperial character of this expansion has often been denied by casting the conquered territories as empty or given to Anglo-American settlers by destiny. Though historians of the American West have long challenged this view, American imperialism is often thought, if at all, to begin with the overseas activities in the Spanish-American War of 1898 (Limerick 1987; Williams 1980). The history of Russian eastward expansion into Siberia, for its part, has generated more ambivalent myths. The laws of serfdom that bound people to the soil obstructed the eastward movement of Russian peasants, but there were state-sponsored resettlement projects. Furthermore, serfdom was not extended to Siberia, a legal situation that tacitly encouraged serfs to run away across the Urals (Shunkov 1968; Yaney 1973:149). Western historians have argued that the frontier concept, so influential in the United States since Frederick Jackson Turner propounded his theory on how the frontier shaped American national character, is also relevant to Russian history (Barrett 1999:4–5; Goehrke 1970:196; Turner 1894). Mark Bassin (1993:475–476) even identifies a Russian inversion of the "frontier hypothesis" in the environmental determinism of the historian Sergei Mikhailovich Solov'ev (1820–1879). Whereas Frederick Jackson Turner argued that the ever-repeated building of society on the advance across vast spaces had a beneficial effect in shaping American love for freedom and independence, Solov'ev, writing in St. Petersburg half a century earlier, saw the need to wrestle with the frontier and the possibility to escape from social problems by moving into open spaces as hindering rather than advancing progress in Russia.

If the concept of continental expansion can be applied to both Russian and U.S. history, Alaska occupies a somewhat anomalous position in both cases. Separated from the Eurasian landmass of the Russian empire by the North Pacific, and from the contiguous United States by Canada, it was connected to both countries by shipping routes during the period under discussion in this book, before the invention of air travel. The overseas location and harsh climate may have brought about some of the colonial experiments I discussed above, such as the "contracting" (Vinkovetsky 2004) of government functions to a commercial company under the Russians and, partially, to trading companies and Protestant missionary organizations under the United States. Intermarriages between Russian and white American men and Native women were also favored by the remoteness of the location, where few white women came.

At the same time, Alaska was not exceptional—the policy of contracting Native schooling to missionary organizations, for instance, was first used on Indian reservations in the contiguous United States under the "peace policy" of President Ulysses S. Grant (Hoxie 1984), and in my discussion of the Russian conquest of Kodiak Island I have pointed out how Shelikhov's strategies of securing peaceful relations with high-ranking families through a combination of hostage taking and gift giving drew on techniques of diplomacy that Russians had developed over centuries of interaction with the steppe peoples of Northern Eurasia (Khodarkovsky 2002). For both Russian and U.S. historiography, Alaska can form a bridge to the histories of other colonial empires, showing that the boundaries between continental expansion and overseas colonialism can be fluid and that states can apply experiences gained in the former when they move to the latter.

One of the most interesting revisions of the frontier concept in American historiography is to understand frontiers as "middle grounds" (White 1991), or zones of encounter rather than as moving lines of white settlement, and to look at the diverse communities and trajectories of change that emerged in frontier regions (Cronon, Miles, and Gitlin 1992; Jameson and Armitage 1997). From the vantage point of the frontier as a zone of many encounters, the history of Russian and U.S. colonization becomes one of Alutiiq interactions not only with Russians and white Americans but also with Native Siberians and Californians and later with Asian and Chicano cannery workers. Comparable to studies of intermarriage between Native Americans and Black slaves (Sturm 2002), there could be a point of contact here between Native American history and studies of race and ethnicity in North America and elsewhere. This widening of focus seems particularly important given the exclusionary interpretations even well-meaning portrayals of Native history and culture can provoke. I would like to close with an anecdote that returns to the theme of nonacademic uses of academic research, showing the diverse and sometimes unpredictable range of users and uses such research can have.

At the Alaska state fair in Fairbanks, in August 1998, I talked to a woman who was campaigning for a citizens' initiative to make English the sole official language of Alaska. Behind her in her booth hung a map representing Native language areas of Alaska, which was published by the University of Alaska and is widely available in bookstores and museums throughout the state, marketed both as educational tool and souvenir (Krauss 1982). I was puzzled what that map was doing among the posters of an organization that called itself "Alaskans for a Common Language" and meant English, not any of the languages of Alaska's Native groups. The woman explained that the map—which shows with the help of blank or partly or completely filled-in dots whether most, some or no children of a village speak the Native language—was a reminder of the fragility of languages, of the need to pay attention to their preservation to make sure they do not disappear.

The initiative aimed at making it illegal for state or local government agencies to use any other language than English in print or speech and to require employees to know or learn other languages than English, except in certain contexts, such as tourism or language teaching (Alaskans for a Common Language n.d.). Organizations pressing for "English Only" laws exist throughout the United States and mainly agitate against the threat to the nation and to public budgets allegedly posed by Spanish-speaking, and to a lesser degree Asian, immigrants. The campaign materials of the Alaskan initiative explicitly stressed that it acknowledged the language rights of Alaska Natives as defined by federal law. The map on the wall may have been a strategy to underline this point, or possibly to gain the votes of Alaska Natives and others sympathetic to Native rights. The subsequent history of the initiative confirms that the campaigners were right to worry about Native reactions: passed by a wide margin in the November 1998 elections, the law was declared unconstitutional by a court decision in 2002, following complaints filed by residents of the Yup'ik village of Togiak (Associated Press 2002). An appeal to the state supreme court was still pending at the time of this writing. But the woman at the campaign booth perceived another meaning in the map. Like those white observers of a hundred years before who blamed Alutiiq poverty at the canneries on Italian and Asian immigrants, she saw her own fears reflected in what she presented as the plight of Alaska Natives and identified English as a language indigenous to America and threatened with extinction by the intrusion of foreign speech.

This encounter with a user of anthropological-linguistic research brings to view how a sensibility for the frontier as a zone of many encounters could help remedy a blind spot in much of the debate about dialogic, responsible research. A good deal of thought and effort is being put into changing the relations between anthropologists and historians and those who have been studied and represented by them, but there is far less discussion of other audiences and other partners in research. Just as ethnohistory has as much to contribute to an understanding of the colonists' aims and actions as to the appreciation of indigenous agency and creativity, so issues of representation in anthropological writings and exhibits have at least two sides: engaging with the responses of mainstream audiences is as important as (and probably a crucial part of) transforming institutional structures to allow for the traditional subjects of anthropological research to represent themselves. In Alaska, a third direction of dialogue and collaboration is opened with the many things that Russian and American scholars could learn from one another, not just in terms of access to museum collections and archival documents but also in terms of theoretical approaches.

With this in mind, I have placed the emphasis of this book not so much on uncovering Native voices or getting beyond western traditions of telling history. Rather I hope that the stories told in the Russian sources have their own value in showing the points of view of long-term sojourners among the Alutiiq, people who were sometimes sympathetic, sometimes disdainful. Interpreted through lenses of American and Russian scholarship, they present pictures of societies that were both dynamically interactive and deliberately segregationalist and that left behind divisions that have not been fully overcome today.

Appendix

Selected Population Figures from Russian Orthodox Church and U.S. Census Sources

Kodiak Parish
(Kodiak Island and Northern Pacific side of the Alaska Peninsula)
from the Clerical Registers (ARCA D252-D253/174), 1843–1895

For a discussion of the meaning of the categories, see Chapter 5. Remember that the Russian church statistics usually count only the Orthodox population and that the figures given for women refer to wives and daughters of men in the given category, regardless of what one might consider these women's own ethnicity. Figures for Russian men also include the minor sons of Russian men and Creole/Native women, who would be considered Creole once they grew up. In listing the figures for individual status groups, I preserve the hierarchical order of the records: first officials, then ordinary Russians, then Creoles, then Aleuts; first men, then women. The totals for each year are given as they appear in the records, except for 1885 and 1895, when I supply the missing totals. When comparing totals, note that the geographic scope of Kodiak parish varies over the years, with places on the Alaska or Kenai Peninsula or Prince William Sound sometimes included, sometimes not.

Abbreviations: m = male, f = female.

1843 (the first year the register contains population figures for individual villages)

St. Paul Harbor:	Company officials	3m	4f
	Russians	46m	29f
	Creoles	80m	77f
	Aleuts	43m	48f
Orlovskoe:	Creoles	4m	9f
	Aleuts	117m	114f
Three Saints:	Creoles	3m	7f
	Aleuts	123m	111f
Aekhtalik:	Aleuts	124m	132f
Akhiok:	Aleuts	49m	50f
Karluk:	Russians	2m	4f
	Creoles	4m	8f
	Aleuts	120m	94f
Katmai:	Russians	1m	3f
	Creoles	5m	1f
	Aleuts	100m	98f
Severnovskoe:	Aleuts	42m	32f
Afognak—Aleut village:	Russians	10m	10f
	Aleuts	69m	24f
Afognak—Seleznevo:	Creoles	39m	41f
Spruce Island:	Russians	14m	8f
	Creoles	12m	15f
Woody Island:	Aleuts	114m	110f
Nikolaevskii redut [Kenai]:	Russians	7m	6f
	Creoles	9m	11f
	Kenaitsy	188m	156f
Konstantinovskii redut and Copper River odinochka:	Russians	5m	7f
	Creoles	16m	18f
	Chugach	200m	136f
Ugalentsy village:	Eyak	13m	7f
Ukamok Island:	Russians	2m	3f
	Creoles	2m	2f
	Aleuts	47m	35f
Total:	Company officials	3m	4f
	Russians	87m	70f
	Creoles	174m	189f
	Aleuts	948m	848f
	Kenaitsy, Chugach, and Ugalentsy	401m	299f

1849 *houses*

St. Paul Harbor:	Company officials	4m	5f	1
	Russians	30m	24f	9
	Creoles	96m	91f	15
	Aleuts	23m	24f	1
	Tlingit	3m	4f	1
	Indians	/	1f	/
Orlovskoe:	Creoles	6m	7f	2
	Aleuts	145m	121f	11
Three Saints:	Creoles	3m	7f	1
	Aleuts	128m	116f	11
Aekhtalik:	Aleuts	131m	123f	13
Akhiok:	Aleuts	46m	48f	5
Karluk:	Russians	2m	4f	1
	Creoles	7m	4f	3
	Aleuts	112m	102f	9
Katmai:	Russians	4m	4f	1
	Creoles	8m	9f	3
	Aleuts	112m	108f	10
Afognak—Aleut village:	Russians	19m	17f	7
	Aleuts	67m	78f	6
Afognak—Seleznevo:	Creoles	75m	75f	20
Spruce Island:	Russians	5m	4f	2
	Creoles	24m	31f	10
	Aleuts	4m	5f	2
Woody Island:	Aleuts	120m	112f	30
Ukamok Island:	Russians	3m	1f	1
	Creoles	3m	3f	1
	Aleuts	41m	29f	5
Total:	Company officials	4m	5f	
	Creoles	222m	228f	
	Aleuts	933m	880f	
	Russians	64m	54f	
	Tlingit	3m	4f	

1860

St. Paul Harbor:	Company officials	1m	/
	Russians	36m	13f
	Creoles	139m	132f
	Yakuts	1m	/
	Aleuts	12m	13f
	Tlingit	3m	5f
Orlovskoe:	Creoles	4m	3f
	Aleuts	140m	158f
Three Saints:	Creoles	4m	8f
	Aleuts	133m	122f
Aekhtalik:	Aleuts	153m	132f
Akhiok:	Aleuts	47m	57f
Karluk:	Creoles	14m	12f
	Aleuts	139m	127f
Katmai:	Creoles	11m	8f
	Aleuts	119m	116f
Afognak—Aleut village:	Russians	22m	24f
	Creoles	56m	72f
	Aleuts	81m	82f
Afognak—Seleznevo:	Creoles	51m	48f
Spruce Island:	Russians	6m	3f
	Creoles	12m	28f
	Aleuts	2m	5f
Woody Island:	Aleuts	114m	99f
Ukamok Island:	Russians	1m	/
	Creoles	4m	2f
	Aleuts	38m	32f
Total:	Company officials	1m	/
	Tlingit	3m	5f
	Russians	65m	39f
	Creoles	295m	314f
	Yakuts	1m	/
	Aleuts	978m	943f

1867

St. Paul Harbor:	Company officials	1m	/
	Russians	2/m	13f
	Creoles	190m	165f
	Aleuts	77m	85f
	Tlingit	8m	11f
Orlovskoe:	Creoles	6m	7f
	Aleuts	136m	132f
Southern villages [Three Saints and Kaguyak?]:	Creoles	7m	8f
	Aleuts	97m	101f
Aekhtalik:	Aleuts	122m	97f
Akhiok:	Aleuts	49m	52f
Karluk:	Creoles	12m	15f
	Aleuts	136m	130f
Katmai:	Creoles	16m	10f
	Aleuts	106m	86f
Afognak—Aleut village:	Russians	7m	2f
	Creoles	59m	69f
	Aleuts	66m	59f
Afognak—Creole village:	Creoles	32m	30f
Spruce Island:	Creoles	52m	42f
Woody Island:	[left blank, see Aleuts at St. Paul Harbor]		
Ukamok Island:	Creoles	8m	5f
	Aleuts	42m	26f
Total:	Company officials	1m	/
	Russians	34m	15f
	Creoles	362m	351f
	Aleuts	831m	786f
	Tlingit	8m	11f

1870

St. Paul Harbor:	U.S. citizens	3m	3f
	Creoles	104m	102f
	Tlingit	9m	10f
Orlovskoe:	Creoles	12m	11f
	Aleuts	133m	118f
Southern villages:	Creoles	16m	12f
	Aleuts	92m	109f
Aekhtalik:	Aleuts	120m	96f
Akhiok:	Aleuts	54m	46f
Karluk:	Creoles	9m	11f
	Aleuts	120m	134f
Katmai:	Creoles	20m	13f
	Aleuts	96m	84f
Afognak—Aleut village:	Russians	8m	3f
	Creoles	71m	77f
	Aleuts	68m	57f
Afognak—Seleznevo:	Creoles	37m	31f
Spruce Island:	Creoles	55m	50f
	Aleuts	3m	3f
Woody Island:	Creoles	53m	54f
	Aleuts	75m	77f
Ukamok Island:	Aleuts	38m	26f
Total:	Clergy	3m	10f
	Russians	8m	3f
	U.S. citizens	3m	3f
	Creoles	377m	361f
	Aleuts	799m	750f
	Tlingit	9m	10f

1877

St. Paul Harbor and Woody Isl.:	U.S. citizens	2m	/
	Creoles	160m	173f
	Tlingit	7m	5f
	Russian	1m	/
Spruce Island:	Creoles	54m	45f
Afognak Island:	Creoles	102m	83f
	Aleuts	69m	58f
Orlovskoe:	Creoles	11m	6f
	Aleuts	109m	98f
Three Saints:	Creoles	12m	9f
	Aleuts	72m	60f
Kaguyak:	Creoles	2m	2f
	Aleuts	53m	38f
Aekhtalik:	Aleuts	91m	78f
Akhiok:	Aleuts	65m	51f
Karluk:	Creoles	12m	12f
	Aleuts	136m	145f
Katmai:	Creoles	19m	18f
	Aleuts	93m	88f
Kamysh'iak village:	Creoles	19m	18f
	Aleuts	93m	88f
Total:	Clergy	7m	6f
	Russians	1m	/
	U.S. citizens	2m	/
	Creoles	372m	348f
	Aleuts	773m	686f
	Tlingit	7m	5f

1885

St. Paul Harbor:	Russians and others	10m	12f
	Creoles	129m	120f
	Tlingit	6m	7f
	Clergy	3m	9f
Woody Island:	Creoles	28m	18f
	Aleuts	44m	52f
Spruce Island:	Creoles	44m	52f
Afognak Island:	Creoles	107m	93f
	Aleuts	65m	46f
Orlovskoe:	Creoles	6m	9f
	Aleuts	90m	90f
Three Saints:	Creoles	9m	7f
	Aleuts	80m	52f
Aekhtalik:	Aleuts	96m	75f
Kaguyak:	Aleuts	54m	50f
Akhiok:	Aleuts	62m	43f
Karluk:	Creoles	7m	9f
	Aleuts	143m	132f
Katmai:	Creoles	20m	19f
	Aleuts	68m	46f
on Cape Douglas:	Aleuts	30m	37f
Total:	Russians and others	10m	12f
	Creoles	350m	327f
	Aleuts	732m	623f
	Tlingit	6m	7f
	Clergy	3m	9f

1895

St. Paul Harbor:	Russians and others	14m	9f
	Creoles	133m	146f
	Tlingit	5m	2f
	Clergy	5m	9f
Woody Island:	Creoles	34m	23f
	Aleuts	28m	23f
Spruce Island:	Creoles	33m	42f
Afognak Island:	Creoles	101m	98f
	Aleuts	48m	40f
Orlovskoe:	Creoles	4m	4f
	Aleuts	24m	23f
Kiliuda:	Aleuts	10m	5f
Three Saints:	Aleuts	50m	35f
Kaguyak:	Creoles	9m	6f
	Aleuts	48m	49f
Aekhtalik:	Aleuts	45m	36f
Pokrovskoe:	Aleuts	10m	13f
Akhiok:	Aleuts	56m	40f
Uganak:	Aleuts	18m	19f
Karluk:	Creoles	5m	6f
	Aleuts	74m	61f
Katmai:	Creoles	21m	17f
	Aleuts	54m	33f
Kugak:	Aleuts	9m	8f
Wrangell:	Aleuts	34m	29f
Douglas:	Aleuts	34m	31f
Wide Bay:	Aleuts	23m	18f
Total:	Russians and others	14m	9f
	Creoles	340m	342f
	Aleuts	565m	408f
	Tlingit	5m	2f
	Clergy	5m	9f

Kodiak and Afognak Parishes, 1912/1910

Kodiak Parish (ARCA D259/179, cumulative census, 1912)				U.S. census, 1910	
Kodiak City:	Russians	2m	1f	*white*	*154*
	Creoles	209m	197f	*mixed*	*258*
				Aleut	*13*
	Japanese	6m	3f	*Japanese 4*	
	Am. Indian	4m	3f	*Kuskwogmiut [Yup'ik]*	*1*
Woody Island:				*white*	*23*
	Creoles	21m	26f	*mixed*	*104*
	Aleuts	32m	36f	*Aleut*	*40*
				Kutchin	*1*
Eagle Harbor/Orlovskoe:	Aleuts	30m	24f	*Aleut*	*56*
Old Harbor:	Aleuts	28m	29f	*Aleut*	*53*
Kaguyak:				*white*	*1*
	Creoles	12m	6f	*mixed*	*15*
	Aleuts	21m	21f	*Aleut*	*43*
Aiakhtalik:	Aleuts	57m	49f	*Aleut*	*86*
Akhiok:				*white*	*1*
	Creoles	6m	7f	*mixed*	*2*
	Aleuts	60m	40f	*Aleut*	*103*
	Japanese	1m	5f		

	Alitak Cannery:	*white*	*15*
		mixed	*8*
		Aleut	*1*
		Japanese	*1*

Afognak Parish (ARCA D261/180, confessional records, 1912)				U.S. census, 1910	
Karluk:	American husbands	4m		*white*	*226*
				mixed	*19*
	Aleuts	48m	41f	*Aleut*	*78*
				Filipino	*81*
				Chinese	*67*
				Mexican	*43*
				Hawaiian	*25*
				Korean	*3*
				Puerto Rican	*3*
				Chilean	*2*
Uganak:				*white*	*2*
				mixed	*10*
	Aleuts	12m	11f	*Aleut*	*18*
Afognak:	Clergy and family	12m+f			
	American husbands	14m		*white*	*38*
	Creoles	139m	140f	*mixed*	*217*
	Aleuts	46m	42f	*Aleut*	*61*
				Yupik	*2*
Little Afognak:	Creoles	13m	9f	*mixed*	*20*
Uzen'koe/Ouzinkie:	American husbands	3m		*white*	*4*
	Creoles	50m	57f	*mixed*	*95*
				Aleut	*2*
				Kutchin	*1*
Douglas:	Aleuts	24m	21f	*Aleut*	*43*
				Aglurmiut	*1*
				Nushagamiut	*1*
Katmai:	American husband	1m			
	Aleuts	47m	35f	*Aleut*	*61*
				Nushagamiut	*1*
Wrangell:	Aleuts	15m	15f	*not listed*	
Kanatak:	Aleuts	13m	8f	*Aleut*	*23*

Prince William Sound/Kenai area, 1858–1910

1858 confessional records, Kenai parish (ARCA D299/201)	
Konstantinovskii redut:	8 Russians, 70 Chugach
Khatliuk:	81 Chugach
Tatitlek:	39 Chugach
Kiniklik:	46 Chugach
Chenega:	61 Chugach
Tsuklok:	136 Chugach, 2 [Creoles?]
Akhmylik:	63 Chugach
Aleksandrovskaia odinochka:	8 Creoles, 117 Chugach

1870 confessional records, Kenai parish (ARCA D294/199)	
Konstantinovskii redut:	88 Creoles and Kenaitsy
Khatliuk:	118 Chugach
Tatitlek:	37 Chugach
Kiniklik:	40 Chugach
Chenega:	93 Chugach
Tsuklok:	43 Chugach
Akhmylik:	50 Chugach
Aleksandrovskoe:	listed, but figures missing

1886 confessional records, Nuchek parish (ARCA D304/204)	
Nuchek:	34 Creoles, 129 Chugach
Tatitlek:	35 Creoles, 67 Chugach
Kiniklik:	54 Chugach
Chenega:	65 Chugach

1894 confessional records, Nuchek and Tatitlek (ARCA D305/204, D306/205)	
Nuchek:	29 Creoles, 38 Chugach
Tatitlek:	105 Chugach and Creoles
Kiniklik:	69 Chugach
Chenega:	83 Chugach

1907 parish census, Tatitlek (ARCA D306/205)		U.S. census, 1910
Nuchek:	54 Creoles, 38 Chugach	*1 white, 45 Aleuts*
Makaka Point, Hawkins Isl.:	not listed	*1 white, 18 mixed, 1 Aleut*
Tatitlek:	86 Creoles, 109 Chugach	*3 whites, 152 mixed, 1 Japanese*
Ellamar:	not listed	*45 whites, 53 Aleuts, 1 Japanese*
Kiniklik:	32 Chugach	*2 whites, 33 Aleuts, 4 mixed*
Chenega:	28 Creoles, 34 Chugach	*26 Aleuts*
		33 Aleuts and 7 mixed people listed near Cordova ("Cordova Unincorporated")

1907 parish census, Kenai (ARCA D300/202)		U.S. census, 1910
Aleksandrovskoe:	94 Aleuts	*3 whites, 8 mixed, 62 Aleuts*
Seldovia:	all Kenaitsy (Denaina)	*42 whites, 38 mixed, 84 Aleuts, 1 Chinese*

Villages from the southern part of the Pacific side of the Alaska Peninsula and from its entire Bristol Bay side (Belkofsky and Nushagak parishes) are not included in these figures. See Partnow (1993:152), Morseth (1998:52), and Dumond (1986) for population figures.

Glossary

ACC: Alaska Commercial Company   Founded in 1868; San-Francisco-based consortium of businessmen who had acquired assets of the Russian-American Company and came to operate most of the RAC's former trading posts in Alaska.

anayugak   Alutiiq term for a hereditary chief on Kodiak Island as reported in Russian sources, possibly derived from *angyaq*, the term for a large skin boat.

artel', pl. *arteli*   Russian term for a group of workers dispatched for a common task and for the work station or post that such a group occupies.

baidara, pl. *baidary*   Russian, Siberian-derived term for a large, open skin boat used for group travel and whaling, known as *angyaq* in Alutiiq.

baidarka, pl. *baidarki*   Russian term for kayak (diminutive of *baidara*).

baidarshchik, pl. *baidarshchiki*   Literally "boatman" (Russian); Russian foreman of an *artel'*.

barabara, pl. *barabary*   Russian, Kamchadal-derived term for a semisubterranean house constructed of wood and insulated with sod, often inhabited by several nuclear families. Known as *ciqluaq* in Alutiiq.

clerical register   Russian *klirovaia vedomost'* ; yearly record of the property, clergy and lay employees, and population figures of a Russian Orthodox parish.

colonial citizen   Russian *kolonial'nyi grazhdanin*; category of Russian-born employees of the RAC released from tax obligations in their home community and allowed to reside permanently in Alaska, created in the third charter of the RAC in 1844.

confessional records   Russian *ispovednye vedomosti* or *ispovednye rospisi*; in the Russian Orthodox Church, register of all the members of a parish, noting their age and whether or not they had attended confession and communion on a particular day, usually during Lent or during the annual visit of the priest to an outlying village. The Russian Orthodox Church was required to keep such records from the church reforms of Peter the Great (1722) up to the Bolshevik Revolution (1917), and to make them available to the imperial government.

Creole   Russian *kreol*, from Spanish *criollo*; in Russian Alaska, a person born of a union between a Russian father and a Native mother or between Creole parents. The legal status of Creoles as exempt from tax obligations in Russia and from work obligations imposed on Natives was defined in the 1821 charter of the RAC.

HBC: Hudson's Bay Company   British trading company active in northern Canada and rival of the RAC in Southeast Alaska. An 1839 agreement giving the HBC rights to a trading post in the Alaska Panhandle in exchange for deliveries of manufactured trade goods alleviated some of the RAC's supply problems.

iasak   Russian word of Turkic origin; tribute as imposed on non-Russian subjects of the Russian empire.

iukola   Russian for dried fish, a staple provision prepared by Alutiiq slaves and conscripted workers for the RAC.

kaiur, pl. *kaiury*   Russian term applied to the slaves whom the Russians expropriated from Alutiiq elites after the conquest of Kodiak. The status of *kaiury* was abolished in the 1821 charter, to be replaced by at least nominally paid laborers.

kamleika, pl. *kamleiki*   Russian term for the waterproof gutskin parkas used during kayak expeditions.

kazhim   Russian term for Alutiiq and Unangan ceremonial houses used for communal winter festivals, known in Alutiiq as *qasgiq*.

lavtak, pl. *lavtaki*   Russian term for the split sea lion skins used to make covers for kayaks and *baidary*.

Novoarkhangel'sk   Russian name for modern-day Sitka, Alaska.

odinochka, pl. *odinochki*   From Russian *odin*, one; small Russian post, often manned by only one Russian with a group of Native workers.

promyshlennik, pl. ***promyshlenniki***   Russian for hunter; a rank-and-file Russian employee of the RAC.

RAC:Russian-American Company   *Rossiisko-Amerikanskaia Kompaniia*; consortium formed by the heirs of the Irkutsk merchant Grigorii Shelikhov, which obtained an imperial monopoly on hunting, trade, and administration of Russia's Alaskan colonies in 1799. The main office was located in St. Petersburg; operations in Alaska were overseen by the Chief Manager (*Glavnyi pravitel'*), whose seat was in St. Paul Harbor on Kodiak until 1805, in Novoarkhangel'sk (Sitka) after that.

redut, pl. ***reduty***   Russian for redoubt, fortified post.

St. Paul Harbor   Russian *Pavlovskaia gavan'*, Russian-period name of the city of Kodiak, Alaska.

starshina, pl. ***starshiny***   In Russian, "elder"; term used to designate both Alutiiq chiefs (*toiony*) and Russian foremen (*baidarshchiki*).

Sugpiaq   The Alutiiq language.

toion, pl. **toiony**   Russian term of Yakut origin; used to designate a Native chief, sometimes one specifically appointed by the Russians.

zakashchik, pl. ***zakashchiki***   Russian term for a second chief in an Alutiiq village, subordinate to the *toion*. Possibly this office was a Russian-era innovation.

zhupan, pl. ***zhupany***   Russian term (of Siberian origin?) for a family sleeping compartment within a *barabara*.

References

Agnot, Ephraim. 1987. Interview conducted by Laurie Mulcahy, August 1986. In *Adaq'wy.* Oral history interviews conducted by Laurie Mulcahy, edited by Kodiak Area Native Association. Ms. on file, Consortium Library, University of Alaska Anchorage: 25–34.

A. K. D. 1899. Po povodu reporta ob aliaskinskom shkol'nom dele za proshlyi uchebnyi god/Remarks suggested by the Report on School Work in Alaska for the past school year. *Pravoslavnyi Amerikanskii Vestnik/Russian Orthodox American Messenger* 3 (22):599–603.

Alaskans for a Common Language. n.d. The Initiative. Flyer. Collection of the author.

Alekseev, Aleksandr Ivanovich. 1975. *Sud'ba russkoi Ameriki.* Magadan: Magadanskoe knizhnoe izdatel'stvo.

Anderson, Benedict. 1983. *Imagined Communities: Reflections on the Origin and Spread of Nationalism.* London: Verso.

Antonii, Ieromonakh. 1900. Shkol'noe delo russkoi pravoslavnoi tserkvi v Aliaske/ Report on the school work of the Russian Orthodox Church in Alaska. *Pravoslavnyi Amerikanskii Vestnik/Russian Orthodox American Messenger* 4 (5):114–118, (7):144–145, (22):444–446.

Anonymous. 1839. Podrobnaia karta chasti uzskago mesta v Prolive Kupreianova. Manuscript map, Rare Map Collection, Elmer E. Rasmuson Library, University of Alaska Fairbanks.

Appadurai, Arjun. 1993. Number in the colonial imagination. In *Orientalism and the Postcolonial Predicament: Perspectives on South Asia*, edited by C. A. Breckenridge and P. van der Veer. Philadelphia: University of Pennsylvania Press, 314–339.

Arndt, Katherine L. 1996. "Released to reside forever in the Colonies:" Founding of a Russian-American Company retirement settlement at Ninilchik, Alaska. In

Adventures Through Time: Readings in the Anthropology of Cook Inlet, Alaska,
edited by N. Y. Davis and W. E. Davis. Anchorage: Cook Inlet Historical Society:
235–250.

———, ed. and trans. 1985 [1861]. Memorandum of Captain 2nd Rank Golovnin on
the condition of the Aleuts in the settlements of the Russian-American Company and on its promyshlenniki. *Alaska History* 1 (2):59–71.

Associated Press. 2002. Alaska English-only law violates free speech, judge rules.
www.freedomforum.org/templates/document.asp?documentID=15965, ac-
cessed March 7, 2007.

Barman, Jean, and Bruce M. Watson. 1999. Fort Colvile's fur trade families and the
dynamics of race in the Pacific Northwest. *Pacific Northwest Quarterly* 90
(3):140–153.

Barrat, Glynn. 1981. Russia in Pacific Waters: A Survey of the Origins of Russia's
Naval Presence in the North and South Pacific. Vancouver: University of British
Columbia Press.

Barrett, Thomas M. 1999. *At the Edge of Empire: The Terek Cossacks and the North
Caucasus Frontier, 1700–1860.* Boulder: Westview.

Barry, Mary J. 1997. *A History of Mining on the Kenai Peninsula, Alaska.* Anchorage:
MJP Barry.

Bassin, Mark. 1993. Turner, Solov'ev, and the "Frontier Hypothesis": The nationalist
signification of open spaces. *Journal of Modern History* 65:473–511.

Befu, Harumi. 1970. An ethnographic sketch of Old Harbor, Kodiak: An Eskimo village. *Arctic Anthropology* 6 (2):29–42.

Berger, Thomas R. 1985. *Village Journey: The Report of the Alaska Native Review
Commission.* New York: Hill and Wang.

Berkhofer, Robert F. 1974. The political context of a new Indian history. In *The
American Indian,* edited by N. Hundley. Santa Barbara: Clio Books, 101–126.

———. 1979. *The White Man's Indian: Images of the American Indian from Columbus
to the Present.* New York: Vintage.

Birket-Smith, Kaj. 1953. *The Chugach Eskimo.* Nationalmuseets skrifter, Etnografisk
række 6. Copenhagen: Nationalmuseets Publikationsfond.

Bitterli, Urs. 1991 [1976]. *Die „Wilden" und die „Zivilisierten": Grundzüge einer
Geistes- und Kulturgeschichte der europäisch-überseeischen Begegnung.* Revised
edition. Munich: C. H. Beck.

Black, Lydia T. 1977a. Ivan Pan'kov – An Architect of Aleut Literacy. *Arctic Anthropology* 14, (1):94–107.

———. 1977b. The Konyag (The inhabitants of the island of Kodiak) by Iosaf [*sic*]
(Bolotov) (1794–1799) and by Gedeon (1804–1807). *Arctic Anthropology* 14
(2):79–108.

———. 1990. Creoles in Russian America. *Pacifica* 2 (2):142–155.

———. 1991. The Russian conquest of Kodiak. *Anthropological Papers of the University of Alaska* 24 (1-2):165–182.

———. 1997. Put' na Novyi Valaam: stanovlenie russkoi pravoslavnoi tserkvi na
Aliaske. In *Istoriia Russkoi Ameriki 1732–1867. Tom I: Osnovanie Russkoi
Ameriki 1732–1799,* edited by N. N. Bolkhovitinov. Moskva: Mezhdunarodnye
otnosheniia, 251–277.

————. 2001. Forgotten Literacy. In *Looking Both Ways: Heritage and Identity of the Alutiiq People*, edited by A. L. Crowell, A. F. Steffian, and G. L. Pullar. Fairbanks: University of Alaska Press, 60–61.

————. 2004. *Russians in Alaska, 1732–1867.* Fairbanks: University of Alaska Press.

Black, Lydia T., and Katherine L. Arndt, eds. 1997. *A Good and Faithful Servant: The Year of Saint Innocent. An exhibit commemorating the bicentennial of the Birth of Ioann Veniaminov 1797–1997.* Fairbanks: University of Alaska and Alaska State Veniaminov Bicentennial Committee.

Bolkhovitinov, Nikolai Nikolaevich. 1996. The sale of Alaska and Russian American relations. In *An Alaska Anthology: Interpreting the Past*, edited by S. W. Haycox and M. C. Mangusso. Seattle: University of Washington Press, 89–101.

————. 1997. Vvedenie. In *Istoriia Russkoi Ameriki 1732–1867. Tom I: Osnovanie Russkoi Ameriki 1732–1799*, edited by N. N. Bolkhovitinov. Moscow: Mezhdunarodnye otnosheniia, 7–11.

————. 1999. Rossiisko-amerikanskaia kompaniia na rubezhe 1860x godov i vopros ee reorganizatsii. In *Istoriia Russkoi Ameriki 1732–1867. Tom III: Russkaia Amerika: ot zenita k zakatu 1825–1867*, edited by N. N. Bolkhovitinov. Moscow: Mezhdunarodnye otnosheniia, 394–424.

Bortnovskii, Ioann. 1901. Putevoi zhurnal Sviashchennika Ioanna Bortnovskago za 1900 god. Kenai, Aliaska. *Pravoslavnyi Amerikanskii Vestnik/Russian Orthodox American Messenger* 5 (13):275–276.

Boxberger, Daniel L. 1988. In and out of the labor force: The Lummi Indians and the development of the commercial salmon fishery of North Puget Sound, 1880–1900. *Ethnohistory* 35 (2):161–190.

Brah, Avatar, and Annie E. Coombes, eds. 2000. *Hybridity and its Discontents: Politics, Science, Culture.* London/New York: Routledge.

Bray, Tamara L., and Thomas W. Killion, eds. 1994. *Reckoning with the Dead: The Larsen Bay Repatriation and the Smithsonian Institution.* Washington, D.C.: Smithsonian Institution Press.

Brody, Hugh. 1988. *Maps and Dreams: Indians and the British Columbia Frontier.* Vancouver: Douglas & McIntyre.

Burbank, Jane. 2006. An Imperial Rights Regime: Law and Citizenship in the Russian Empire. *Kritika*, n.s., 7 (3):397–431.

Bychkov, Oleg V. 1992. Osobennosti promyslovogo byta russkikh v vostochnoi Sibiri v XVII veke. In *Russkie pervoprokhodtsy na Dal'nem Vostoke v XVII–XIX vekakh: Istoriko-arkheologicheskie issledovaniia*, vol. 1, edited by Rossiiskaia Akademiia Nauk, Dal'nevostochnoe Otdelenie. Vladivostok: RAN, 105–122.

Case, David S. 1984. *Alaska Natives and American Laws.* Fairbanks: University of Alaska Press.

Chaffin, Yule, Trisha Hampton Krieger, and Michael Rostad. 1983. *Alaska's Konyag Country.* Kodiak: Chaffin, Inc.

Clark, Donald W. 1974. *Koniag Prehistory: Archaeological Investigations at Late Prehistoric Sites on Kodiak Island, Alaska.* Stuttgart: Kohlhammer.

————. 1984. Pacific Eskimo: Historical Ethnography. In *Handbook of North American Indians. Vol. 5: Arctic*, edited by D. Damas. Washington, D.C.: Smithsonian Institution Press, 185–197.

———. 1987. On a misty day you can see back to 1805: Ethnohistory and historical archaeology on the southeastern side of Kodiak Island, Alaska. *Anthropological Papers of the University of Alaska* 21 (1-2):105–132.

———. 1989. The Russian Three Saints Bay Colony, Alaska: Its history and archaeology. Unpublished manuscript on file at the Smithsonian Arctic Studies Center, Anchorage office.

Clifford, James. 2004. Looking several ways: Anthropology and Native heritage in Alaska. *Current Anthropology* 45 (1):5–23.

Cole, Terence M. 1996. Jim Crow in Alaska: The passage of the Alaska Equal Rights Act of 1945. In *An Alaska Anthology: Interpreting the Past*, edited by S. W. Haycox and M. C. Mangusso. Seattle: University of Washington Press, 314–335.

Cook, Linda, and Frank Norris. 1998. *A Stern and Rock-Bound Coast: Kenai Fjords National Park Historic Resource Study.* Anchorage: National Park Service.

Cracraft, James. 1971. *The Church Reform of Peter the Great.* Stanford: Stanford University Press.

Cronon, William, George Miles, and Jay Gitlin, eds. 1992. *Under an Open Sky: Rethinking America's Western Past.* New York: Norton.

Crowell, Aron L. 1992. Postcontact Koniag ceremonialism on Kodiak Island and the Alaska Peninsula: Evidence from the Fisher Collection. *Arctic Anthropology* 29 (1):18–37.

———. 1997. *Archaeology and the Capitalist World System: A Study from Russian America.* New York: Plenum Press.

Crowell, Aron L., and Sonja Luehrmann. 2001. Alutiiq culture: Views from archaeology, anthropology, and history. In *Looking Both Ways: Heritage and Identity of the Alutiiq People*, edited by A. L. Crowell, A. F. Steffian, and G. L. Pullar. Fairbanks: University of Alaska Press, 21–71.

Crowell, Aron L., and Daniel H. Mann. 1998. *Archaeology and Coastal Dynamics of Kenai Fjords National Park, Alaska.* Research/Resources Management Report ARRCR/CRR-98/34. Anchorage: National Park Service.

Crowell, Aron L., Amy F. Steffian, and Gordon Pullar, eds. 2001. *Looking Both Ways: Heritage and Identity of the Alutiiq People.* Fairbanks: University of Alaska Press.

Curtis, E. S. 1868. Military reservation of Fort Kodiak. Manuscript map, Rare Maps Collection, Elmer E. Rasmuson Library, University of Alaska Fairbanks.

Dauenhauer, Nora Marks, and Richard L. Dauenhauer. 1987. Introduction. In *Haa Shuká, Our Ancestors: Tlingit Oral Narratives*, edited by N. M. and R. L. Dauenhauer. Seattle: University of Washington Press, 3–59.

Dauenhauer, Richard L. 1996. Two missions to Alaska. In *An Alaska Anthology: Interpreting the Past*, edited by S. W. Haycox and M. C. Mangusso. Seattle: University of Washington Press, 76–88.

Davis, Nancy Yaw. 1984. Contemporary Pacific Eskimo. In *Handbook of North American Indians. Vol. 5: Arctic*, edited by D. Damas. Washington, D.C.: Smithsonian Institution Press, 198–204.

———. 1986. *A Sociocultural Description of Small Communities in the Kodiak-Shumagin Region.* U.S. Department of the Interior Technical Report 121.

Davydov, Gavriil Ivanovich. 1810. *Dvukratnoe puteshestvie v Ameriku Morskikh Ofit-serov Khvostova i Davydova, pisannoe sim poslednim.* Vol.1. Saint Petersburg: Morskaia Tipografiia.

———. 1812. *Dvukratnoe puteshestvie v Ameriku Morskikh Ofitserov Khvostova i Davydova, pisannoe sim poslednim.* Vol. 2. Saint Petersburg: Morskaia Ti-pografiia.

———. 1977. *Two Voyages to Russian America, 1802–1807.* Translated by Colin Bearne and edited by R. A. Pierce. Kingston, Ont.: Limestone Press.

de Laguna, Frederica. 1956. *Chugach Prehistory: The Archaeology of Prince William Sound, Alaska.* Seattle: University of Washington Press.

Desson, Dominique. 1995. Masked rituals of the Kodiak Archipelago. Ph.D. diss., University of Alaska Fairbanks.

Dmytryshyn, Basil, and E. A. P. Crownhart-Vaughan, eds. and trans. 1979. *The End of Russian America: Captain P. N. Golovin's Last Report, 1862.* Portland: Oregon Historical Society.

Dmytryshyn, Basil, E. A. P. Crownhart-Vaughan, and Thomas Vaughan, eds. 1988. *To Siberia and Russian America: Three Centuries of Russian Eastward Expansion. Vol. 2: Russian Penetration of the North Pacific Ocean, 1700–1797.* Portland: Oregon Historical Society.

———. 1989. *To Siberia and Russian America: Three Centuries of Russian Eastward Expansion. Vol. 3: The Russian American Colonies, 1798–1867.* Portland: Oregon Historical Society.

Dridzo, A. D., and R. V. Kinzhalov, eds. 1994. *Russkaia Amerika: Po lichnym vpechatleniiam missionerov, zemleprokhodtsev, moriakov, issledovatelei i drugikh ochevidtsev.* Moscow: Mysl'.

Drucker, Philip. 1939. Rank, wealth, and kinship in Northwest Coast Society. *American Anthropologist*, n.s. 41:55–64.

Dumond, Don E. 1986. *Demographic Effects of European Expansion: A Nineteenth-Century Native Population on the Alaska Peninsula.* University of Oregon Anthropological Papers 35. Eugene: Department of Anthropology.

———. 1994. The Uyak site in prehistory. In *Reckoning with the Dead: The Larsen Bay Repatriation and the Smithsonian Institution*, edited by T. Bray and T. W. Killion. Washington, D.C.: Smithsonian Institution Press, 43–53.

Dumond, Don E., and James W. VanStone. 1995. *Paugvik: A Nineteenth-Century Native Village on Bristol Bay, Alaska.* Fieldiana, Anthropology, n.s. 24. Chicago: Field Museum of Natural History.

Dzeniskevich, Galina I. 1977. Tavaroobmen u atapaskov Aliaski v pervoi polovine XIX v. In *Problemy istorii i etnografii Ameriki*, edited by Akademiia nauk SSSR, Institut etnografii im. N. N. Miklukho-Maklaia. Moscow: Nauka, 254–264.

Efimov, A.V., ed. 1964. *Atlas geograficheskikh otkrytii v Sibiri i v severo-zapadnoi Amerike: XVII-XVIII vv.* Moscow: Nauka.

Ellanack, Katie. 1987. Interview conducted by Laurie Mulcahy, February 1986. In *Adaq'wy.* Oral history interviews conducted by Laurie Mulcahy, edited by Kodiak Area Native Association. Ms. on file, Consortium Library, University of Alaska Anchorage, 35–38.

Elliott, Charles P. 1900. Salmon fishing grounds and canneries. In *Compilation of Narratives of Exploration in Alaska.* US Senate Report No. 1023. Washington, D.C.: Government Printing Office, 738–741.

Erlandson, Jon, Aron Crowell, Christopher Wooley, and James Haggarty. 1992. Spatial and temporal patterns in Alutiiq Paleodemography. *Arctic Anthropology* 29 (2):42–62.

Fall, James A. 1993. Subsistence. In *Exxon Valdez Oil Spill Symposium: Abstract Book*, edited by Exxon Valdez Oil Spill Trustee Council. Anchorage: 16–18.

Fedorova, Svetlana G. 1971. *Russkoe naselenie Aliaski i Kalifornii: konets XVIII v. – 1867 g.* Moscow: Nauka.

Fienup-Riordan, Ann. 2005. *Yup'ik Elders at the Ethnologisches Museum Berlin: Fieldwork Turned on Its Head.* Yup'ik translations by Marie Meade, German translations by Sonja Luehrmann, Anja Karlson, and Adelaide Pauls. Seattle/London: University of Washington Press.

Fisher, William J. 1880. Kadiak Island. *Alaska Appeal* 1 (20):2–3.

Forsyth, James. 1992. *A History of the Peoples of Siberia: Russia's North Asian Colony, 1581–1990.* Cambridge: Cambridge University Press.

Fortuine, Robert. 1989. *Chills and Fever: Health and Disease in the Early History of Alaska.* Fairbanks: University of Alaska Press.

Francis, Daniel, and Toby Morantz. 1983. *Partners in Furs: A History of the Fur Trade in Eastern James Bay, 1600–1870.* Kingston/Montreal: McGill-Queen's University Press.

Freeburn, Lawrence. 1976. *The Silver Years of the Alaska Canned Salmon Industry.* Anchorage: Alaska Northwest Publishing.

Friday, Chris. 1994. *Organizing Asian American Labor: The Pacific Coast Canned Salmon Industry, 1870–1942.* Philadelphia: Temple University Press.

Fried, Morton H. 1967. *The Evolution of Political Society: An Essay in Political Anthropology.* New York: Random House.

Gedeon, Hieromonk (Gideon). 1989. *The Round the World Voyage of Hieromonk Gideon, 1803–1809.* Translated, with introduction and notes by Lydia T. Black, edited by R. A. Pierce. Kingston, Ont.: Limestone Press.

———. 1994. Zapiski ieromonakha Gedeona o Pervom russkom krugosvetnom puteshestvii i Russkoi Amerike, 1803–1808 gg., edited by R. G. Liapunova. In *Russkaia Amerika: Po lichnym vpechatleniiam missionerov, zemleprokhodtsev, moriakov, issledovatelei i drugikh ochevidtsev*, edited by A. D. Dridzo and R. V. Kinzhalov. Moscow: Mysl', 27–121.

Geyer, Dietrich. 1973. Rußland als Problem der vergleichenden Imperialismusforschung. In *Das Vergangene und die Geschichte. Festschrift für Reinhard Wittram zum 70. Geburtstag*, edited by R. von Thadden, G. von Pistohlkors, and H. Weiss. Göttingen: Vandenhoeck & Ruprecht, 337–368.

———. 1977. *Der russische Imperialismus. Studien über den Zusammenhang von innerer und auswärtiger Politik 1860–1914.* Göttingen: Vandenhoeck & Ruprecht.

Gibson, James R. 1976. *Imperial Russia in Frontier America: The Changing Geography of Supply of Russian America, 1784–1867.* New York: Oxford University Press.

———. 1987. Russian expansion in Siberia and America: Critical contrasts. In *Russia's American Colony*, edited by S. F. Starr. Durham: Duke University Press, 32–40.

———. 1996. Russian dependence on the Natives of Alaska. In *An Alaska Anthology: Interpreting the Past*, edited by S. W. Haycox and M. C. Mangusso. Seattle: University of Washington Press, 21–42.

———. 1998. Sitka versus Kodiak: Countering the Tlingit threat and situating the colonial capital in Russian America. *Pacific Historical Review* 67 (1):67–98.

Goehrke, Carsten. 1970. Geographische Grundlagen der russischen Geschichte. *Jahrbücher für Geschichte Osteuropas*, n.s., 18 (2):161–204.

Grinev, Andrei Val'terovich. 1994. Nekotorye tendentsii v otechestvennoi istoriografii rossiiskoi kolonizatsii Aliaski. *Voprosy Istorii*, no. 11:163–167.

———. 1996. "Kolonial'nyi politarizm" v Novom svete. *Etnograficheskoe obozrenie*, no. 4:52–64.

———. 1997. Russkie promyshlenniki na Aliaske v kontse XVIII v. Nachalo deiatel'nosti A. A. Baranova. In *Istoriia Russkoi Ameriki 1732–1867. Tom I: Osnovanie Russkoi Ameriki 1732–1799*, edited by N. N. Bolkhovitinov. Moscow: Mezhdunarodnye otnosheniia, 154–196.

———. 1999. Russkie kolonii na Aliaske na rubezhe XIX v. In *Istoriia Russkoi Ameriki 1732–1867. Tom II: Deiatel'nost' Rossiisko-Amerikanskoi Kompanii 1799–1825*, edited by N. N. Bolkhovitinov. Moscow: Mezhdunarodnye otnosheniia, 15–52.

———. 2000. Tuzemtsy Aliaski, russkie promyshlenniki i Rossiisko-amerikanskaia kompaniia: sistema ekonomicheskikh otnoshenii. *Etnograficheskoe obozrenie*, no. 3:74–88.

Harvey, Lola. 1991. *Derevnia's Daughters: Saga of an Alaskan Village*. Manhattan, KS: Sunflower University Press.

Haycox, Stephen. 2002. *Alaska: An American Colony*. Seattle/London: University of Washington Press.

Holmberg, Heinrich Johann. 1855. *Karte des russischen Amerika. Nach den neuesten Quellen*. Helsingfors: F. Liewendal.

———. 1856. Ethnographische Skizzen über die Völker des Russischen Amerika. *Acta Societatis Scientarium Fennicae* 4:281–422.

Hoxie, Frederick E. 1984. *A Final Promise: The Campaign to Assimilate the Indians, 1880–1920*. Lincoln: University of Nebraska Press.

Huggins, Eli Lundi. 1981. *Kodiak and Afognak Life, 1868–1870*. Kingston, Ont.: Limestone Press.

Hulley, Clarence C. 1958. *Alaska: Past and Present*. Portland: Binfords & Mort.

Hussey, John A. 1971. *Embattled Katmai: A History of Katmai National Monument*. San Francisco: National Park Service.

Immigration Commission. 1911. *Japanese and Other Immigrant Races in the Pacific Coast and Rocky Mountain States. Vol. 3: Diversified Industries*. Reports of the Immigration Commission. Immigrants in Industries, part 25. Washington, D.C.: Government Printing Office.

Innokentii, Bishop. 1905. "Priemyshi". *Pravoslavnyi Amerikanskii Vestnik/Russian Orthodox American Messenger* 9 (5):91–92, (6):104–107, (7):125–131.

Innokentii, Metropolitan of Moscow and Kolomna [Ioann Veniaminov]. 1888 [1840]. *Zapiski ob ostrovakh Unalashkinskago otdela*. Vol. 3 of *Tvoreniia Innokentiia*

Mitropolita Moskovskago. Compiled by Ivan Barsukov. Moscow: Sinodal'naia tipografiia.

Istomin, Alexei A. 1992. *The Indians at the Ross Settlement: According to the Censuses by Kuskov, 1820–1821.* Jenner: Fort Ross Interpretive Association.

Ivanov, S. V. 1949. Sidiachie chelovecheskie figurki v skul'pture aleutov. *Sbornik muzeia antropologii i etnografii* 12:195–212.

Jackson, Sheldon. 1898. Report on Education in Alaska, 1885–1895. In *Seal and Salmon Fisheries and General Resources of Alaska.* Vol. 3. Washington, D.C.: Government Printing Office, 539–560.

Jacobs, Jane, ed. 1997. *A Schoolteacher in Old Alaska: The Story of Hannah Breece.* New York: Vintage Books.

Jameson, Elizabeth, and Susan Armitage, eds. 1997. *Writing the Range: Race, Class, and Culture in the Women's West.* Norman: University of Oklahoma Press.

Kan, Sergei. 1985. Russian Orthodox brotherhoods among the Tlingit: Missionary goals and Native response. *Ethnohistory* 32 (3):196–223.

———. 1996. Clan mothers and godmothers: Tlingit women and Russian Orthodox Christianity, 1840–1940. *Ethnohistory* 43 (4):613–641.

———. 1999. *Memory Eternal: Tlingit Culture and Russian Orthodox Christianity through Two Centuries.* Seattle/London: University of Washington Press.

Kangas, Hana Yasuda. 1990. Interview for the Alaska Japanese Pioneer Research Project conducted by Ron Inouye. Oral History Department, Elmer E. Rasmuson Library, University of Alaska Fairbanks.

Kaplan, Amy. 1993. "Left alone with America": The absence of empire in the study of American culture. In *Cultures of United States Imperialism*, edited by A. Kaplan and D. E. Pease. Durham: Duke University Press, 3–21.

Kappeler, Andreas. 2001. *The Russian Empire: A Multiethnic History.* Translated by Alfred Clayton. Harlow/London: Longman.

Kardulias, P. Nick. 1990. Fur production as a specialized activity in a world system: Indians in the North American fur trade. *American Indian Culture and Research Journal* 14 (1):25–60.

Kashevarov, Nikolai. 1898. Afognakskaia tserkov' Rozhdestva Bogoroditsy: Istoriko-statisticheskoe opisanie. *Pravoslavnyi Amerikanskii Vestnik/Russian Orthodox American Messenger* 2 (17):508.

———. 1907. Pokhodnyi dnevnik Sviashchennika Nikolaia Kashevarova. *Pravoslavnyi Amerikanskii Vestnik/American Orthodox Messenger* 11 (11):208–210.

Ketz, James A., and Katherine Arndt. 1990. *Calendar of Russian-American Company and Alaska-Commercial Company Documents Relating to Nuchek, Alaska (1818–1905).* Anchorage: Chugach Heritage Foundation.

Khisamutdinov, Amir A. 1993. *The Russian Far East: Historical Essays.* Honolulu: Center for Russia in Asia.

Khlebnikov, Kirill T. 1994. *Notes on Russian America. Part I: Novo-Arkhangel'sk.* Edited by Svetlana G. Fedorova, translated by Serge LeComte and Richard Pierce. Kingston, Ont.: Limestone Press.

Khodarkovsky, Michael. 2002. *Russia's Steppe Frontier: The Making of a Colonial Empire, 1500–1800.* Bloomington: Indiana University Press.

Khotovitskii, Dmitrii. 1916. Kad'iak: Iz vpechatlenii ochevidtsa. *Pravoslavnyi Ameri-kanskii Vestnik/Russian Orthodox American Messenger* 20 (14):217–220.

Knecht, Richard A., Sven Haakanson, and Shawn Dickson. 2003. Awa'uq: Discovery and excavation of an eighteenth-century refuge rock in the Kodiak Archipelago. In *To the Aleutians and Beyond: The Anthropology of William S. Laughlin*, edited by B. Frohlich, A. Harper, and R. Gilbert. Ethnographical Series 20. Copenhagen: National Museum of Denmark, 177–191.

Knecht, Richard A., and Richard H. Jordan. 1985. Nunakakhnak: An historic period Koniag Village in Karluk, Kodiak Island, Alaska. *Arctic Anthropology* 22 (2):17–35.

Knight, Nathaniel. 1998. Science, empire, and nationality: Ethnography in the Russian Geographical Society, 1845–1855. In *Imperial Russia: New Histories for the Empire*, edited by J. Burbank and D. L. Ransel. Bloomington/Indianapolis: Indiana University Press, 108–141.

Kodiak Area Native Association, ed. 1987. *Adaq'wy*. Oral history interviews conducted by Laurie Mulcahy. Ms. on file, Consortium Library, University of Alaska Anchorage.

Krauss, Michael E. 1982 [1974]. Native Peoples and Languages of Alaska. Revised edition. Map. Fairbanks: Alaska Native Language Center.

Kushner, Howard I. 1975. "Seward's Folly"? American commerce in Russian America and the Alaska Purchase. *California Historical Quarterly* 54 (1):5–26.

———. 1987. The significance of the Alaska purchase to American expansion. In *Russia's American Colony*, edited by S. F. Starr. Durham: Duke University Press, 295–315.

Langsdorff, Georg Heinrich von. 1812. *Bemerkungen auf einer Reise um die Welt in den Jahren 1803 bis 1807. Zweiter Band: Reise von Kamtschatka nach der Insel St. Paul, Unalaska, Kodiak, Sitcha, Neu-Albion, Kamtschatka, Ochotsk und durch Sibirien nach St. Petersburg.* Frankfurt on Main: Friedrich Wilmans.

Lantis, Margaret. 1947. *Alaskan Eskimo Ceremonialism.* Monographs of the American Ethnological Society 11. New York: J. J. Augustin.

LeDonne, John P. 1991. *Absolutism and Ruling Class: The Formation of the Russian Political Order, 1700–1825.* New York: Oxford University Press.

Lee, Molly. 1996. Context and contact: The history and activities of the Alaska Commercial Company, 1867–1900. In *Catalogue Raisonné of the Alaska Commercial Company Collection, Phoebe Apperson Hearst Museum of Anthropology*, edited by N. H. H. Graburn, M. Lee, and J.-L. Rousselot. Berkeley/Los Angeles: University of California Press, 19–38.

———. 1999. Tourism and taste cultures: Collecting Native art in Alaska at the turn of the twentieth century. In *Unpacking Culture. Art and Commodity in Colonial and Postcolonial Worlds*, edited by R. B. Phillips and C. B. Steiner. Berkeley/Los Angeles: University of California Press, 267–281.

Lethcoe, Jim, and Nancy Lethcoe. 1994. *History of Prince William Sound, Alaska.* Valdez: Prince William Sound Books.

Liapunova, Roza G. 1977. Zapiski ieromonakha Gedeona (1803–1807) – odin iz istochnikov po istorii i etnografii Russkoi Ameriki. In *Problemy istorii i etnografii Ameriki*, edited by Akademiia nauk SSSR, Institut etnografii im. N. N. Miklukho-Maklaia. Moscow: Nauka, 215–228.

———. 1987. *Aleuty: Ocherki etnicheskoi istorii.* Leningrad: Nauka.

———. 1994. O Russkoi Amerike. In *Russkaia Amerika: Po lichnym vpechatleniiam missionerov, zemleprokhodtsev, moriakov, issledovatelei i drugikh ochevidtsev,* edited by A. D. Dridzo and R. V. Kinzhalov. Moscow: Mysl', 7–25.

Liapunova, Roza G., and Svetlana G. Fedorova, eds. 1979. *Russkaia Amerika v neo-publikovannykh zapiskakh K. T. Khlebnikova.* Leningrad: Nauka.

Liljeblad, Sue Ellen. 1979. Ethnic evolution of the "China Crew." Paper submitted for "The Sea in Alaska's Past: A Maritime History Conference," September 7–8, 1979. Ms. on file, Consortium Library, University of Alaska Anchorage.

Limerick, Patricia N. 1987. *The Legacy of Conquest: The Unbroken Past of the American West.* New York: Norton.

Lisianskii, IUrii F. [Urey Lisiansky]. 1812. Kad'iak s okruzhaiushchimi ego ostrovami (Kodiak with surrounding islands). Plate 7 in folio accompanying IU. Lisianskii, *Puteshestvie vokrug sveta v 1803, 4, 5, i 1806 godakh po poveleniu Ego Imperatorskago Velichestva Aleksandra Pervago na korable Neve.* Saint Petersburg: Drechsler.

———. 1814. *A Voyage Round the World, in the Years 1803, 4, 5, & 6; performed, by order of His Imperial Majesty Alexander the First, Emperor of Russia, in the Ship Neva.* Translated by the author. London: John Booth.

———. 1947. *Puteshestvie vokrug sveta na korable "Neva" v 1803–1806 godakh.* Abridged edition. Moscow: Ogiz.

———. 1994. Pis'mo kapitana 2-go ranga IU.F. Lisianskogo N. P. Rumiantsevu o merakh po uluchsheniiu uslovii zhizni mestnogo naseleniia Russkoi Ameriki, 20 Dekabria 1806 g. In *Rossiisko-amerikanskaia Kompaniia i izuchenie tikhookeanskogo severa, 1799–1815. Sbornik dokumentov,* edited by A. I. Narochnitskii and N. N. Bolkhovitinov. Moscow: Nauka, 163–165.

Litke, Fedor P. [Friedrich Lütke]. 1835. *Puteshestvie vokrug sveta, sovershennoe po poveleniiu Imperatora Nikolaia I, na voennom shliupe Seniavin, v 1826, 1827, 1828 i 1829 godakh.* Saint Petersburg.

———. 1948. *Puteshestvie vokrug sveta na voennom shliupe "Seniavin", 1826–1829.* Moscow: Ogiz.

Littlefield, Alice. 1993. Learning to labor: Native American education in the United States, 1880–1930. In *The Political Economy of North American Indians*, edited by J. H. Moore. Norman: University of Oklahoma Press, 43–59.

Luehrmann, Sonja. 2005. Russian colonialism and the Asiatic mode of production: (Post-)Soviet ethnography goes to Alaska. *Slavic Review* 64 (4):851–871.

Martysh, Vasilii. 1902. Putevoi zhurnal Sviashchennika Afognakskago prikhoda Vasiliia Martysha za 1901 god. *Pravoslavnyi Amerikanskii Vestnik/Russian Orthodox American Messenger* 6 (20):430–434.

Masson, Jack, and Donald Guimary. 1981. Asian labor contractors in the Alaskan canned salmon industry: 1880–1937. *Labor History* 22 (3):377–397.

Meillassoux, Claude. 1975. *Femmes, greniers, et capitaux.* Paris: Maspero.

————. 1998 [1986]. *Anthropologie de l'esclavage: le ventre de fer et d'argent.* Paris: Quadrige/Presses Universitaires de France.

Merck, Carl Heinrich. 1980. *Siberia and Northwestern America 1788–1792: The Journal of Carl Heinrich Merck, Naturalist with the Russian Scientific Expedition Led by Captains Joseph Billings and Gavriil Sarychev.* Translated by Fritz Jaensch. Kingston, Ont.: Limestone Press.

Michael, Henry N., ed. and trans. 1967. *Lieutenant Zagoskin's Travels in Russian America, 1842–1844.* Arctic Institute of North America Anthropology of the North: Translations from Russian Sources 7. Toronto: University of Toronto Press.

Mishler, Craig, and Rachel Mason. 1996. Alutiiq Vikings: Kinship and fishing in Old Harbor, Alaska. *Human Organization* 55 (3): 263–269.

Mitchell, Donald Craig. 1997. *Sold American: The Story of Alaska Natives and Their Land, 1867–1959.* Hanover: University Press of New England.

Mobley, Charles M., et al. 1990. *The 1989 Exxon Valdez Cultural Resource Program.* Anchorage: Exxon Shipping Company and Exxon Co., USA.

Morseth, Michele. 1998. *Puyulek Pu'irtuq! The People of the Volcanoes. Aniakchak National Monument and Preserve Ethnograpahic [sic] Overview & Assessment.* Anchorage, AK: National Park Service.

Morskoe Ministerstvo, ed. 1847. Merkatorskaia karta vostochnago okeana i Beringova Moria s Poluostrovom Aliaskoiu i Aleutskimi ostrovami. Sostavlena iz raznykh zhurnalov i kart. Saint Petersburg. Rare Map Collection, Elmer E. Rasmuson Library, University of Alaska Fairbanks.

Moser, Jefferson F. 1898. The salmon and salmon fisheries of Alaska. Report of the operations of the United States Fish Commission Steamer Albatross for the year ending June, 1898. *Bulletin of the United States Fish Commission* 18:1–178.

Moss, Madonna L., and Jon M. Erlandson. 1992. Forts, refuge rocks, and defensive sites: The antiquity of warfare along the North Pacific coast of North America. *Arctic Anthropology* 29 (2):73–90.

Mousalimas, S. A. 1995. *The Transition from Shamanism to Russian Orthodoxy in Alaska.* Providence/Oxford: Berghahn Books.

Muszynski, Alicia. 1988. Race and gender: Structural determinants in the formation of British Columbia's salmon cannery labor forces. *Canadian Journal of Sociology/Cahiers Canadiens de Sociologie* 13 (1-2):103–120.

Nash, Marie Matsuno. 1991. Interview for the Alaska Japanese Pioneer Research Project conducted by Ron Inouye. Oral History Department, Elmer E. Rasmuson Library, University of Alaska Fairbanks.

Naske, Claus-M. 1983. The relocation of Alaska's Japanese residents. *Pacific Northwest Quarterly* 74 (3):124–132.

National Park Service. 1997. Sitka. Official Map and Guide. Sitka National Historical Park, Alaska. Washington, D.C.: Government Printing Office.

Norris, Frank. 1984. *North to Alaska: An Overview of Immigrants to Alaska, 1867–1945.* Alaska Historical Commission Studies in History 121. Anchorage.

Okladnikova, Elena A. 1987. Science and education in Russian America. In *Russia's American Colony*, edited by S. F. Starr. Durham: Duke University Press, 218–248.

Okun', Semën B. 1939. *Rossiisko-Amerikanskaia Kompaniia.* Moscow/Leningrad: Gosudarstvennoe Sotsial'no-ekonomicheskoe izdatel'stvo.

Oleksa, Michael. 1987. Introduction. In *Alaskan Missionary Spirituality*, edited by M. Oleksa. New York/Mahwah: Paulist Press, 3–35.

Orbach, Michael K., and Beverly Holmes. 1986. The Pribilof Island Aleuts: Tentative players in a hybrid economy. In *Contemporary Alaskan Native Economies*, edited by S. J. Langdon. Lanham: University Press of America, 71–99.

Osborn, Sannie Kenton. 1997. Death in the daily life of the Ross Colony: Mortuary behavior in frontier Russian America. Ph.D. diss., University of Wisconsin Milwaukee.

Oswalt, Wendell H. 1967a. *Alaskan Eskimos.* San Francisco: Chandler.

———. 1967b. *Alaska Commercial Co. Records: 1868–1911.* Register. Fairbanks: University of Alaska Library.

Partnow, Patricia H. 1993. Alutiiq ethnicity. Ph.D. diss., University of Alaska Fairbanks.

———. 2001. *Making History: Alutiiq/Sugpiaq Life on the Alaska Peninsula.* Fairbanks: University of Alaska Press.

Pascoe, Peggy. 1997. Race, gender and intercultural relations: The case of interracial marriage. In *Writing the Range. Race, Class, and Culture in the Women's West*, edited by E. Jameson and S. Armitage. Norman: University of Oklahoma Press, 69–80.

Pels, Peter. 1997. The anthropology of colonialism: Culture, history, and the emergence of western governmentality. *Annual Review of Anthropology* 26:163–183.

Peterson, Jacqueline, and Jennifer S. H. Brown, eds. 1985. *The New Peoples: Being and Becoming Metis in North America.* Lincoln: University of Nebraska Press.

Petroff, Ivan. 1884. *Report on the Population, Industries, and Resources of Alaska.* Department of the Interior, Census Office. Washington, D.C.: Government Printing Office.

Petrov, Aleksandr IUr'evich. 2006. *Rossiisko-amerikanskaia kompaniia: Deiatel'nost' na otechestvennom i zarubezhnom rynkakh (1799-1867).* Moscow: IVI RAN.

Petrov, Aleksandr IUr'evich, and L. M. Troitskaia. 1997. Osnovanie postoiannykh poselenii na Severo-Zapade Ameriki. Deiatel'nost' G. I. i N. A. Shelikhovykh. In *Istoriia Russkoi Ameriki 1732–1867. Tom I: Osnovanie Russkoi Ameriki 1732–1799*, edited by N. N. Bol-khovitinov. Moscow: Mezhdunarodnye otnosheniia, 109–153.

Pierce, Richard. 1990. *Russian America: A Biographical Dictionary.* Kingston, Ont.: Limestone Press.

Polanyi, Karl. 1944. *The Great Transformation.* New York: Farrar & Rinehart.

Porter, Robert P. 1893. *Report on Population and Resources of Alaska at the 11th Census: 1890.* Washington, D.C.: Government Printing Office.

Pracht, Max, J. K. Luttrell, and J. Murray. 1898. Salmon fisheries of Alaska. Reports of special agents Pracht, Luttrell, and Murray for the years 1892, 1893, 1894, 1895. In *Seal and Salmon Fisheries and General Resources of Alaska*, vol. 2. Washington, D.C.: Government Printing Office, 383–459.

Pravoslavnyi Amerikanskii Vestnik. 1897. Defects of American statistics: Orthodox population of Alaska. *Pravoslavnyi Amerikanskii Vestnik/Russian Orthodox American Messenger* 2 (8):262–265.

———. 1939. Byloe i nastoiashchoe: Ocherki Pravoslavnoi Aliaski. *Pravoslavnyi Amerikanskii Vestnik/Russian Orthodox American Messenger* 35 (7):108–110.

Prisadskii, A. 1939. Iz kadiakskoi stariny. *Pravoslavnyi Amerikanskii Vestnik/Russian Orthodox American Messenger* 35 (5):75–78.

Pullar, Gordon L. 1992. Ethnic identity, cultural pride, and generations of baggage: A personal experience. *Arctic Anthropology* 29 (2):182–191.

———. 1994. Alutiiq. In *Native America in the Twentieth Century: An Encyclopedia*, edited by M. B. Davis. New York: Garland, 29–31.

Rathburn, Robert E. 1981. The Russian Orthodox Church as a Native institution among the Koniag Eskimo of Kodiak Island, Alaska. *Arctic Anthropology* 18 (1):11–22.

Ray, Arthur J., and Donald Freeman. 1978. *"Give Us Good Measure": An Economic Analysis of Relations Between the Indians and the Hudson's Bay Company Before 1763.* Toronto/Buffalo: University of Toronto Press.

Roppel, Patricia. 1986. *Salmon from Kodiak: An History of the Salmon Fisheries of Kodiak Island, Alaska.* Anchorage: Alaska Historical Commission.

Roscoe, Fred. 1992. *From Humboldt to Kodiak, 1886–1895.* Edited by Stanley N. Roscoe. Kingston, Ont.: Limestone Press.

Roseberry, William. 1989. *Anthropologies and Histories: Essays in Culture, History, and Political Economy.* New Brunswick: Rutgers University Press.

Rostad, Michael. 1988. *Time to Dance: Life of an Alaska Native.* Anchorage: A. T. Publishing.

Russian-American Company. 1849. Merkatorskaia karta kad'iakskago arkhipelaga, sostavlena Rossiiskoiu-Amerikanskoiu Kompanieiu po noveishim svideniiam. Map. Saint Petersburg. Baranov Museum collection, Kodiak.

Sahlins, Marshall. 1972. *Stone Age Economics.* Chicago/New York: Aldine Atherton, Inc.

Sarafian, Winston Lee. 1970. Russian-American Company employee policies and practices, 1799–1867. Ph.D. diss., University of California Los Angeles.

Sarychev, Gavriil A. 1802. *Puteshestvie Flota Kapitana Sarycheva po severo-vostochnoi chasti Sibiri, Ledovitomu moriu i Vostochnomu okeanu, v prodolzhenie os'mi let, pri Geografi-cheskoi i Astronomicheskoi morskoi ekspeditsii, byvshei pod nachal'stvom Flota Kapitana Billingsa, s 1785 po 1793 god.* Saint Petersburg: Tipografiia Shnora.

———. 1826. *Atlas severnoi chasti vostochnago okeana, sostavlen v chertezhnoi gosudarstvennago Admiralteiskago Departamenta s noveishikh opisei i kart.* Saint Petersburg.

Sauer, Martin. 1802. *An Account of a Geographical and Astronomical Expedition to the Northern Parts of Russia for Ascertaining the Degrees of Latitude and Longitude of the Mouth of the River Kolyma, of the Whole Coast of the Tshutski, to East Cape, and of the Islands in the Eastern Ocean, Stretching to the American Coast.* London: T. Cadell, Junior.

Schmeckebier, Laurence F. 1927. *The Office of Indian Affairs: Its History, Activities and Organization.* Baltimore: Johns Hopkins Press.

Service, Elman R. 1962. *Primitive Social Organization: An Evolutionary Perspective.* New York: Random House.

Shalamov, Tikhon. 1898. Kratkoe tserkovno-istoricheskoe opisanie Kad'iakskago prikhoda. *Pravoslavnyi Amerikanskii Vestnik/Russian Orthodox American Messenger* 2 (11):340–341.

Shelikhov, Grigorii I. 1981 [1791]. *A Voyage to America, 1783–1786.* Translated by Marina Ramsay, edited by R. A. Pierce. Kingston, Ont.: Limestone Press.

Shubin, Valerii O. 1992. Russkie poseleniia na Kuril'skikh ostrovakh v XVIII-XIX vekakh. In *Russkie pervoprokhodtsy na Dal'nem Vostoke v XVII-XIX vekakh: Istoriko-arkheologicheskie issledovaniia,* vol. 1, edited by Rossiiskaia Akademiia Nauk, Dal'nevostochnoe Otdelenie. Vladivostok: RAN, 54–78.

Shunkov, V. I., ed. 1968. *Istoriia Sibiri. Tom II: Sibir' v sostave feodal'noi Rossii.* Leningrad: Nauka.

Sider, Gerald M. 1986. *Culture and Class in Anthropology and History: A Newfoundland Illustration.* Cambridge: Cambridge University Press.

Slezkine, Yuri. 1994. *Arctic Mirrors: Russia and the Small Peoples of the North.* Ithaca: Cornell University Press.

Sloss, Frank H. 1977. Who owned the Alaska Commercial Company? *Pacific Northwest Quarterly* 68 (3):120–130.

Sloss, Frank H., and Richard A. Pierce. 1971. The Hutchinson, Kohl Story: A fresh look. *Pacific Northwest Quarterly* 62 (1):1–6.

Smolitsch, Igor. 1964. *Geschichte der russischen Kirche, 1700–1917,* vol. 1. Leiden: E. J. Brill.

Spicer, Edward H. 1962. *Cycles of Conquest: The Impact of Spain, Mexico, and the United States on the Indians of the Southwest, 1533–1960.* Tucson: University of Arizona Press.

Stafeev, Vladimir. ms. Journal, 1880–1895. Alaska State Historical Archives, Juneau.

Stephan, John J. 1994. *The Russian Far East: A History.* Stanford: Stanford University Press.

Stoler, Ann Laura. 1989. Rethinking colonial categories: European communities and the boundaries of rule. *Comparative Studies in Society and History* 31 (1):134–161.

———. 1991. Carnal knowledge and imperial power: Gender, race, and morality in colonial Asia. In *Gender at the Crossroads of Knowledge: Feminist Anthropology in the Postmodern Era,* edited by M. di Leonardo. Berkeley/Los Angeles: University of California Press, 51–101.

Sturm, Circe. 2002. *Blood Politics: Race, Culture, and Identity in the Cherokee Nation of Oklahoma.* Berkeley/Los Angeles: University of California Press.

Takaki, Ronald. 1989. *Strangers from a Different Shore: A History of Asian Americans.* New York: Penguin.

———. 1990 [1979]. *Iron Cages: Race and Culture in Nineteenth-Century America,* expanded edition. New York: Oxford University Press.

Taylor, Kenneth I. 1966. A demographic study of Karluk, Kodiak Island, Alaska, 1962–1964. *Arctic Anthropology* 3 (2):211–240.

Teben'kov, Mikhail D. 1981 [1852]. *Atlas of the Northwest Coasts of America, from Bering Strait to Cape Corrientes and the Aleutian Islands with several sheets on the Northeast Coast of Asia.* Translated and edited by Richard A. Pierce. Kingston, Ont.: Limestone Press.

ten Broek, Jacobus, Edward N. Barnhart, and Floyd W. Matson. 1968. *Prejudice, War and the Constitution*. Berkeley/Los Angeles: University of California Press.

Thornton, Russell, Jonathan Warren, and Tim Miller. 1992. Depopulation in the Southeast after 1492. In *Disease and Demography in the Americas*, edited by J. W. Verano and D. H. Ubelaker. Washington, D.C.: Smithsonian Institution Press, 187–195.

Tikhmenev, Petr Aleksandrovich. 1978 [1861]. *A History of the Russian-American Company*. Translated and edited by Richard A. Pierce and Alton S. Donnelly. Seattle: University of Washington Press.

———. 1979. *A History of the Russian-American Company. Volume 2: Documents*. Translated by Dmitri Krenov and edited by Richard A. Pierce and Alton S. Donnelly. Kingston, Ont.: Limestone Press.

Townsend, Joan B. 1980. Ranked societies of the Alaska Pacific Rim. *Senri Ethnological Studies* 4:123–156.

Turner, Frederick Jackson. 1894. The significance of the frontier in American History. *Annual Report of the American Historical Association for the Year 1893*. Washington, D.C.: Government Printing Office.

Vakhtin, Nikolai, Evgenii Golovko, and Peter Schweitzer. 2004. *Russkie starozhily Sibiri: sotsial'nye i simvolicheskie aspekty samosoznaniia*. Moscow: Novoe izdatel'stvo.

Van Kirk, Sylvia. 1980. Many Tender Ties: Women in Fur-Trade Society, 1670–1870. Norman: University of Oklahoma Press.

Vinkovetsky, Ilya. 2001. Circumnavigation, empire, modernity, race: The impact of round-the-world voyages on Russia's imperial consciousness. *Ab Imperio*, no. 1–2:191–210.

———. 2004. The Russian-American Company as a colonial contractor for the Russian empire. In *Imperial Rule*, edited by A. Miller and A. J. Rieber. Budapest: Central European University Press, 161–175.

Wall, Wendy L. 1997. Gender and the "Citizen Indian." In *Writing the Range: Race, Class, and Culture in the Women's West*, edited by E. Jameson and S. Armitage. Norman: University of Oklahoma Press, 202–229.

Wallerstein, Immanuel. 1974. *The Modern World-System: Capitalist Agriculture and the Origins of the European World-Economy in the Sixteenth Century*. New York/San Francisco: Academic Press.

———. 1989. *The Modern World-System III. The Second Era of Great Expansion of the Capitalist World-Economy, 1730–1840s*. San Diego: Academic Press.

Welch, Richard E. 1996. American Public Opinion and the Purchase of Russian America. In *An Alaska Anthology: Interpreting the Past*, edited by S. W. Haycox and M. C. Mangusso. Seattle: University of Washington Press, 102–117.

White, Richard. 1991. *The Middle Ground: Indians, Empires, and Republics in the Great Lakes Region, 1650–1815*. Cambridge: Cambridge University Press.

Williams, Walter L. 1980. United States Indian policy and the debate over Philippine annexation: Implications for the origins of American imperialism. *Journal of American History* 66 (4):810–832.

Woldt, Adrian, ed. 1884. *Capitain Jacobsen's Reise an der Nordwestküste Amerikas 1881–1883*. Leipzig: Max Spohr.

Wolf, Eric R. 1982. *Europe and the People Without History.* Berkeley/Los Angeles: University of California Press.

Wolff, Eberhard. 1995. „Triumph! Getilget ist des Scheusals lange Wuth": Die Pocken und der hindernisreiche Weg ihrer Verdrängung durch die Pockenschutzimpfung. In *Das große Sterben: Seuchen machen Geschichte,* edited by H. Wilderotter and M. Dorrmann. Berlin: Jovis, 158–189.

Woodhouse-Beyer, Katharine. 2001. Gender relations and socio-economic change in Russian America: An archaeological study of the Kodiak Archipelago, Alaska, 1741–1867 A.D. Ph.D. diss., Brown University.

Wooley, Christopher B. 1995. Alutiiq culture before and after the Exxon Valdez oil spill. *American Indian Culture and Research Journal* 19 (4):125–153.

Yaney, George L. 1973. *The Systematization of Russian Government: Social Evolution in the Domestic Administration of Imperial Russia, 1711–1905.* Urbana/Chicago: University of Illinois Press.

Yerbury, J. Colin. 1986. *The Subarctic Indians and the Fur Trade, 1680–1860.* Vancouver: University of British Columbia Press.

Znamenski, Andrei A. 1999. *Shamanism and Christianity: Native Encounters with Russian Orthodox Missions in Siberia and Alaska, 1820–1917.* Westport: Greenwood Press.

———, ed. 2003. *Through Orthodox Eyes: Russian Missionary Travels to the Dena'ina and Ahtna, 1850s–1930s.* Rasmuson Library Historical Translation Series 13. Fairbanks: University of Alaska Press.

Index

(Page numbers in *italics* refer to illustrations; villages and geographical features are listed under their most recent name, alternative names or nearby locations are in parentheses.)